CATEGORY
FRAUD

About the Author

Brian Lindsay was awarded a PhD from the University of New South Wales for his thesis "Darkening Frontier, Vanishing Outback: Film, Landscape and National Identities in Australia and the United States". His articles about the Academy Awards have appeared in *The Sydney Morning Herald* and *The Australian*. Passionate about film and theatre history, he lives in Sydney, Australia with his partner, Simon.

CATEGORY FRAUD

Brian Lindsay

Tranter Ward Books

Tranter Ward Books
Sydney NSW Australia
www.tranterward.com

First Edition 2016

ISBN: 978-0-9804909-1-6 (paperback)
ISBN: 978-0-9804909-2-3 (e-book)

Cover design by Simon Moore, Elton Ward Creative

National Library of Australia Cataloging-in-Publication Data

Creator: Lindsay, Brian, author.
Title: Category Fraud / Brian Lindsay.
ISBN: 978098040916 (paperback)
Notes: Includes bibliographical references and index.
Subjects: Academy Awards (Motion pictures)
          Motion picture industry--History.

For my parents,

Penny, Alan & Lorraine

Contents

Prologue

Going My Way

In early 1936 the Academy of Motion Picture Arts and Sciences was on the verge of collapse and its annual awards were in danger of being consigned to history. "No one can respect an organization with the high-sounding title of the Academy of Motion Picture Arts and Sciences which has failed in every single function it has assumed," declared the newly established Screen Directors Guild in its newsletter. "The sooner it is destroyed and forgotten, the better for the industry."[1] Within weeks the eighth awards ceremony faced a boycott by the industry's leading actors, writers and directors.[2] Meanwhile, Academy membership had fallen from six hundred to just forty.[3] The cause of the crisis: industrial relations.

The Academy was founded in 1927 in the wake of the signing of the Studio Basic Agreement between nine Hollywood studios and five labour unions late the previous year.[4] The contract provided protections to studio craftsmen such as carpenters, painters, electricians and musicians. Fearful that the agreement would galvanize efforts by Actors Equity to introduce standardized contracts and ultimately result in the unionization of actors, writers and directors, Louis B. Mayer, the head of Metro-Goldwyn-Mayer, moved quickly to establish a prestigious industry body that could mediate disputes between the studios and their principal talent. Within a fortnight, the Academy was founded at a dinner at the Ambassador Hotel in Los Angeles and articles of incorporation were drafted.

The aims of the Academy were published in June 1927. At the top of the list was a determination to "take aggressive action in meeting outside attacks that are unjust". This was followed by the promotion of "harmony and solidarity among the membership and among the different branches" and the reconciliation of "internal differences that exist or arise". The adoption of "ways and means as are proper to further the welfare and protect the honor and good repute of the profession" was listed next. It was not until the fifth paragraph that "awards of merit for distinctive achievements" rated a mention and even then they appeared secondary to "the interchange of constructive ideas" as means by which the Academy would encourage "the improvement and advancement of the arts and sciences of the profession". That the presentation of awards for excellence in filmmaking was initially a low priority for the Academy is demonstrated by the fact that a year later no action had been taken to implement the idea of handing out accolades.[5]

The new Academy was formed "to stem the tide of unionization by workers in the fledgling industry," says historian Steve Pond.[6] And it was a manoeuvre that worked, for a time. As historians Larry Ceplair and Steven Englund concluded, the creation of the Academy "managed to forestall serious labor organizing among the Hollywood artists for over five years."[7]

Mayer had been most concerned about the unionization of actors and it was among actors that the new Academy had the greatest appeal in its early years, principally because of the impact of one film: *The Jazz Singer*. Promoted as the first talking picture, Warner Bros.' *The Jazz Singer* was released just months after the establishment of the Academy. The studios were soon undergoing an awkward transition to films with synchronised soundtracks, and actors found themselves at the centre of the industry's growing pains. Numerous silent movie stars nervously made their first appearance in talking pictures in the early years of the Academy's existence and many were anxious to maintain their pre-eminent position in the industry in the face of theatrical luminaries arriving from Broadway. What better way than to be declared the year's best actor or actress and receive a prestigious award?

"All members of the Academy are urged as a special duty and privilege to fill in their nominations for the Academy Awards of Merit with full recognition of the importance and responsibility of the act," proclaimed the Academy's rulebook. "Academy Awards of Merit should be considered the highest distinction attainable in the motion picture profession".[8] Membership of the Academy rose dramatically from 369 in November 1928 to 601 in November

1930.[9] The substantial part of that increase occurred in the acting branch where membership swelled from 93 to 246. At the second awards ceremony in April 1930, the Best Actress prize was handed to Mary Pickford, the most popular silent film actress in America, for her performance in *Coquette*, her first talking picture.

The Awards were "almost incidental"[10] and "an afterthought"[11] for the Academy in its early years. Its *raison d'être* was as an arbiter of labour disputes between producers and talent. As the Depression hit hard, however, its role in industrial relations came under sustained attack. In the wake of the four-day national Bank Holiday declared on March 5, 1933 by President Franklin D. Roosevelt, the Academy formed an emergency committee. Eager to avoid a suspension of production, the committee proposed an across-the-board pay cut for all studio employees for a two-month period of 50 per cent of earnings. The labour unions decried the plan, arguing that technicians on a $50-per-week wage should not face the same percentage cut as major stars and studio executives taking home weekly salaries in four figures. Two weeks later, the stagehands went on strike and every studio in Hollywood was closed down. A compromise was quickly reached: there would be no cut for anyone on $50-per-week and a sliding scale of cuts up to a maximum of 50 per cent for everyone on more than $50-per-week. While most in the industry begrudgingly went along with the revised deal, screenwriters resigned from the Academy en masse and formed the Screen Writers Guild.[12]

Just four months later, the actors followed suit. The Roosevelt Administration introduced the National Industrial Recovery Act in June 1933 requiring the introduction of industrial self-regulation codes. Amid fears that producers would draft a new code for Hollywood that favoured the studios at the expense of talent, many leading performers left the Academy and established the Screen Actors Guild. The exodus of acting talent accelerated in the months that followed when it was revealed that the new industry code capped the salaries of writers, actors and directors, but not studio executives. The new guild condemned the Academy in its newsletter as a company union and its president told the *Los Angeles Times*, "We believe our members should have nothing to do with it under any circumstances."[13] By the time that the turmoil was over, only ninety-five actors remained in the Academy.[14]

When the directors created their own guild in January 1936, the fears that had prompted Mayer to create the Academy nine years earlier had come to pass: the writers, directors and actors had all become unionized. All three guilds were on the warpath, not only forbidding members to join the Academy but urging them to boycott the upcoming awards ceremony. In his memoirs, then Academy President Frank Capra said he felt at the time that "the odds were ten to one the Academy would fold."[15]

With a stroke of genius and considerable good luck, Capra managed to blunt the boycott and avert disaster in the short-term by turning the 1935 Oscar ceremony into a testimonial dinner for D. W. Griffith, the revered silent film director considered by many as the father of American cinema.[16] Soon after, Capra had the Board of Governors formally vote to remove itself from the industrial relations sphere.[17] But to keep the Academy alive into the future, he knew that reforms were also necessary and that winning back the support of the actors had to be his principal goal.

To address criticism that the major studios pressured their contract employees to nominate certain films and particular performers in order to complement publicity campaigns and drive box office receipts, it was announced that nominees for the ninth Academy Awards would be chosen by a special Awards Nominating Committee of fifty members selected from across all the branches of the Academy.[18] "We feel that this committee of fifty will be able to give the various achievements of the year more individual discussion and consideration than could be done by the old method," Capra explained. The committee included high-profile actors Clark Gable, Carole Lombard, Lionel Barrymore and Ronald Colman.[19]

In the technical categories, Capra had the Academy dispense with the xenophobic rules that had limited the field of films eligible for the Cinematography and Interior Decoration awards to those made in the United States. The qualification requirement had been introduced several years earlier when cinematographers had argued that sound films made in the United States under the technical and budgetary limitations imposed by the nascent sound-recording technology were at a disadvantage compared to silent films which could be made on stunning locations and utilise impressive visual effects. Advances in technology meant that any such disadvantage had since vanished and that the eligibility rules had become archaic.[20]

Capra introduced two other changes, each designed to appease actors, the largest group in the industry. He increased the number of nominees in the acting categories from three to five, and doubled the number of awards for which actors would be eligible.[21] Both these changes have remained with the Academy ever since.

In the first eight years of the Academy Awards, statuettes were handed out for Best Actor and Best Actress. During that period, the two categories were dominated by major box office stars nominated for performances in leading roles. Only a handful of actors were recognised for their work in supporting roles, such as Lewis Stone in *The Patriot*, Frederic March in *The Royal Family of Broadway* and Franchot Tone in *Mutiny on the Bounty*; none of them won.

From the 1937 ceremony onwards, Oscars were presented for Best Actor, Best Actress, Best Actor in a Supporting Role and Best Actress in a Supporting Role. From the very outset, the distinction between the categories was opaque.

In the studio era, actors were divided into three tiers: stars, featured players and contract players (also known as bit players and often grouped with casually-employed extras). In major, prestige studio productions, stars had leading parts and carried the narrative while featured and contract players, in different ways, provided support to the stars. Studios also churned out numerous cheap productions, known as 'programmers', which were designed to play in cinemas prior to the main attraction and had featured players in the main parts with contract players filling out the cast. The status of performers in this hierarchy was clearly defined in annual directories issued by studios and the Academy in which artists were classified as either "leading men", "leading women" or "characters and comedians."

At the 1937 Oscar ceremony, comedic actor George Jessel introduced the winners of the two new awards with a homily about the vital importance to the motion picture industry of *supporting players* (as opposed to players in *supporting roles*).[22] The new prizes, in the view of the Academy and the studios, were for featured and contract players regardless of whether they were appearing in a supporting role in a prestige production or headlining a programmer. In a move that symbolised their lower rank in the studios' hierarchy of thespians, the winners would receive plaques rather than the famous golden statuettes.[23] It would not be until the sixteenth ceremony in 1944 that supporting players received Oscar statuettes.

The Best Actor and Best Actress categories, meanwhile, were for movie stars. The Academy and studio executives regarded the prestigious golden statuettes as reserved for famous, high-paid actors and actresses regardless of whether they were playing the main characters in the film or had been cast in a role of secondary importance by their studio for one reason or another (reasons included multiple parts in a film for performers of the same gender, the casting of an older star in a substantial but secondary role as the parent of a young, rising star etc.).

It was understood by industry powerbrokers that nominees would be classified in accordance with their status as a star or featured player within the studio hierarchy regardless of the size or nature of their role in a particular film. This is demonstrated by several key decisions that Capra's elite, fifty-strong nominating committee made when making their selections in the acting categories for the ninth Academy Awards.

Stuart Erwin, a featured player recently signed by Twentieth Century-Fox, headlined *Pigskin Parade*, a B-grade musical comedy programmer about a melon farmer who is turned into a college football star by a husband and wife coaching team. Erwin played the film's central character and was given top billing in the film's credits. The nominating committee, however, included him on the ballot for the very first Best Supporting Actor Academy Award. The reason: he was a featured actor, not a movie star.

Meanwhile, M-G-M was keen to establish two of the latest additions to its stable of top movie stars by securing them nominations in the main categories even though they had given performances in supporting roles. Former Fox player Spencer Tracy appeared in three vehicles in 1936: as a newspaper editor in the screwball comedy *Libeled Lady* starring William Powell, as a man who swears revenge after narrowly surviving being lynched by a mob in the drama *Fury* and as the priest in the big-budget disaster film *San Francisco* starring Clark Gable. With its climactic ten-minute earthquake sequence, *San Francisco* became the year's high-grossing film at the box office and a frontrunner for Academy Awards recognition. Even though he had a supporting role with only seventeen minutes of screen time, the Academy's nominating committee listed Tracy among the contenders for the year's Best Actor Oscar. The reason: he was a rising star being given a major build up by his new studio.

Similarly, young Austrian actress Luise Rainer had been given a pivotal supporting role in M-G-M's extravagant musical biopic *The Great Ziegfeld* starring William Powell as Broadway impresario Florenz Ziegfeld. Rainer was cast as the showman's first wife, actress Anna Held, and gave a scene-stealing portrayal with a particularly notable scene in which Held tearfully speaks to her former husband over the telephone congratulating him on his second marriage. Despite appearing in less than one third of the nearly three-hour film, the Academy's nominating committee listed Rainer among the contenders for the year's Best Actress Oscar. The reason: she was a rising star being given a major build up by her new studio. Some weeks earlier, the New York Film Critics' Circle had provided the committee with some cover for their decision by selecting Rainer as their choice as Best Actress of the Year. The group did not, however, give out awards for performers in supporting roles in those days so their prize was for the best performance in any role. On Oscar night, Rainer took home the first of her consecutive Best Actress statuettes.

Capra's gamble paid off. Following his reforms, the Screen Actors Guild decided not to repeat its calls for a boycott of the Academy Awards ceremony, telling its membership:

> Last year the Screen Actors Guild asked its members to stay away from the Academy dinner. Despite the fact that the request was at the eleventh hour, it was almost uniformly honoured. Since that time the Academy has largely kept out of producer-actor relations. It should do so entirely, since this is the function of the Guild – the organization chosen by the actors to represent them. The Guild this year intends to offer no objection to its members attending the dinner, reserving the right, however, to change its attitude in future years as the situation warrants.[24]

For the Academy, the introduction of the Academy Awards for Best Actor in a Supporting Role and Best Actress in a Supporting Role was a ploy designed to win back support for the Academy among Hollywood's actors. The studios embraced the move as a way to secure accolades for their second-tier performers, thus simultaneously appealing to their vanity and bolstering their status with the public, while continuing to hand statuettes to their top talent (whether they be established stars in headlining roles or rising stars in secondary or showcase parts). And the arrangement worked while there was a nominations committee that placed nominees in one or the other category accordingly. But the special Awards Nominating Committee was disbanded after only one year.

For the tenth Academy Awards, Capra further pursued his agenda to win over the guilds and secure the future of the Academy and its annual awards. The new Academy charter formally abandoned involvement in industrial relations negotiations between labour and management.[25] And the nominations process was again overhauled with the Academy inviting all guild members to complete ballots regardless of whether they were members of the Academy.[26]

The select committee of fifty was swept aside in favour of an electorate of fifteen thousand, of whom twelve thousand were bit players and extras on the membership rolls of the Screen Actors Guild.[27]

The disconnect between the ostensible reason for the two new acting awards (rewarding performances by any actors and actresses appearing in supporting roles) and the thinking behind their introduction by the Academy and the studios (rewarding players who were not major stars for performances in any role regardless of billing or size) was quickly thrown into sharp relief by the broadening of the nomination franchise. There was soon confusion and a chaotic history has unfolded since.

The Academy invited the studios to issue reminder lists along with the nominations ballots, which historian Emanuel Levy noted gave the studios "tremendous power" [28]. The accompanying voting guidelines stated that "Actors marked in the Reminder List by a star are considered Leads and can be nominated only for the General Best Acting Awards" while those completing ballots were able "to nominate any supporting player for both the Supporting Award and the General Performance Award"[29].

When the nominees for the eleventh Academy Awards were announced in early 1938, featured player Fay Bainter became the first person to receive nominations in both the lead and supporting categories in the same year. It was only the third year of the new supporting awards and only the second year that nominations for the Oscars had been made by the dramatically broadened franchise. Bainter was an established Broadway star appearing opposite Walter Huston as the title character's wife in the original production of 'Dodsworth' in 1934 when courted by Hollywood to make her film debut. Four years later she appeared in the supporting role of Aunt Belle in *Jezebel*, Warner Bros.' most prestigious production of the year starring Bette Davis and Henry Fonda, and took on a leading part in Warner Bros.' small-budget family drama *White Banners* as a kindly woman who becomes the cook and housekeeper to an inventor's family. Taking the wording on the ballot paper literally, the membership of the guild included Bainter on the Best Supporting Actress ballot for *Jezebel* and on the Best Actress ballot for *White Banners* even though she was a featured player rather than a movie star and was without a long-term studio contract (appearing in films for RKO in 1937, for Warner Bros. in 1938 and for Paramount in 1939). On Oscar night, Bainter triumphed in the secondary category, taking home a plaque.

History repeated itself, four years later at the fifteenth Academy Awards when newcomer and featured player Teresa Wright, scored nominations in the lead and supporting category (her second and third nominations in just two years, having been a nominee in the supporting category the previous year). Wright was recognised in the Best Supporting Actress category for her performance in the supporting role of a young, upper-class woman who falls in love with an air force pilot from a local middle-class family in *Mrs Miniver* and in the Best Actress category for her performance in the leading role of Lou Gehrig's wife in *The Pride of the Yankees* opposite Gary Cooper. Like Bainter before her, Wright collected a plaque as Best Supporting Actress on Oscar night.

A further two years later, less than a decade after the introduction of the two new acting categories, the underlying confusion about the categories resulted in one of the most quixotic situations in the Academy's history: the nomination of Barry Fitzgerald's performance in *Going My Way* for both the Best Actor and Best Supporting Actor prizes for 1944. Fitzgerald was a veteran featured player with a secondary lead role in *Going My Way* in support of the movie's star, Bing Crosby. He had been named Best Actor of the Year by the New York Film Critics' Circle but, as had been the case with Luise Rainer's win in New York as Best Actress for *The Great Ziegfeld* eight years earlier, Fitzgerald's selection was not made in the context of a separate prize for the best performance in a supporting role. The New York critics were simply declaring that he gave the best performance, leading or supporting, by any actor during the year. Shortly prior to the announcement of the Oscar nominees, Fitzgerald had won the Hollywood Foreign Press Association's Golden Globe Award as Best Supporting Actor for his performance.

On Oscar night, Fitzgerald was declared Best Supporting Actor by the Academy and his co-star Crosby was named Best Actor. Fitzgerald was the second winner in the category to receive a statuette following a change in practice by the Academy the previous year. His award was only made of plaster though as were all Oscar statuettes during the Second World War years. In what has now become a well-known part of Oscar lore, he promptly decapitated his trophy by accident while practicing his golf swing at home with friends. He received a golden statuette retrospectively after the war ended.[30]

The double nomination of Fitzgerald for the same performance drew criticism and demonstrated the need for the Academy to better define the delineation between the acting prizes and provide clearer guidelines. During the nine years following the introduction of the additional categories, the studios used the annotated Reminder Lists to ensure nominations were meted out in accordance with the studio player hierarchy as they had intended. There were several instances in which performances in supporting roles by rising studio stars had been shortlisted in the top acting categories while featured players headlining lesser productions appeared on the ballot in the supporting category in accordance with their status at the studios rather than the size of their role. As far back as 1937 *The New York Times* had sourly proclaimed, "The principal trouble with the Academy Awards is the lurking suspicion of logrolling and political dealing."[31] *Photoplay*, meanwhile, had greeted the news of Fitzgerald's double nomination with "no one can, in the same picture, be both [lead and support] – any more than a man in uniform can simultaneously be a lieutenant and a corporal – but the Academy achieved the impossible"[32].

Frustratingly, however, the Academy chose to make minimal change in the wake of Fitzgerald's double nomination. The rules were amended the following year to state that a "performance by an actor or actress in any leading role shall be eligible for nomination only for the General Awards for acting achievement" while a "performance by an actor or actress in any supporting role may be nominated for either the General Best Performance or the Awards for Supporting Players"[33]. Under the revised rules, Fitzgerald's performance was still eligible for both categories, but could only secure a nomination in one category or the other, not both. The studios continued to determine which performances would be classified as leading parts through the Reminder Lists mailed out with the ballots.

Five years later the rules were further modified to read if "a performance by an actor or actress should receive sufficient votes to be nominated for both the Best Actress Award and the Award for Supporting Player, only the achievement which, in the preferential tabulation process, first received the quota shall be placed on the ballot."

When studios orchestrated a succession of controversial nominations in the mid-1950s raising the ire of *The New York Times* and leading figures in the Screen Actors Guild, the Academy finally embraced the sort of reform that should have followed in the wake of Fitzgerald's double nod for *Going My Way* over a decade earlier. In 1957 it was announced that while the Academy would consider the designation by the studios, a special committee would ultimately determine the appropriate classification of any screen role, albeit only if the studio designation was questioned.[34]

Unfortunately, the Academy backtracked on this reform in 1964 declaring "determination of whether a role was a lead or supporting is made individually by members of the Acting branch at the time of balloting."[35]

The Academy has maintained the same position ever since. The current rules of the Academy state:

> A performance by an actor or actress in any role shall be eligible for nomination either for the leading role or supporting role categories. If, however, all the dialogue has been dubbed by another actor, the performance shall not be eligible for award consideration. Singing that is dubbed will not affect the performer's eligibility unless it constitutes the entire performance. The determination as to whether a role is a leading or supporting role shall be made individually by members of the branch at the time of balloting.

> The leading role and supporting role categories will be tabulated simultaneously. If any performance should receive votes in both categories, the achievement shall be placed only on the ballot in that category in which, during the tabulation process, it first receives the required number of votes to be nominated. In the event that the performance receives the number of votes required to be nominated in both categories simultaneously, the achievement shall be placed only on the ballot in that category in which it receives the greater percentage of the total votes.

A reminder list prepared by studios and distributors continues to be sent to Academy members along with the ballots.

In recent decades the confusion over whether performances should be in the lead or supporting category has turned into frustration and hostility as the disconnect between the nomenclature and practice of the prizes has become exploited by campaigns designed to maximize the chances of a particular performer's chances of a nomination or a win.

The Academy's rules provide clear guidelines regarding eligibility for the screenplay and music categories and allow for executive committees of the Writers and Music branches to resolve questions of eligibility in their relevant fields, but the same guidelines and arbitration process is absent from the rules covering the acting categories. The special rules for the acting categories remain so astonishingly vague as to invite flagrant manipulation.

In recounting the history of confusion and rising resentment surrounding the supporting categories, the following pages make the case for why the Academy needs to bring the rules for the acting categories into line with those circumscribing other fields of achievement and put an end to the awards season practice that has become known as category fraud.

Act One

One Flew Over the Cuckoo's Nest

In the aftermath of the Academy Awards ceremony in March 1937, the *Hollywood Citizen-News* reported, "Critics were generally of the opinion that [had] Spencer Tracy as the priest in *San Francisco* been placed in the category of Supporting Actor he might have won that hands down".[1]

Tracy appears on screen for just seventeen minutes in the nearly two-hour long disaster film that M-G-M released to coincide with the thirtieth anniversary of the earthquake that devastated San Francisco in 1906. His character, Father Mullin, appears fifteen minutes into the film as the hero's boxing partner and childhood friend. In this and all his subsequent scenes, Father Mullin appears in relation to one or other of the film's two main characters, played by Clark Gable and Jeanette MacDonald. Mullin's interaction with the hero and heroine advances their inter-connected storyline but he has no narrative of his own and does not demonstrate any character development. He is a consistent and stable plot device included to support the two main characters. In the finale sequence in which the citizens of the city march up a hill singing the 'Battle Hymn of the Republic' and look out over the ruins, Gable and MacDonald are placed front and centre of the frame, while Tracy appears behind them, slightly out of focus. There is no doubt about whose show it is.

San Francisco was assembled as a blockbuster vehicle for Gable and MacDonald. He was coming off hits *It Happened One Night* and *Mutiny on the*

Bounty while she was riding high after *Naughty Marietta* and *The Merry Widow*. The stars received joint top billing in the film's credits, above the title, and the publicity focussed on their first pairing: the tagline "They were born to fall in love!" appeared in newspaper advertisements and on lobby posters.[2] Given the small size of his part, Tracy was "needed only occasionally" during the shooting of the film and according to biographer James Curtis, "seemed to regard his time on the picture as something of a vacation."[3]

M-G-M had recently signed Tracy to be a new star and, having lured him over from Fox, carefully used *San Francisco* to establish a new screen image for him and raise his profile with the public. Casting him as a Catholic priest was a calculated move to disassociate him from the string of tough guy roles he had played at Fox over the previous five years.[4] The film's pressbook declared "It's News When Spencer Tracy, Screen's 'Toughest Guy,' Enacts a Priest!".[5]

Although Tracy was ultimately billed beneath the film's title, M-G-M positioned him as a star and leading actor from the outset. When his casting was announced on 24 January 1936, the *Los Angeles Times* reported, "Instead of two stars of the first magnitude, *San Francisco*, [a] depiction of the old days in the great west coast city, is to have three luminaries. As is known, Clark Gable and Jeanette MacDonald for some time have been assigned to this cast, and yesterday Spencer Tracy was added … Start of *San Francisco* is programmed as soon as Gable returns from Mexico, which will be in about a week. Gable and Miss MacDonald have never previously appeared in a picture together, and casting Tracy with the stars is also an innovation."[6] The innovation was putting a leading man in a featured role in support of two other stars. Curtis argues that it was "a bold move, giving the conflict over Mary a sizzling undercurrent of sexual tension."[7] The fact that Tracy was cast so close to the beginning of production (which started on Valentine's Day) is further indication that Father Mullin was a supporting role and one that had originally been intended for a featured player.

Upon its release, *San Francisco* was a huge box office success and was well received by critics. Frank Nugent in *The New York Times* singled out "another brilliant portrayal by Spencer Tracy" and, noting that the film was opening just a month after the release of *Fury* in which he had an acclaimed leading role, opined "[he is] heading surely toward an award for the finest performances of the year."[8]

Despite the acclaim, Curtis reveals that Tracy hadn't considered the possibility of an Academy Award nomination as he had been among the many actors who resigned from the Academy to form the Screen Actors Guild. According to Curtis, when Tracy was shortlisted for his supporting role in *San Francisco* alongside actors he admired such as Walter Huston and Paul Muni for leading roles in the dramas *Dodsworth* and *The Story of Louis Pasteur*, respectively, he "seemed a little embarrassed by the whole thing".[9]

The studio strategy that landed a Best Actor nomination for Spencer Tracy also scored a Best Actress statuette that year for another M-G-M rising star appearing in a supporting role in a prestige production and box office hit: Luise Rainer.

> *Alternate Nominee* – If Spencer Tracy had instead been considered for the Best Supporting Actor category for *San Francisco*, who might have been in the race for the Best Actor statuette? While historians regard the most glaring omission from the list of nominees to be Charlie Chaplin for *Modern Times*, it's more likely that M-G-M would have ensured Spencer Tracy was on the ballot nonetheless by backing his acclaimed lead performance in *Fury*.

With Swedish actress Greta Garbo already under contract as one of the studio's biggest stars, Louis B. Mayer instructed his employees to import new European talents who could be promoted as 'The New Garbo'. One of their discoveries was Luise Rainer, a twenty-five-year-old member of Max Reinhardt's theatrical troupe in Vienna and Berlin. An M-G-M talent scout signed her to a seven-year studio contract and she made her debut for M-G-M opposite William Powell as a countess' innocent companion in *Escapade*, a remake of the Austrian film *Maskerade*. As with Tracy, her second film for the studio was a big budget production in which she has a featured role in support of an established star: *The Great Ziegfeld*, an extravagant musical biopic about Broadway producer Florenz Ziegfeld.

Costing more than $2 million, *The Great Ziegfeld* was the studio's most lavish undertaking since *Mutiny on the Bounty*.[10] In addition to sheer spectacle, its success was predicated on the popularity of leading man William Powell and his reteaming with Myrna Loy, with whom he had starred in the hugely successful comedy *The Thin Man* two years earlier (in the same year as *The Great Ziegfeld*, M-G-M would also pair Powell and Loy together in *Libeled Lady* and *After the Thin Man*). Rainer and Loy were cast in showcase parts with limited screen time as the showman's first and second wives, actresses Anna Held and Billie Burke, respectively. Given her status as one of the studio's major talents and keen to exploit the reunion of the *Thin Man* stars in the publicity for the film, Loy was given second billing even though her character only appears in the last third of the movie. Eager to establish their recent discovery as a star, M-G-M gave Rainer third billing on the same title card as Powell and Loy, ahead of the film's title.

Although she has the largest female role in *The Great Ziegfeld*, Rainer's part "was so small by today's standards she would have been nominated for a featured role" wrote historian Emanuel Levy.[11] She first appears at the half hour mark but once the plot has covered the section of Ziegfeld's life during which he made Held a star, she has few scenes. Rainer disappears from the narrative at the two-thirds mark, apart from one post-script scene in which Held tearfully congratulates Ziegfeld on his marriage to Burke: the lachrymose scene many point to as the key to Rainer's Oscar win. In total, Rainer appears on screen in the three-hour *The Great Ziegfeld* for about forty minutes playing a character that is entirely secondary to the narrative centred on the title character. She plays a character defined by her evolving relationships with Ziegfeld; his discovery, his star, his wife.

"If the picture overcrowds its screen, at least we must admit it is an impressive kaleidoscope", critic Frank Nugent wrote in *The New York Times* upon the film's premiere in April 1936. He went on to comment, "Miss Rainer continues to justify the epithet winsome, but is inclined to emotional excesses which are not entirely justified and frequently were extremely trying". Despite mixed reviews, *The Great Ziegfeld* delivered a substantial return on the studio's investment and the when the New York Film Critics Circle convened in early January 1937, it was Rainer who they selected for their Best Actress prize. A month later, the fifty-strong Awards Nominating Committee included her among the five nominees for the Best Actress Oscar and the studio began to manoeuvre to secure a golden statuette for its latest star.

Sympathy following the sudden death of producer Irving Thalberg only a few months earlier was expected to carry his widow, actress Norma Shearer, to victory in the Best Actress category for *Romeo and Juliet*. The reigning queen of M-G-M with one Oscar on her mantelpiece already, Shearer had been absent from the silver screen for two years following the birth of their second child and Thalberg had fashioned *Romeo and Juliet* as a prestigious comeback vehicle for her. The film brought her a record fourth Oscar nomination. M-G-M stars and contract players made up the bulk of the voting membership and *Variety* reported, "For the best performance of actresses, indications are that Norma Shearer will get the statuette for *Romeo and Juliet* unless the studio group has a last-minute change of heart and tosses its ballots toward Luise Rainer, also Metro."[12]

The Hollywood Reporter predicted a win for Rainer, but noted that she had "surprised Hollywood two months ago by marrying, without preliminary fanfare or ballyhoo, the brilliant young playwright, Clifford Odets."[13] Mayer's antipathy towards Odets, whom he referred to as "that rotten Communist"[14] was well known, as was the studio's practice of controlling every aspect of their stars' lives, especially nuptials which proffered numerous opportunities for publicity. Had Rainer's private wedding and her choice of spouse raised the ire of the studio mogul enough for him to sink her Oscar chances?

Although the winners were now chosen by the membership of the guilds, historians argue that the studio bosses at M-G-M and Warner Bros. still held considerable sway over the result of the voting because their employees dominated the guilds' rank and file through sheer weight of numbers. It is rumoured that Louis B. Mayer and Jack Warner struck a deal in which Warner Bros. backed *The Great Ziegfeld* for Best Picture and M-G-M supported Paul Muni as Best Actor for Warners Bros.' *The Story of Louis Pasteur*.[15] Warner Bros. had loaned Muni to M-G-M to star opposite Luise Rainer in *The Good Earth*, which had just been released into cinemas. An Oscar victory for the Warner Bros.' leading man would assist M-G-M to promote their latest prestige drama. Of course, having both of the reigning Academy Award winners headlining *The Good Earth* would be even better and Warner Bros. did not have a star on the ballot for Best Actress that year.

When the nominees gathered at the Biltmore Hotel in Los Angeles for the ninth Academy Awards banquet, Rainer was not in attendance. Known as shy and somewhat reclusive, and convinced that Shearer was going to win, Rainer had stayed at home with Odets. Although the winners were scheduled to be announced at the conclusion of the banquet at around 11.00pm, the Academy had arranged to brief the press at 8.00pm under a strict embargo to enable the results to appear in the newspapers the following morning. Rumours were soon circulating out of the pressroom that Rainer had indeed secured the statuette and Mayer issued orders that she "put on some makeup and get downtown"![16] Rainer made an entrance shortly before the award presentations.

As expected, *The Great Ziegfeld* was named as Best Picture and Muni was declared the winner of the Best Actor prize for his portrayal of the French scientist Louis Pasteur. The Best Actress category was the last to be announced that evening and host George Jessel confirmed that Rainer had won the statuette making her the first person to win an Academy Award as Best Actor or Best Actress for a performance in a supporting role. As historian Steve Pond concluded, Mayer and Warner "had sewn up the evening between them".[17]

In the year that the Academy Awards for Best Supporting Actor and Best Supporting Actress were introduced, the fifty-strong select Awards Nominating Committee established by Academy President Frank Capra, steered the performances of Spencer Tracy in *San Francisco* and Luise Rainer in *The Great Ziegfeld* into the Best Actor and Best Actress categories, even though they both had supporting roles, because they were rising M-G-M stars. The studio wanted Tracy and Rainer in the prestigious main categories to underscore their status as top-ranked, headlining performers distinct from the many featured and contract players that filled most of the studios' payrolls. The studios invested heavily in their stars, both in terms of salary and publicity, and carefully managed all aspects of their on-screen careers and off-screen images. Having worked hard to establish performers as popular or glamorous movie stars, the studios ensured that they were recognised only in the prestigious lead categories at the Academy Awards, regardless of the size of their roles. M-G-M followed the same approach three years later with another newly imported star: Greer Garson.

> *Alternate Winner* – If Luise Rainer had instead been considered for the Best Supporting Actress category for *The Great Ziegfeld*, who might have won the Oscar as Best Actress of 1936? Buoyed by sympathy following the untimely death that year of her husband, the talented producer Irving G. Thalberg, it is likely that Norma Shearer would have collected an unprecedented second Oscar for *Romeo and Juliet*. On the morning of the ceremony, trade paper *Variety* had predicted Shearer would win narrowly ahead of Rainer.

> *Alternate Nominee* – If Luise Rainer had instead been considered for the Best Supporting Actress category for *The Great Ziegfeld*, who might have been in the race for the Best Actress statuette?

Given the film received nominations for Best Picture, Director, Actor and Supporting Actress, it is likely that Ruth Chatterton, runner-up for the New York Film Critics' Best Actress accolade that year, would have been nominated for *Dodsworth*.

When Greer Garson read the script for *Goodbye, Mr Chips* she was dismayed and disillusioned.[18] The role of the charming young wife of the eponymous schoolteacher was as slight as she recalled from reading James Hilton's original story in the *British Weekly* magazine some years earlier. It was just the latest in a series of supporting roles offered to her by M-G-M which she felt inappropriate as her Hollywood film debut.[19]

Following a run of successful plays such as 'The Golden Arrow', 'Accent on Youth' and 'Mademoiselle', thirty-three-year-old Garson was heralded by the *London Express* as "The Most Sought After Young Actress in London". [20] Intrigued by the press coverage, Louis B. Mayer attended a performance of her latest production, a costume melodrama at the prestigious St James Theatre called 'Old Music', while visiting London in August 1937 to inspect his studio's recently leased facilities in the north of the city. Biographer Michael Troyan reports that Mayer "admired her elegant manner"[21] and thought her ideal for playing nurturing mothers and refined ladies in the kinds of prestige dramas that M-G-M excelled at making with its top leading ladies. Garson was offered a lucrative seven-year contract at $500 per week and was in Hollywood by the end of the year.

She arrived to discover the studio had no particular role lined up for her, only a series of screen and makeup tests which led to offers from directors which left her unimpressed. According to Troyan, director Sam Wood saw one of her tests and wanted to cast her as the villainess in the latest Marx Brothers movie, *A Day at the Races*. Garson objected to Mayer himself, declaring that she did not wish to play a mere supporting character nor appear in a zany comedy.[22]

And yet, a supporting role was precisely what M-G-M had in mind, albeit one in a more prestigious film. Following the same formula used to launch Spencer Tracy and Luise Rainer three years earlier, the studio intended to introduce Garson in a showcase supporting role in a major production headlined by an established star. She was tested for the role of Louise, the heroine's good-hearted sister in *The Toy Wife*, a melodrama about a plantation heiress in the antebellum South starring Luise Rainer, but complained to producer Merian C. Cooper, "I was a star in London. I did not come to Hollywood to play supporting roles! Please, don't harness me to the chariot wheels of another star!"[23] The role went to Barbara O'Neill, a featured player best remembered today for her Oscar-nominated role supporting Bette Davis and Charles Boyer in *All This, and Heaven Too*.

The role Garson coveted was that of Lady Edwina Esketh in *The Rains Came*, an adaptation of Louis Bromfield's best-selling novel in pre-production at Twentieth Century-Fox as a vehicle for Tyrone Power.[24] As M-G-M was borrowing Power to appear opposite Norma Shearer in *Marie Antoinette*, a loan-out to Fox for *The Rains Came* was a distinct possibility. But Mayer vetoed the idea, not wanting his latest discovery to make her first appearance in an American film for a rival studio. M-G-M star Myrna Loy was loaned instead.

With the casting of Loy as Lady Esketh in *The Rains Came*, the role of Katherine in *Goodbye, Mr Chips* became available as the part had previously been assigned to Loy.[25] Garson was not, however, happy to be presented with another supporting role in another star's vehicle. "How can I do anything with that sparrow of a woman!" she apparently complained to a friend at the studio. "The role is a first act curtain."[26] Garson was also apprehensive because the film was to be shot in England and she felt humiliated at returning to London to appear in a supporting role only a year after she had been a West End star and the toast of theatre society. Aware of her burgeoning reputation as a difficult actress and that the studio had already come close to terminating her contract, however, she swallowed her pride and accepted the part.[27]

The leading role in *Goodbye, Mr Chips* was played by Robert Donat, the star of *The 39 Steps* who was enjoying the critical and commercial success of *The Citadel* while shooting *Goodbye, Mr Chips*. He would receive an Academy Award nomination as Best Actor a few months later, just as *Goodbye, Mr Chips* was about to open in cinemas in the United States. Garson's character functions to humanize Mr Chips, progress his character development and give the drama an element of tragedy. Her role, while memorable and the only significant role for an actress, is brief.

Garson first appears just over half an hour into *Goodbye, Mr Chips* when her character, Katherine Ellis, encounters Mr Chips while vacationing in the Austrian Alps. She plays a modern-thinking young woman who is charmed by the shy, older schoolteacher and quickly agrees to becomes his wife. Her warmth and love gives the hero confidence and enables him to reach his potential as a great teacher. But their happy marriage is brief. Garson's final scene is about half way through the film, her character dying in childbirth off-screen shortly after. In all, Garson appears in about one quarter of the movie's running time. She angrily dismissed it as "an almost infinitesimal part" in a telegram to Mayer after the film opened.[28]

Critics hailed *Goodbye, Mr Chips* as one of the year's best films and many singled out Garson's performance for praise, some noting also the brevity of her role. *Variety* said that she played her sentimental part "with rare understanding and tenderness" and the *New York Herald Tribune* applauded "a performance of enormous sincerity which makes her relatively brief appearance in the film electric and haunting".

M-G-M seized on the strong response to Garson's performance. She was rushed into a co-starring role opposite Robert Taylor in *Remember?*, for which the publicity material referred to her portrayal of 'Mrs Chips'. And her work in *Goodbye, Mr Chips* was pushed for recognition by the Academy in the main rather than supporting category. It was the same strategy the studio had successfully pursued with Tracy and Rainer three years earlier.[29]

When the nominations were announced in February 1940, Garson's name was included on the shortlist for the Best Actress Oscar alongside Bette Davis, Irene Dunne, Greta Garbo and Vivien Leigh. Exactly as M-G-M had hoped, the nomination not only vaulted Garson into the ranks of leading ladies in the minds of the public but it marked her as a talented star on a par with her illustrious fellow nominees. As Troyan commented, "With one picture, Greer was suddenly on an equal footing with Greta Garbo, Metro's only other nominated star."[30]

The surprise inclusion of Garson resulted in the exclusion from Oscar contention that year of performances by two M-G-M leading ladies: Loy in *The Rains Came*, the role Garson had wanted for herself, and Shearer in *The Women*.

As widely expected, the Academy Award for Best Actress that year was won by Vivien Leigh for her portrayal of Scarlett O'Hara in *Gone with the Wind*. Echoing the sentiments of the *Hollywood Citizen-News* about Spencer Tracy's nomination for *San Francisco* three years earlier, the *Chicago Sunday Tribune* declared, "Greer Garson might have won an Oscar except for an error; she was nominated in the star performance division, but she was only a featured player. She might have won in the featured division."[31] Given her anger at being offered secondary parts in the first place, including her role in *Goodbye, Mr Chips*, it would have been inconceivable for the studio to have placed Garson in the

Best Supporting Actress category that year at the Oscars: she would have found it humiliating. And besides, M-G-M was building Garson up to be a major new star, not a featured player and therefore, regardless of her limited screen time and the fact that her role was a supporting part, the studio and the Academy felt she belonged in the top category along with the other movie stars.

> *Alternate Nominee* – If Greer Garson had instead been considered for the Best Supporting Actress category for *Goodbye, Mr Chips*, who might have been in the race for the Best Actress statuette? While some think Norma Shearer would have made the list for *The Women*, nominations for *Mr Smith Goes to Washington* in the Best Picture, Director, and Actor categories strongly suggest the Academy would have recognised Jean Arthur for her performance in that film.

A decade later, Anne Baxter was equally determined to be regarded as a star rather than a featured player and saw a Best Actress nomination as a chance to cement a more prestigious status in Hollywood.

The granddaughter of acclaimed architect Frank Lloyd Wright, Baxter was raised in New York City where she was a student of the legendary acting teacher Maria Ouspenskaya. At seventeen she signed a seven-year studio contract with Twentieth Century-Fox as a featured player and made her screen debut in a loan-out deal to M-G-M in *20 Mule Team*.

Following parts in forgettable films such as *The Great Profile*, *Charley's Aunt* and *Swamp Water*, Baxter was cast in supporting roles in Orson Welles' *The Magnificent Ambersons* in 1942 and Billy Wilder's *Five Graves to Cairo* in 1943. Her appearance in these major productions led to a series of top-billed parts in B-grade movies like *The North Star*, *The Eve of St Mark*, *Sunday Dinner for a Soldier* and *Guest in the House*. Significant supporting roles in two further prestige productions followed when she was cast as Countess Jaschikoff in Otto Preminger's *A Royal Scandal* starring Tallulah Bankhead and as Sophie in Edmund Goulding's *The Razor's Edge* starring Tyrone Power and Gene Tierney.

The role of Sophie in the 1946 adaptation of the W. Somerset Maugham novel gave Baxter a unique opportunity to demonstrate her range. The character is charming and likeable before her life is shattered by a terrible tragedy that results in a self-destructive spiral into alcoholism and renders her pathetic and pitiable. While *The New York Times* complained that she indulged in pathos, *Variety* lauded her for a "personal hit". Baxter earned both the Golden Globe Award and the Academy Award for Best Supporting Actress for her performance.

While an Oscar for her flashy role in *The Razor's Edge*, did not transform Baxter in a major movie star, she nonetheless found herself cast in top tier productions, often as the leading lady opposite a male matinee idol. She was billed above the title for her supporting role in the Clark Gable and Lana Turner vehicle *Homecoming*, appeared as one of the four leads in *The Walls of Jericho* with Cornel Wilde, Linda Darnell and Kirk Douglas, and then co-starred opposite Tyrone Power, Gregory Peck and Dan Dailey in *The Luck of the Irish*, *Yellow Sky* and *You're My Everything*, respectively. Her career as a featured actress was behind her.

Consistent with the status of secondary leading lady which Baxter had enjoyed since her Academy Award win, she was cast in the early months of 1950 in the role of the ambitious understudy Eve Harrington in *All About Eve*. That studio head Darryl F. Zanuck considered the part of Eve to be a lead rather than a supporting role is evident from the fact that he had wanted Jeanne Crain to play the part.[32] Although unknown to the general public today, Crain was a popular, rising star at the time and Zanuck would never have considered placing her in a supporting role. She had been one of the nominees for the Best Actress Academy Award twelve months earlier for her performance in *Pinky* and was one of the three co-leads in the acclaimed *A Letter to Three Wives* at the time that casting decisions for *All About Eve* were being made. Studio archives reveal that other actresses considered for the role by casting directors, either briefly or seriously, included Elizabeth Taylor, June Allyson and Olivia de Havilland.[33] All were established or rising stars and not names that would have been shortlisted for a supporting role.

Officially, Crain dropped out of the production because she was pregnant, a plausible explanation given her third child was born that year. Baxter herself always maintained that she was cast because Crain became pregnant just as production approached.[34] In an interview twenty years later, however, the film's writer-director, Joseph L. Mankiewicz, revealed that he had vetoed Crain's casting because he had been unimpressed when working with her on *A Letter to Three Wives* and felt that she lacked the "bitch virtuosity" required for the role.[35] "I could only rarely escape the feeling that Jeanne was, somehow, a visitor to the set," he told writer Gary Carey. "She worked hard. Too hard at times, I think, in response to my demands, as if trying to compensate by sheer exertion for what I believe must have been an absence of emotional involvement with acting."[36]

With Crain out of the picture, Baxter was cast, partly because she had a physical resemblance to Claudette Colbert, the Academy Award winning star chosen by Zanuck and Mankiewicz to play the role of the insecure theatre legend Margo Channing. "Joe's idea originally was that Anne Baxter as a young girl looked very much like me," Colbert explained many years later. "And that was the point of it – that this young girl had a fixation about the older actress. She looked like her, and she thought she could be better. When Bette did the role, it became a whole different thing."[37]

The decision to cast Bette Davis in the star role when Colbert injured her back filming *Three Came Home* did indeed make *All About Eve* a whole different thing. As film historian Sam Staggs has explained, "Davis was brass; Colbert platinum". With the switch from Colbert to Davis, the character of Margo was transformed from an elegant theatrical queen with hints of Lynn Fontanne into a tough theatrical diva with a resemblance to Tallulah Bankhead.

The screenplay's exploration of an actress coming to terms with getting older was also muted. Mankiewicz later said, "The question of aging would have been emphasized if Claudette had played Margo. Margo can't play her usual roles because she's too old. But, in the eyes of the pubic, Bette Davis was never really young. And so that dimension of the aging actress is somewhat eclipsed with Bette playing Margo Channing."[38]

Also somewhat eclipsed is the character of Eve Harrington. On paper there should be no doubt that Eve Harrington, the title character, is one of two leading roles in *All About Eve*. The film's narrative agency lies almost entirely with Eve: it is her arrival that marks the start of the story; it is her presence in Margo's inner circle that creates tension, disrupts marriages and professional relationships (even entirely displacing characters such as Birdie); it is she who pushes to be made Margo's new understudy; it is she who convinces Karen to ensure Margo misses a performance by tampering with the car; it is she who then blackmails Karen to secure the role in the play within the film 'Footsteps on the Ceiling'; and the story ends when her lies are revealed by Addison DeWitt and she becomes the target of a young student's schemes. It is Eve's ambition and machinations that drive the plot of *All About Eve*.

And Anne Baxter as Eve has about the same amount of screen time as Bette Davis does as Margo and is often the focal point of the film's direction, cinematography and editing. The two women share some sequences in the film and divided others between them. In the long scene in Margo's dressing room shortly after the film's beginning, Margo and Eve are the two main characters that the others revolve around and Mankiewicz ensures that Eve is the centre of the audience's attention as she tells her back story by making her the focus of the other characters' attention with shots of Eve alone on a chair cut with shots of the other four characters assembled like an audience and listening to her speak. In the long cocktail party sequence, Margo is the focus of the scenes in the drawing room and the kitchen while Eve is the centre of the scenes in the upstairs bedroom and the stairway. Similarly, at the restaurant sequence towards the film's end, Margo is the focus at the main table but Eve is the centre of the scene in the ladies' room. And while Eve disappears from the film for nearly half an hour from around the one-hour mark, Margo is almost entirely absent from the last twenty-five minutes of the movie.

Anecdotal evidence, however, suggests that most viewers regard Eve as a supporting character in *All About Eve*. This is mainly because of Davis and her tour de force performance as Margo. She dominates the film and Baxter is simply unable to compete. During Eve's prolonged absence from the screen, the audience is captivated by Davis in the theatre scene with Gary Merrill as Bill Sampson and the scene in the stranded car with Celeste Holm as Karen Richards. In contrast, the absence of Margo is particularly noticeable during the last part of the movie. The audience keeps waiting for her to reappear.

Eve Harrington's ambition and machinations drive the plot of *All About Eve*, which both starts and ends with her rather than with Margo Channing. As written by Mankiewicz and played by Davis, however, it is Margo who is the film's emotional focus. While the plot is about Eve's ambition, the film is really about the insecurities Margo harbours about her career and her love life now that she has turned forty. It is the scene in the stranded car in which Margo opens up to her old friend about her fears and misgivings that remains with audiences. While fans love to quote arch lines from the cocktail party sequence, it is Davis' moving portrayal of Margo's vulnerability in the scene in the car that is the heart of the movie. In essence, Mankiewicz's screenplay is an exploration of the aging star's emotional life and the part of Eve is merely a narrative device. Despite her screen time, Baxter seems like a supporting player as a result. As Staggs has commented, "the part of Eve Harrington seemed less important than the role of Margo Channing. It still does."[39]

Having landed a secondary leading role in a prestigious picture, Baxter was determined to secure an Academy Award nomination in the Best Actress rather than the Best Supporting Actress category. She knew that it was the studios that determined the placement of performers in the two categories with the annual reminder list and that decisions were routinely made on the basis of star status regardless of a performer's billing or the importance of the role. At the time of *All About Eve*, Baxter was on her second seven-year contract at Twentieth Century-Fox and was paid $40,000 for the eight-week production, only slightly more than supporting player Celeste Holm who earned $35,000 and well short of the $130,000 taken home by Bette Davis.[40] Fearful that the studio would baulk at the idea of entering a contract player in the Oscar contest on an equal footing with a Hollywood legend, Baxter relentlessly lobbied Zanuck to be considered in the Best Actress category alongside Davis.[41] It didn't take much to convince the studio boss that a nomination in the lead category would enhance the value of his contract player and he owed nothing to Davis and felt no need to protect her Oscar chances. "I was not under contract to Fox. Miss Baxter was," Davis explained to Johnny Carson during an appearance on the 'Tonight' show in 1986. "The studio got the word out that it was throwing its weight behind their contract player. That's the way they did it in those days."[42] When the nominations were announced in February 1951, Baxter and Davis were named as the first pair of Best Actress nominees from the same film in Oscar history.

"It was Anne Baxter's fault that Bette didn't win the Oscar," says Staggs in his book 'All About "All About Eve"'. "If Anne hadn't insisted on running against Bette for Best Actress, Baxter herself might well have gotten the Academy Award as Best Supporting Actress, and Bette might have won another Oscar, her third, for her performance as Margo Channing."[43] This has now become one of the core stories in popular Oscar lore and is referenced in most discussions of female co-stars in contention for an Academy Award. In a recent article about Oscar campaigns, Tom O'Neil commented "Davis was the sympathetic center of *All About Eve*. Baxter was the bad-girl spoiler both on screen and off. Had Baxter moved down to supporting, she wouldn't have drawn away *Eve* votes and Davis might've triumphed, deservedly, for one of her greatest performances."[44]

The same view has been expressed repeatedly for years. In the mid-1980s, Emanuel Levy argued in 'And the Winner Is', "Baxter persuaded Twentieth Century-Fox to back her nomination for the lead award in *All About Eve*, thereby running against Bette Davis, who clearly was the film's star and had the major role. Had Baxter been nominated for a featured role, as many believed she should have, Davis would have won Best Actress and she a second, supporting award. Baxter had already earned a supporting Oscar in 1946 for *The Razor's Edge*, which was precisely her reason to compete for the Best Actress Oscar."[45]

Given the film won the Academy Awards for Best Picture, Best Director and Best Supporting Actor, categories in which it had only a single nomination, but failed to take home either the Best Actress or Best Supporting Actress statuettes, categories in which it had two nominees, the received wisdom is that the *All About Eve* vote was split resulting in nominees in other films claiming the gold. "Bette lost *because* Annie was nominated. Annie lost *because* Bette Davis ditto," Mankiewicz later said. "Celeste Holm lost because Thelma Ritter was nominated, and *she* lost *because* Celeste ditto."[46]

It is impossible to know what would have happened had Baxter been included among the Best Supporting Actress nominees (either alongside Holm and Ritter or at the expense of one of them) rather than in the Best Actress category. Many argue that Davis would not have won the Oscar anyway because she had become an unpopular figure with many in Hollywood because of her diva behaviour on set and her infamous feuds with co-stars and directors. [47] And others argue that it was actually the nominations of Hollywood legends Bette Davis and Gloria Swanson in comeback roles as aging thespians in the dramas *All About Eve* and *Sunset Blvd.* that resulted in young newcomer Judy Holliday winning the statuette for her comedic turn in *Born Yesterday*. The inclusion of Baxter on the ballot, it is suggested, made no difference at all.

Despite the nomination, Baxter never became a major film star. She was cast as the female lead opposite Cary Grant in *People Will Talk*, Joseph L. Mankiewicz's follow up to *All About Eve*, but had to withdraw from the production when she became pregnant with her first child. Ironically, she was replaced by Jeanne Crain. Twenty years later she took over the role of Margo Channing from Lauren Bacall in the Broadway production of 'Applause', a musical adaptation of *All About Eve*, and played the part for a year.

In an interview in the early 1980s, Baxter remarked, "I've decided recently that I was wrong. I *should* have accepted another supporting Oscar and then Bette would have undoubtedly gotten hers."[48]

Alternate Nominee – If Anne Baxter had instead been considered for the Best Supporting Actress category for *All About Eve*, who might have been in the race for the Best Actress statuette? The Academy would most likely have nominated the popular Betty Hutton for the hit musical *Annie Get Your Gun* for which she was a Golden Globe Award nominee.

From the mid-1930s to the mid-1940s, Rosalind Russell was a leading lady and movie star. She was popular with both critics and the public, enjoying success in both comedies such as *The Women, His Girl Friday* and *My Sister Eileen* (for which she earned her first Best Actress Oscar nomination) and dramatic pictures such as *Craig's Wife, The Citadel* and *Sister Kenny* (for which she received her second Best Actress Oscar nomination). In 1947, Russell was the strong favourite to take home the Academy's statuette for her work in *Mourning Becomes Electra*, an adaptation of the Eugene O'Neill play. But in one of the greatest surprise upsets in Oscar history she lost to rank outsider Loretta Young. Russell was forty-years-old at the time, the age that Margo Channing would bemoan in *All About Eve* just a couple of years later. She soon discovered that Hollywood had few worthwhile roles for middle-aged women and so turned to the theatre, appearing in the touring production of 'Bell, Book and Candle'.

In her autobiography, Russell stated that the success of the 'Bell, Book and Candle' tour gave her the courage to pursue a second career on Broadway, but that she nonetheless had grave reservations when she was offered the lead role in 'Wonderful Town', a musical version of one of her earlier film successes, *My Sister Eileen*.[49] Although she had no experience as a singer, she decided to take the role after speaking late one night with theatre director Joshua Logan, the husband of one of her closest friends.[50] 'Wonderful Town' was a hit, running on Broadway for over five hundred performances during an eighteen month run. It won five Tony Awards, including Best Musical and Best Actress in a Musical for Russell, who played the role of Ruth Sherwood for nearly a year.

Russell's late night confidant, Joshua Logan, also won a Tony Award that same season, taking home the Best Director prize for 'Picnic', a new play by William Inge. The play lost the Tony Award for Best Play to Arthur Miller's 'The Crucible', but garnered Inge the Pulitzer Prize

When Columbia tackled a film adaptation of 'Picnic' two years later, movie stars William Holden and Kim Novak took over the lead roles from Ralph

Meeker and Janice Rule, but studio boss Harry Cohn hired Logan to direct, hoping that he'd have the same success with the material that he'd enjoyed on Broadway. Surprisingly, Logan chose to retain only three supporting players from the original cast. Among those who he decided to replace was Eileen Heckart who had originated the role of Rosemary Sydney, the aging schoolteacher desperate to secure a husband before the end of another summer break and the start of the new school year.

Logan wanted his wife's friend for the part but feared that she would baulk at a supporting role after so many years as a movie star. But Russell jumped at the opportunity. "Josh Logan, who was directing, came to me," she later wrote in her autobiography, "and said 'Would you like to do *Pic-*' and I said 'Yes' so fast he never got the *nic* out."[51]

Heckart had won a Theatre World Award for her performance and Russell knew that "the frustrated schoolteacher [was] an awfully good part."[52] Over twenty years later she explained, "Producers think in limited terms, and they almost always saw me as a sophisticated Park Avenue creature. That was why I leaped to do *Picnic* ... why I inclined toward character acting, where you could get a hold of something."[53] Russell was apparently so excited about playing the role she told Logan not to hide her wrinkles but rather let her "look like a real leathery Kansas dame."[54]

Despite her excitement about the role, biographer Bernard F. Dick argues "there was no doubt, even in Rosalind's mind, that Rosemary was not the female lead."[55] She did regard her role as a significant one, however. Later she claimed that it was more substantial in the shooting script than in the final edit. "A lot of the schoolteacher's stuff was cut out of *Picnic*. It made me unhappy, but I understood the reasons. The studio was introducing Kim Novak, they thought they had a big star, they wanted to protect her. And because Bill Inge knew and wrote her so well, Rosemary is sneaky, she can take over."[56]

The screenplay by Daniel Taradash, however, retains the character's subplot with minimal changes. And all of Rosemary's memorable lines and significant business from the stage play are included in the film. There is no evidence that the part of Rosemary was diminished in either the adaptation of the play or in the editing of the film. Russell's recollection is most likely a face-saving myth to gloss over a former movie star's embarrassment at appearing in supporting role, albeit a significant and flashy character part.

Buoyed by her recent success on Broadway in 'Wonderful Town', including a prestigious Best Actress Tony Award, Russell was certainly not going to allow her star status to be tarnished in the film's billing. Unable to justify star billing with William Holden and Kim Novak (whose names appear alone before and immediately after the title, respectively), her agent arranged for her to be listed after the supporting players with the credit "and co-starring Rosalind Russell as Rosemary, the school teacher".

When the film was screened for critics in December 1955, Russell received the best reviews among the cast. "Although Rosalind Russell's delineation of the school teacher is uneven," wrote *The New York Times*, "it is powerful and genuinely moving." *Variety* commented, "Russell is a standout, moving in her plea for marriage, amusing as she pretends indifference to men and pitiable in her whiskey-inspired outburst against Holden." And *The Hollywood Reporter* stated, "Roz is hilariously funny, touchingly pathetic and, in her drunk scene, as horrifyingly menacing as a Greek Harpy, in her portrayal of this desperate woman who fears that life is passing her by."

Cohn wanted to mount an Oscar campaign for Russell in the Best Supporting Actress category, but she refused to co-operate. "Now, hold on a minute, Harry," the actress is reputed to have told the studio head of Columbia. "I've been a star for a good many years and I don't intend to change to a supporting actress now simply in hopes of winning an Oscar."[57] Consistent with the tradition of the previous two decades, Russell regarded herself as a star and leading lady who belonged in the Best Actress category regardless of the size of the role she was playing. To be included in the Best Supporting Actress, even though hers was a supporting role, would have been both inappropriate and a loss of status. She declined to permit Columbia to include her name on that year's studio reminder list.

Her biographer regarded the decision as "a mistake" and argues that "Rosalind probably would have received a supporting actress nomination if she had agreed" to Cohn's campaign "if for no other reason than for being gracious enough to take on a supporting role in a movie after conquering Broadway and making the cover of *Time* magazine."[58]

It is likely, however, that Russell never regretted her decision to maintain the veneer of studio stardom by insisting on co-star billing in *Picnic* and refusing consideration for the Best Supporting Actress Oscar. Within three years she was enjoying one of the biggest successes of her career as the titular character in the Broadway production of 'Auntie Mame' and the subsequent Hollywood film adaptation. Her portrayals earned her Tony and Academy Award nominations as Best Actress. And she was a leading lady and star again in 1962 when she played Rose opposite Natalie Wood in the major Hollywood production of the musical *Gypsy*.

While Columbia didn't attempt to secure a Best Actress for Rosalind Russell for her supporting role in *Picnic* in the way that M-G-M had for Greer Garson in *Goodbye, Mr Chips* or Twentieth Century-Fox had for Anne Baxter in *All About Eve*, Russell's refusal to allow her name to be put into consideration for the supporting actress statuette demonstrated the enduring view across Hollywood that, regardless of a player's billing or the significance of their role in terms of screen time or narrative importance, stars belonged in the main categories at the Oscars and the secondary awards were for contract and featured players.

Rosalind Russell was not alone in harbouring concerns about the impact a nomination in the supporting categories at the Oscars might have on the career of an ageing movie star. The fear that such a nomination would signal to Hollywood that a career as a leading performer was over was widespread. Many stars believed that only smaller character parts would be offered following a nomination in a supporting category.

Peter Finch, for example, was furious when his publicist, Michael Maslansky, suggested mounting a campaign for the season's Best Supporting Actor awards for his work as a veteran newsreader whose angry outburst on air garners him a cult following in *Network*. "Absolutely not!" he reportedly screamed at Maslansky, "Howard Beale was not a supporting role." [59] The part had originally been offered to Henry Fonda so the producers evidently considered it to be a part for a 'name' actor rather than a character player.

Many film historians, however, disagree. In *Network*, the third-billed Finch creates "a larger than life satirical caricature figure" who initiates and sustains the plot's central drama, but who is one-note and secondary to the film's two protagonists played by William Holden and Faye Dunaway. [60] As critic and historian Danny Peary commented, "Finch's role is a supporting one – he turns up every twenty minutes or so to rant and rave on television and then he disappears. William Holden, as Beale's best friend, is *Network*'s leading man and a much more legitimate candidate for Best Actor." [61]

Like so many of his contemporaries in the 1970s, Finch was cynical about awards for acting but was acutely aware of their practical significance for an actor's career, especially as they got older. "I hate the politics of the whole thing, but the nomination is a big help," he once said. "I'm not even sure that winning is that important, but a nomination lets people know you're there."[62] At sixty-years-old, Finch was keen to secure a second Best Actor Oscar nomination for *Network*, which he considered his best work. He wanted to remind the industry that he was still "there". As biographer Trader Faulkner explained, Finch "did realise [the Oscar's] importance and value for future choice of films and salary bargaining ... he felt he'd rather go for the top award or be out of the competition altogether."[63]

Furthermore, Finch wanted a nomination in the Best Actor category in order to reconfirm his status as a leading man. He had been a star of British cinema for the previous twenty years and collected a record four British Academy Awards as Best British Actor for leading roles in *A Town Like Alice*, *The Trials of Oscar Wilde*, *No Love for Johnnie* and *Sunday, Bloody Sunday* (the drama for which he'd earned his only previous Oscar nomination), as well as further nominations for *Windom's Way* and the Hollywood production *The Nun's Story*. His work on *Network* brought him an unprecedented fifth British Academy Award. He was so worried that a nomination as Best Supporting Actor would result in offers only for character parts for the remainder of his career that he made it very clear to Maslansky that he'd prefer to have no nomination than a supporting nod.

Finch also retained the traditional view that the lead category was for film stars, regardless of the size of their role, and the supporting categories were for featured players and character actors. As a star, he believed he belonged in the Best Actor category while "the lesser Oscar categories ... could be left to *Network*'s fine supporting actors: Robert Duvall, Ned Beatty and Beatrice Straight."[64]

The aversion to supporting categories felt by stars had begun to soften following Ingrid Bergman's victory as Best Supporting Actress for *Murder on the Orient Express* two years earlier, but the view of the supporting prizes as secondary and of lesser value endured, as comments by Bette Davis made evident. "I'm not proud – a supporting Oscar would be fine," she told friends. "Ingrid won two Best Actress Oscars and then that one, and two and a half would be gratefully received in my case, too."[65] Peter Finch, however, was not interested in 'a half Oscar'.

In the two months following *Network*'s November 1976 release, Finch gave hundreds of television and print media interviews as he promoted the film and campaigned for Best Actor accolades. "Peter wanted to win that Oscar," Maslansky later said. "It was an obsession with him."[66]

During that period, however, momentum was building behind other contenders. The Los Angeles and New York Film Critics groups and the National Society of Film Critics all gave their Best Actor awards to Robert De Niro for his portrayal of a sociopath in Martin Scorsese's *Taxi Driver*, while the National Board of Review named David Carradine as folksinger Woodie Guthrie in *Bound for Glory*. Carradine had been the runner-up for the prize in New York and Finch's co-star in *Network*, William Holden, had placed third. Some critics felt Finch was "miscast"[67] and not as strong as Holden.

The dynamics of the season changed dramatically, however, when Finch died of a heart attack in mid-January. Two weeks later, he was declared the winner of the Golden Globe for Best Actor in a Motion Picture (Drama) and the Academy Award and British Academy Award soon followed. Peter Finch was the first posthumous winner in the acting categories in Oscar history.

Alternate Winner – If Peter Finch had instead been considered for the Best Supporting Actor category for *Network*, who might have won the Oscar as Best Actor of 1976? Robert De Niro was the overwhelming choice of the major critics groups for his performance in *Taxi Driver*, but perhaps because he had won a statuette only two years earlier, the favourite heading into the ceremony that year was Sylvester Stallone for *Rocky*, the eventual Best Picture winner, and he is most likely to have taken home the Academy Award.

Alternate Nominee – If Peter Finch had instead been considered for the Best Supporting Actor category for *Network*, who might have been in the race for the Best Actor statuette? It's plausible to think that either Dustin Hoffman or Robert Redford would have made the list for *All the President's Men*, one of the year's Best Picture nominees, but perhaps the Academy would have included David Carradine, a Golden Globe nominee and winner of the National Board of Review prize for his performance in *Bound for Glory*, another of that year's Best Picture Oscar contenders.

When *The Silence of the Lambs* opened in North American cinemas on Valentine's Day in 1991, it captured the public's imagination and stormed to the top of the box office. *People* magazine reported, "Not since 1960, when Janet Leigh turned on the shower in *Psycho*, has a film quite touched off the seismic tremors of terror which have accompanied *The Silence of the Lambs*. Hannibal Lecter has become the Norman Bates of the '90s, and moviegoers are flocking to see him."

Key to the film's success was indeed the performance by Anthony Hopkins as Dr Hannibal Lecter, an imprisoned serial killer. *Variety* said he "makes the role the personification of brilliant, hypnotic evil, and the screen jolts with electricity whenever he is on" and the *New York Post* declared, "Hopkins will just blow you away with the quiet energy in his portrayal." The *Los Angeles Times* concluded that with an "insinuating performance ... he very nearly owns the film."

Just six weeks after the film's release, Hopkins and co-star Jodie Foster attended the Academy Awards ceremony where they were the co-presenters of the screenplay awards. On the red carpet, a local television interviewer told Hopkins, "This is your rehearsal for next year" as the crowds cheered. "If you say so," the actor replied.[68] A short time later, with everyone seated inside the Shrine Auditorium, the telecast began with close-ups of some of the assembled celebrities. When the camera picked out Hopkins, the official announcer Les Marchak called him a "sure nominee for next year's Oscars."[69] Following the rapturous applause Hopkins and Foster were accorded upon appearing onstage to hand out the screenplay statuettes, "backstage scuttlebutt ... marked [Hopkins] down as a longshot for the 1991 supporting award."

Although his portrayal had indelibly touched the collective psyche and won acclaim from critics, historian Anthony Holden argued that Hopkins' chances of Oscar glory were tempered by the film's early release date. "No film in the history of the Academy Awards had lasted more than a year in the notoriously fickle memories of the Oscar electorate," he explained. "This one had been released six weeks before the *previous* year's show ... *The Silence of the Lambs* would be out on video and cable TV well before most of the big 1991 Oscar movies had even opened."[70] That the film remained strongly in contention for the various film prizes at the end of the year was, in Holden's view, "thanks especially to the dark, dream-invading stillness of Hopkins's performance."[71]

On 16 December 1991, the National Board of Review rewarded Hopkins with their Best Supporting Actor prize for his role in *The Silence of the Lambs*. A day later, the performance garnered him the Best Actor award from the New York Film Critics Circle.

Hopkins appears on screen for just sixteen minutes in *The Silence of the Lambs* and, apart from the brief telephone scene which is the film's denouement, he is absent from the last quarter of the film's two hour running time. He nonetheless steals the film. It was Hannibal Lecter that lingered in viewers' minds and haunted them long after they had left the cinema. As Holden commented, Hopkins had "created a classic movie monster to rival Perkins' Norman Bates in the collective film-going consciousness."[72]

Following the result in New York, Hopkins insisted the film's distributors promote him for the lead category. Like Finch fifteen years earlier, Hopkins was a respected leading man in the theatre and appreciated how inclusion in the Best Actor field could give him access to better roles and allow him to command higher salaries. Although many felt it would have "been smarter to go for the Supporting category, where the competition looked so much weaker", Orion acquiesced.[73] The decision was met with "some controversy",[74] but when the nominations for the Golden Globes and the Oscars were announced, Hopkins was indeed shortlisted for the Best Actor awards.

While most leading commentators predicted that Nick Nolte would win the Oscar for *The Prince of Tides*, on the big night it was Hopkins who triumphed.[75] There was a roar of approval from the press gathered backstage and the audience gave him a standing ovation which historian Danny Peary has said "indicated that his election was a runaway".[76]

Over two decades later, many still consider the selection of Hopkins as Best Actor that year as a "debatable lead win"[77] because of how little he actually appears during the film. Others, however, point out that "screen time isn't the only metric."[78] David Sims, an editor on *The Atlantic*, argued "Hopkins barely appears in *The Silence of the Lambs*, but his Lead Actor win in 1991 was hailed as well-deserved because his Hannibal Lecter so dominated the movie". Lecter looms much larger in *The Silence of the Lambs* than his screen time would suggest because Hopkins makes him compelling (and because director Jonathon Demme shoots the character in unsettlingly intense close-ups).

Another important way to measure whether a performance should be promoted for the lead or supporting film awards, however, is the relation of the role to the film's main plotline. Is it central or peripheral to the principal action? When considering the movie's plot, Dr Hannibal Lecter is clearly an ancillary character. "Some would argue that Hopkins' Hannibal Lecter is a focal point of the film, but that's a tenuous position to hold as the film really is about Clarice Starling and her attempts to catch Buffalo Bill," blogger Steve Katz recently wrote. "Certainly the Lead Actor statue is more prestigious than Supporting … [but] the role is pretty clearly designed for the Supporting category."[79] While Lecter's knowledge assists trainee FBI agent Clarice Starling solve her case, the mind-games he plays with her are an aside. The film is centred on Starling and her investigation. When the plot reaches its climax, Lecter is completely absent from the film (having escaped his imprisonment). *The Silence of the Lambs* is about Starling and her investigation. As terrifying and unforgettable as he is, Lecter is neither the protagonist nor the antagonist. Hopkins' "role was much smaller and obviously in support of best-actress winner Jodie Foster," concluded Richard Natale in the *Chicago Tribune*.[80]

While the dominance of his unforgettable characterisation was the justification for including Hopkins in the lead category, the motivation, as it had been with Finch in 1976, was the actor's own ambition. Hopkins himself pressed Orion to elevate him into the Best Actor stakes in order to reaffirm (or in some ways reclaim) his leading man status. It was Laurence Olivier who singled out Hopkins early in his theatrical career as a performer of "obviously exceptional promise", selecting him to be his understudy at the Royal National Theatre in London in the late 1960s.[81] In the two decades that followed he was lauded as the successor to Richard Burton as British theatre's leading actor and appeared in starring roles both on Broadway in Peter Shaffer's 'Equus' and in the West End in David Hare and Howard Brenton's 'Pravda' and opposite Judi Dench in 'Anthony and Cleopatra'.

Hopkins, however, found the repetition of theatrical performing to be tiring and preferred film and television work. He had several leading roles in films such as *The Elephant Man*, *The Bounty* and *84 Charing Cross Road* but was unable to achieve the film success that he had hoped for. At the end of the 1980s he returned to London, having all but given up on a career as a Hollywood movie star. "Well that part of my life's over; it's a chapter closed," he said at the time. "I suppose I'll just have to settle for being a respectable actor poncing around the West End and doing respectable BBC work for the rest of my life."[82]

The phenomenal success of *The Silence of the Lambs* and the reaction to his performance as Hannibal Lecter in particular, suddenly presented Hopkins with the opportunity to attain the height of film stardom that he coveted. Like Anne Baxter and Peter Finch before him, he insisted on a campaign for the lead prize at the Academy Awards because of the enhanced prestige and because he was determined to be counted among the leading men rather than the character actors. In the wake of *The Silence of the Lambs* he wanted to be a leading man in movies, not play supporting parts. Inclusion in the Best Actor category at the Oscars was the ideal way to position himself in the eyes of Hollywood for the kinds of roles he coveted.

His ploy succeeded. In the half dozen years that followed his win at the Academy Awards, Hopkins enjoyed leading roles in major productions on both sides of the Atlantic, including *The Remains of the Day*, *Shadowlands* and *Nixon*. Had he been recognised in the supporting category for *The Silence of the Lambs*, perhaps his career would have featured only supporting roles like those he played in *Bram Stoker's Dracula*, *Howards End*, *Legends of the Fall* and *Amistad*.

Alternate Winner – If Anthony Hopkins had instead been considered for the Best Supporting Actor category for *The Silence of the Lambs*, who might have won the Oscar as Best Actor of 1991? Ahead of the ceremony, most experts were predicting that Golden Globe winner Nick Nolte would receive the Academy Award for *The Prince of Tides* and it is hard to imagine any other outcome.

Alternate Nominee – If Anthony Hopkins had instead been considered for the Best Supporting Actor category for *The Silence of the Lambs*, who might have been in the race for the Best Actor statuette? A strong campaign had been mounted for Harrison Ford in *Regarding Henry* and National Society of Film Critics prize winner River Phoenix had been lauded for his work in *My Own Private Idaho*, but given the film's nominations for Best Picture and Director, it's most likely the Academy would have shortlisted Golden Globe nominee Kevin Costner for a second year in a row for his performance in *J.F.K.*.

The argument that Anthony Hopkins merited inclusion in the Best Actor category because he created an iconic character and was a commanding presence throughout *The Silence of the Lambs* despite his limited screen time, was reminiscent of the reasons many used to justify the inclusion of Marlon Brando in the Best Actor category twenty years earlier for his performance in *The Godfather.*

As Don Vito Corleone, the ageing head of an organized crime family, Brando dominates the first forty-five minutes of Francis Ford Coppola's masterpiece. During the long opening sequences concerning the wedding of his daughter and the scenes that follow, Don Vito is the main focus of the narrative and Brando's performance commands the viewer's attention. All events and characters revolve around him.

But *The Godfather* is not about Don Vito Corleone. Forty-five minutes into the film, Brando's character is gunned down in the street by a drug baron's henchmen and it is more than an hour before he has any further dialogue. Even in the last third of the film, Brando appears in only a handful of scenes. By then his character is no longer the driving force of either the Corleone family or the film's plot. By that stage *The Godfather* has become the story of how young Michael Corleone reluctantly takes over as the head of the family and assumes the bloody mantle of a ruthless godfather. Half an hour before the film's end credits roll, Don Vito Corleone is dead and Brando vanishes from the screen. As biographer Peter Cowie has noted, it is Michael Corleone, played by Al Pacino, who "steadily envelops" *The Godfather.*[83]

By the end of 1972, *The Godfather* had become a massive box office success and was poised to add numerous accolades to the widespread acclaim bestowed on it by film critics. Eyeing a major Oscar haul, Paramount decided to campaign for Brando to be rewarded in the Best Actor category. The decision "really doesn't hold up to scrutiny," argues film blogger Joe Reid. "Don Corleone gets some memorable lines, but he's bedridden and absent for one huge chunk of the movie and dead for another."[84] But the decision was "understandable" says Reid because "Marlon Brando was the huge movie star at the time" while Pacino, who played "the film's true lead", was just "a young upstart" from Broadway with limited screen credits. The studio believed Brando belonged in the main category at the Oscars because he was an established movie star.

In order to secure the part of Don Vito Corleone in *The Godfather*, Brando was required to submit to a screen test because he hadn't appeared in a commercially successful release in over a decade and had earned a reputation as "notoriously difficult to work with". Although Brando was the first choice of both Coppola and Mario Puzo, the writer of the best-selling novel upon which the movie was based, Paramount executives preferred Laurence Olivier,

Gregory Peck or Ernest Borgnine for the role. Frank Sinatra had also publically expressed interest in the part. Resistance to the casting of Brando was so strident at one stage that Stanley Jaffe, president of Paramount, declared categorically at a meeting of executives that Brando would definitely not be appearing in the film.[85]

However, the series of hit films Brando had made in the 1950s, many of them classics of American cinema, had secured him an enduring place in the top ranks of Hollywood stars. An icon of the method approach to acting, his 1950s performances had garnered him a Best Actor Oscar and a further four nominations (Brando remains the only male actor to have been in contention for the Academy Award in the lead category over four consecutive years). Despite a decade of box office flops, Brando was still regarded as a great actor and the principal marquee attraction for a prestige production like *The Godfather*. Soon after Jaffe resigned from Paramount, Coppola got his man. Brando received top billing in the film's credits and became the centre of the film's publicity campaign.

When the film was released in March, Brando's performance was acclaimed as a brilliant comeback and one of the greatest of his illustrious career. *Variety*, for example, proclaimed that he was "truly remarkable" in a "tour de force". Interestingly, several prominent critics also chose to comment on the size of his role. In *The New York Times* film reviewer Vincent Canby wrote "It's not a large role, but he is the key to the film". Meanwhile in her essay 'Alchemy' in *The New Yorker*, critic Pauline Kael praised a "marvellous" performance but concluded, "Brando isn't the whole show".[86]

Over the intervening years, the view of Brando's performance as iconic but secondary has become commonplace. While Brando "doesn't exactly embody the screen time aspect that most follow" when determining whether someone has a lead or supporting role, writes commentator Clayton Davis, he "is an undeniable presence throughout Francis Ford Coppola's masterpiece."[87]

It was the screen presence of a major star that saw voters overlook a lack of screen time and an absence from the main narrative arc of the film when rewarding Brando with the Golden Globe Award for Best Actor in a Motion Picture (Drama) and then his second Academy Award for Best Actor. As Kael noted "Brando doesn't dominate the movie, yet he gives the story the legendary presence needed to raise it above gang warfare to archetypal tribal warfare".[88]

Ironically, Brando refused to accept either prize.

Alternate Winner – If Marlon Brando had instead been considered for the Best Supporting Actor category for *The Godfather*, who might have won the Oscar as Best Actor of 1972? Of the other nominees, the New York Film Critics' Beat Actor Award winner Laurence Olivier seems the most likely for *Sleuth*, but it is quite possible that the Academy would have chosen Al Pacino for *The Godfather* as he would certainly have been on the ballot had Brando been a Best Supporting Actor nominee instead.

Alternate Nominee – If Marlon Brando had instead been considered for the Best Supporting Actor category for *The Godfather*, who might have been in the race for the Best Actor statuette? Almost certainly Al Pacino would have been nominated in the lead category for *The Godfather* instead of being shortlisted for the Best Supporting Actor prize. At the Golden Globes, Pacino had been nominated alongside Brando on the Best Actor (Drama) and he was the National Society of Film Critics choice as Best Actor.

At the Cocoanut Grove in Los Angeles on 11 March 1964, Margaret Rutherford won the Golden Globe Award for Best Supporting Actress in a Motion Picture for her performance in *The V.I.P.s*. Among the seven other nominees was Patricia Neal for her portrayal of the housekeeper in *Hud*. The Hollywood Foreign Press Association had placed Neal in the supporting category despite both the National Board of Review and the New York Film Critics' Circle naming her Best Actress earlier in the awards season for the same performance. Two weeks prior to the Golden Globe Awards ceremony, the Academy named Neal among the contenders for the Best Actress Oscar.

And Neal wasn't the only actress nominated in the Best Actress category by the Academy that year for a performance in a supporting part. Also included on the ballot was Rachel Roberts for her role as the widowed landlady in the drama *This Sporting Life*. Roberts had been one of the eight nominees for the Best Actress in a Motion Picture (Drama) at the Golden Globes.

Neal and Roberts have the only significant female role in their respective films. Both play women in a domestic environment dominated by a sexually aggressive man: Paul Newman as the disaffected rancher's son in *Hud* and Richard Harris as the ambitious rugby player in *This Sporting Life*. Both women are victimised and the threat of alcohol-fuelled violence overshadows their lives. In both films, the characters played by Neal and Roberts are excluded from the principal plot (the impact of disease on an isolated ranch's stock in *Hud* and a miner's struggle to earn a professional rugby contract in *This Sporting Life*) and are subjects in scenes that explore the inner turmoil of the protagonists played by Newman and Harris. Consequently, both actresses are absent from long sequences and their characters have neither a plot line of their own nor significant development. Apart from a wordless twenty-second scene in a cemetery early in *This Sporting Life*, Roberts' character never appears without sharing the screen with Harris. As a result, both Neal and Roberts have limited screen time. Roberts is in approximately one-third of *This Sporting Life*, appearing in forty-seven minutes of the movie's two hours and eight minutes. Neal, meanwhile, is in less than a quarter of *Hud* and features in only twenty-six of the film's one hour and forty-seven minutes duration.

When *This Sporting Life* was made, Roberts was thirty-five-years-old, the wife of the respected actor and film star Rex Harrison, and one of Britain's leading actresses. Trained at the Royal Academy of Dramatic Art, she had won acclaim both on stage and in film, taking home the 1960 British Academy Award as Best British Actress for her performance as the married woman having an affair with a young factory worker in *Saturday Night and Sunday Morning*. In the credits of *This Sporting Life* she is billed separately after the title (only Harris is listed before the title) ahead of the rest of the supporting cast who are credited in groups.

Paul Newman receives star billing above the title in the opening credits of *Hud*. The first to be listed after the title is Melvyn Douglas, winner of the Academy Award for Best Supporting Actor for his performance as the old rancher. Neal is credited third, after Douglas. Thirty-six-years-old when *Hud* was filmed, Neal was already a Hollywood veteran making a comeback. She had been a leading lady in the early 1950s but her career had been interrupted by a nervous breakdown. She enjoyed a series of triumphs on Broadway as the leading lady in prestigious plays, most notably, in 'The Miracle Worker' in 1959, which perhaps accounts for the decision of the New York Film Critics to vote for her in the leading actress category rather than the supporting actress category for *Hud*. "Miss Neal's triumph in a small role was as unusual as Mr Finney's victory in a comedy," commented critic Bosley Crowther in *The New York Times* when the results of the balloting became known.[89]

A fortnight before the Academy Awards ceremony, Neal and Roberts both won British Academy Awards in the lead performance categories. A fixture in the British culture scene at the time as a result of her marriage to British novelist Roald Dahl, with whom she resided in Buckinghamshire, Neal was named Best Foreign Actress for *Hud*. The status of Roberts as one of Britain's leading thespians was underscored when she collected her second Best British Actress prize in four years for *This Sporting Life*.

As would be the case with Brando nearly a decade later, it was their status as lead actresses that saw Neal and Roberts considered for prizes in the leading rather the supporting category. Both women played supporting parts in terms of screen time, narrative importance and character development. That Neal was understood to be a supporting player in *Hud* was underscored by her placement in the credits below the title and after Melvyn Douglas. Both women were nominated in the lead category, however, because of their professional standing at the time. While not top-rank movie stars, they were lead actresses with a high level of name recognition with the public and marquee value, especially in the theatre.

On Oscar night, Neal emulated Luise Rainer's victory a quarter of a century earlier and took home the golden statuette.

> *Alternate Winner* – If Patricia Neal had instead been considered for the Best Supporting Actress category for *Hud*, who might have won the Oscar as Best Actress of 1963? Almost certainly, Leslie Caron would have won the Academy Award that year for *The L-Shaped Room*. At the Golden Globe Awards, where Neal was up for the Best Supporting Actress prize (she lost), Caron was the winner of the Best Actress (Drama) trophy.

> *Alternate Nominees* – If Patricia Neal and Rachel Roberts had instead been considered for the Best Supporting Actress category for *Hud* and *This Sporting Life*, who might have been in the race for the Best Actress statuette? Given the film received nine Oscar nominations, including Best Picture and Best Actor, it is hard to imagine that the Academy would not have included previous winner Elizabeth Taylor for *Cleopatra* and are likely to have also nominated Geraldine Page, a Golden Globe nominee that year, for *Toys in the Attic*.

The understanding within Hollywood that the Oscars for Best Actor and Best Actress were for established and rising movie stars regardless of whether they played leading or supporting roles lies behind such nominations as Spencer Tracy for *San Francisco*, Luise Rainer for *The Great Ziegfeld*, Greer Garson for *Goodbye, Mr Chips*, Patricia Neal for *Hud* and Marlon Brando for *The Godfather*.

Anne Baxter and Anthony Hopkins, meanwhile, were encouraged to push for their work in *All About Eve* and *The Silence of the Lambs* to be considered for the main awards by an appreciation of the impact that inclusion in the lead rather than supporting category could have on achieving their ambition to have careers as film stars. Conversely, knowing the significance for movie stars of a certain age of being listed among the nominees for the supporting prizes motivated Rosalind Russell and Peter Finch to steadfastly refuse to have their work in *Picnic* and *Network* be put forward in the secondary categories regardless of their screen time and the relative importance of their character to the plot and narrative arc of their film.

What connects them all is film stardom. They were either established film stars, emerging film stars subject to a studio publicity campaign or were performers who'd previously appeared in leading roles and were determined to leverage Oscar recognition into stardom.

But one case of a supporting performance earning recognition from the Academy in the lead categories was an important departure from all these other examples: an unknown actress with no standing in the industry and no name recognition with the public. Her's was a different form of category fraud: a manipulation of the rules designed to maximise the reward for a particular film with no pretence of the categorisation being an acknowledgement of a film star's status. The campaign to reward Louise Fletcher's supporting performance in *One Flew Over the Cuckoo's Nest* with a Best Actress Oscar was a seminal example of what would become commonplace in Oscar campaigns in the decades that followed: favouring a category on the basis of better chances of success regardless of what was appropriate for the role.

"Do Any of These Actresses Rate an Academy Award?" asked a headline in *The New York Times* on 8 February 1976, just days ahead of the announcement by the Academy of its annual list of Oscar nominees. "There are so few surefire candidates this year that the list may be downright embarrassing," explained Judy Klemesrud in the ensuing article. "Studios and producers have been flailing around trying to come up with somebody, anybody, to push for the award in trade paper ads."[90]

The awards season had kicked off in late December with prizes from the National Board of Review, the National Society of Film Critics and the New York Film Critics Circle. All three groups had given their Best Actress accolade to twenty-year-old newcomer Isabelle Adjani for her portrayal of the tragically love-struck young woman in *L'Histoire d'Adèle H.*, a French-language historical drama directed by François Truffaut. At the meeting of the New York film critics, Adjani outpolled Brazilian-born actress Florinda Bolkan for her work in *Una breve vacanza*, an Italian-language melodrama directed by Vittorio de Sica. Bolkan subsequently received the Best Actress prize from the newly-formed Los Angeles Film Critics Circle.

Klemesrud downplayed the chances of either Adjani or Bolkan taking home the Oscar noting, "Commendable as their performances may have been … their movies are foreign imports – a genre which has not swept away all that many Oscars for Best Actress in past years." Indeed, only once before had a performance in a foreign-language film been rewarded with a Best Actress Academy Award when Sophia Loren had triumphed for *La ciociara*. Tellingly, neither Adjani nor Bolkan had been included among the candidates for the Best Actress in a Motion Picture (Drama) Award at the previous month's Golden Globes.

Molly Haskell, a film critic for the *Village Voice*, explained to Klemesrud, that there just weren't any good women's roles in Hollywood. "You just look at the Best Actress list and your heart sinks," said Haskell. "It really makes you realize the paucity of roles for women. Usually when a year has been miserable for women, there has always been at least one really good contender. But this year, no one stands out."

The film distribution companies quickly recognised that such a weak field of candidates created an opportunity for them to secure prestigious Best Actress nominations for actresses in significant supporting roles. And they were further motivated to pursue such an opportunity by the unusually large number of strong contenders for the Best Supporting Actress prize, which included four from Robert Altman's *Nashville* alone. Paramount pushed Faye Dunaway for her "small part as Robert Redford's love interest" in *Three Days of the Condor*, a role which Klemesrud dismissed as "largely gratuitous", while United Artists promoted Louise Fletcher for her portrayal of the cold, unyielding nurse in *One Flew Over the Cuckoo's Nest*, an independently financed movie that they had picked up for distribution only after it had been completed. Both women were nominated for the Golden Globe (Drama) and when the awards were presented in late January, Fletcher emerged victorious. As a result of "the dearth of Best Actress contenders, Louise Fletcher, who was acclaimed as the wretched Nurse Ratched in *One Flew Over the Cuckoo's Nest* has been elevated from what, in any normal year, would be the supporting actress category, into a leading contender for Best Actress," wrote Klemesrud.

Fletcher had indeed earned strong reviews. Pauline Kael lauded her "masterly performance" in *The New Yorker*, [91] while *Variety* declared her "excellent". Aljean Harmetz in *The New York Times* wrote "It is Louise Fletcher's achievement that her Nurse Ratched is so close to being a human being that she is totally oblivious to the fact that she is a monster." [92] But Fletcher was widely regarded at the time, and over the decades since, as a supporting actress in *One Flew Over the Cuckoo's Nest* because of her limited screen time and the fact that the narrative focus is squarely on the character of Randle Patrick McMurphy, played by Jack Nicholson. At the meeting of the New York Film Critics' Circle, Fletcher finished as the runner-up for the Best Supporting Actress prize for her performance. More recently, film historian John Harkness dismissed Fletcher's role as "actually a supporting performance." [93]

Director Milos Forman offered the role of Nurse Ratched to established leading ladies such as Anne Bancroft, Geraldine Page and Ellen Burstyn, as well as to respected character actresses like Angela Lansbury and Colleen Dewhurst. Apparently, most turned the role down because the character was a grotesque monster and a one-dimensional supporting part. As film historian Emmanuel Levy noted, the "character is not written or played on the same level of realism as her patients; she is more of an abstract symbol of sexual inhibition and repressive authority." [94] When a friend suggested that he consider Shelley Duvall for the role, Forman screened Robert Altman's *Thieves Like Us* and instead found himself fascinated by the performance of Fletcher in a small role. "I was caught by surprise when Louise came on the screen," he later said. "I couldn't take my eyes off her. She had a certain mystery which I thought was very, very important for Nurse Ratched." [95]

While Paramount could justify promoting Faye Dunaway's performance in *Three Days of the Condor* for a Best Actress nomination on the basis that she was an established movie star with two Oscar nominations in the Best Actress category already under her belt for *Bonnie and Clyde* and *Chinatown*, the same could not be said for United Artists' decision to push Fletcher in the lead rather than supporting category for her turn in *One Flew Over the Cuckoo's Nest*. Fletcher's small role in Altman's *Thieves Like Us*, a film produced by her husband, was her only acting job in over a decade. She was essentially an unknown and did not even have an agent when Forman cast her in the role of Nurse Ratched. Her elevation to the lead category was thus a departure from the tradition of recognising supporting performances by established or rising stars, such as Luise Rainer, Greer Garson, Anne Baxter and Patricia Neal, in the main category. With the old-fashioned studio system in the past, Oscar campaigns had become the domain of distributors, producers and individual artists. The campaign for Fletcher as Best Actress rather than Best Supporting Actress was entirely opportunistic given the weakness of the field. It is unlikely that United Artists would have pursued such a strategy for Fletcher if there had been a significant number of acclaimed performances by well-known stars in contention.

When the Academy announced its slate of nominees in mid-February, Fletcher was included on the ballot in the Best Actress category. Isabelle Adjani was also nominated for *L'Histoire d'Adèle H.*, but Faye Dunaway and Florinda Bolkan were both overlooked. The previous year's winner, Ellen Burstyn, attracted further attention to the weakness of the field when she commented on television that Academy members shouldn't vote for Best Actress in protest over the lack of good roles for women. "Later, Ellen and I talked about what she had said," Fletcher revealed to Guy Flatley in *The New York Times*. "She hadn't meant anything personal, but it was personal, and my feelings were hurt ... She hadn't even seen *Cuckoo's Nest* because she felt it would be too painful an experience. I told her that I thought it would have been nicer if she had said what she said in a year when she had been nominated."[96]

Burstyn wasn't the last person to hurt Fletcher's feelings that season. Despite the acclaim for her performance and victories at both the Golden Globes and the Academy Awards, she was unable to escape the persistent complaints that her part really belonged in the Best Supporting Actress category. On Oscar night, when she fronted the media backstage with the golden statuette in her hands, a journalist asked her to comment on the category fraud issue. "That's a terrible question and a terrible way to end the evening," she responded defensively.[97] Decades later, the question still lingers.

> *Alternate Winner* – If Louise Fletcher had instead been considered for the Best Supporting Actress category for *One Flew Over the Cuckoo's Nest*, who might have won the Oscar as Best Actress of 1975? Despite her youth, it's difficult to imagine the Academy overlooking Isabelle Adjani for *L'Histoire d'Adèle H.* for which she had won three of the four major critics prizes as Best Actress that year. She would have been the second woman to win an Oscar for a performance in a foreign language.

> *Alternate Nominee* – If Louise Fletcher had instead been considered for the Best Supporting Actress category for *One Flew Over the Cuckoo's Nest*, who might have been in the race for the Best Actress statuette? The Academy might have embraced a second foreign-language performance and nominated Florinda Bolkan, winner of the Los Angeles Film Critics' prize, for *Una breve vacanza*, but it is more likely that either Karen Black in *Day of the Locust* or Marilyn Hassett in *The Other Side of the Mountain* would have made the list. Both were Golden Globe nominees that year.

When the Academy revised its rules following the double nomination of Barry Fitzgerald in 1944, it made reference to "the General Awards for acting achievement" and to "the Awards for Supporting Players". This made clear the understanding throughout Hollywood that the Best Actor and Best Actress categories were for the recognition of established and rising stars in any role (leading or supporting) as well as for featured players performing leading roles in lesser productions.

Consistent with this view of the intended purpose of the awards, several movie stars have been recognised in the lead categories over the course of the Academy's history despite limited screen time or their character's peripheral relationship to the principal plot. Some were newcomers like Luise Rainer and Greer Garson while others were established headliners such as Marlon Brando. Anne Baxter convinced executives to elevate her into the top category in the hopes of breaking into the ranks of top movie stars, while in the post-studio era actors like Peter Finch and Anthony Hopkins insisted on being promoted for the main prize with a view to transferring their leading man status in theatre and British cinema into new careers in Hollywood. Rosalind Russell refused the chance to compete for the Best Supporting Actress Oscar for much the same reasoning.

Some commentators, such as *Variety* editor Tim Gray, argue that "there's no reason to worry" about the increasingly prevalent practice of producers campaigning for stars in co-lead roles to be recognised in the supporting category because category fraud is "not just a one-way street [and] ... the Oscar ecosystem balances things out."[98] The instances of performers in genuinely supporting roles securing nominations in the lead categories at the Oscars, however, have actually been quite rare: less than a dozen in over eighty years. As blogger Nathaniel Rogers explains, where Gray "goes wrong is in suggesting that it all balances out, citing the meager lot of arguably supporting roles that went lead of which there are very, very few."[99]

As the following chapters illustrate, the number of performances in lead roles that have yielded nominations in the supporting categories at the Oscars massively outnumber the instances covered in this chapter of supporting turns garnering mentions in the lead categories. Like most of the examples covered above, many have actually been consistent with the original vision for the awards: the main prizes for stars in any sized role and for featured players appearing as leads in lesser productions, and the secondary prizes for contract players only.

Far too many, however, have been blatant category fraud in which established movie stars in lead or co-lead roles have been promoted for the supporting category in order to improve their chances of a nomination and/or to improve the chances of an Oscar victory for the film by avoiding an *All About Eve* style double nomination for co-stars of the same gender. These cases are a total departure from both the purpose for which the supporting categories were established and the majority of the Academy's history.

Act Two

Ordinary People

While the prestigious Best Actor and Best Actress Academy Awards were for the famous movie stars, the Oscar statuettes for Best Supporting Actor and Best Supporting Actress were for the ordinary movie folk: the studio's featured players. Only a handful of actors were recognised for their work in supporting roles in the first half dozen years of the Academy Awards and none of them won. The introduction of the two additional prizes, for which winners received plaques rather than statuettes, allowed for contract players to be recognised and was a central part of the Academy's efforts to win the support of Screen Actors Guild members at a time of strained industrial relations in Hollywood.

That the two new awards were for featured and contract players regardless of whether they were appearing in a supporting role in a prestige production or headlining a lesser production, known as a 'programmer', was made abundantly clear at the 1937 Oscar ceremony where the awards for Best Supporting Actor and Best Supporting Actress were presented for the first time. Comedic actor George Jessel introduced the new categories with a speech about the vital importance to the motion picture industry of *supporting players* (as distinct from players in *supporting roles*).

Among the nominees for the Best Supporting Actor prize that year was Stuart Erwin for *Pigskin Parade*, a B-grade musical comedy about a melon farmer who is turned into a college football star by a husband and wife coaching team. A featured player recently signed by Twentieth Century-Fox,

Erwin played the film's central character and was given top billing in the film's credits. The Academy's fifty-strong nominating committee, however, included him on the ballot for the very first Best Supporting Actor Academy Award in the same year that Spencer Tracy and Luise Rainer were put in line for the main accolades for their supporting turns in *San Francisco* and *The Great Ziegfeld*, respectively.

Although he headlined the film and played the main character, Erwin was shortlisted for the new Best Supporting Actor category because he was a *supporting player*. The fact that he was the film's star and played the lead character was irrelevant. It was his secondary status in the studio hierarchy that counted. Over the following seven years, three other featured actors were similarly shortlisted for the Best Supporting Actor award for performances in lead roles on the basis of their status, one of them twice!

> *Alternate Nominee* – If Stuart Erwin had instead been considered for the Best Actor category for *Pigskin Parade*, who might have been in the race for the Best Supporting Actor statuette? Spencer Tracy should have been in contention for his supporting role in *San Francisco* but was included on the Best Actor list. One possible nominee is Oscar Homolka for *Rhodes* and some believe Paul Robeson could have been a contender for *Show Boat* even though no African American performer had been nominated to that date.

Keen to break into feature-length productions after a successful series of low-budget comedy short films, producer Hal Roach found the screwball comedy elements for which he was looking in a 1926 novel called 'The Jovial Ghosts' and secured the rights from author Thorne Smith. The novel was adapted into a script about the ghosts of a wealthy, married couple recently killed in a car accident who endeavour to liberate a friend from his dull and regimented lifestyle as the president of a bank. The production was entitled *Topper*, the surname of the unhappy bank president.

For the trio of starring roles, Roach sought three box office commodities: W.C. Fields as Topper, and Cary Grant and Jean Harlow as the ghosts (they had just appeared together in the box office hit *Suzy*). Although he initially harboured reservations about the film's supernatural aspects, Grant accepted the role. Both Fields and Harlow, however, declined due to ill health. As an alternative to Harlow, Roach cast Constance Bennett, who had been among the highest-paid stars a few years earlier, but he struggled to find a major talent willing to take on the role of the bank president. In the end, the part was given to Roland Young, an English character actor who had briefly been under contract with M-G-M as a featured actor in the early 1930s, but who was working on a freelance basis at the time of his casting in *Topper*. Grant, Bennett and Young were listed in the credits together, above the title.

A sizeable hit with audiences upon its release in July, *Topper* was recognised in two categories by the Academy: Best Sound Recording and Best Supporting Actor for Roland Young. Like Erwin the previous year, Young was included in the supporting category because he was a character actor rather than a movie star. The fact that he played a lead part, arguably the film's principal part, was overlooked.

Young has more screen time than either Grant or Bennett. The ghosts are often invisible because, as they explain to Topper, they don't want to "waste any ectoplasm". Consequently, there are numerous sequences in which Young appears without his co-stars. He is seen talking to nobody, being carried through a hotel lobby by invisible hands, and riding in a car that has nobody at the wheel. Young carries these parts of the film on his own, with Grant and Bennett merely providing dialogue laid over at a later stage.

In addition to being the title character, Topper is also the film's principal protagonist. His life is the centre of the narrative and he is the character to whom the supporting cast relates. Billie Burke as Topper's social-climbing wife, Hedda Hopper as their neighbour and Eugene Palette as the hotel detective all interact with Young rather than Grant and Bennett. Although not on par with Grant and Bennett in terms of fame or salary, Young merited the above the title billing he shares with them because he has the film's main role. His amusing, physical performance is also the heart of the film. As *The New York Times* wrote at the time, Young is "responsible for whatever success ... [the] film enjoys."

The Academy, however, was never going to include a featured player in the Best Actor category, particularly one without a studio contract. M-G-M was the distributor of *Topper*, but the film was made independently, by Roach. The studio had no compelling reason to advance Young in the prestigious Best Actor category ahead of its own stable of leading stars. That year, the studio's focus was on securing the Best Actor statuette for Spencer Tracy for his performance in *Captains Courageous*.

In terms of billing, screen time and plot, Young has a lead role in *Topper*. But without a studio interested in promoting him for commercial interests of its own, and because of his long standing in Hollywood as a featured player, it was on the ballot paper for the Best Supporting Actor award that Young's name appeared in early 1938.

> *Alternate Nominee* – If Roland Young had instead been considered for the Best Actor category for *Topper*, who might have been in the race for the Best Supporting Actor statuette? The most likely candidate is Walter Connelly for *The Good Earth*, a nominee for Best Picture and Director for which Luise Rainer won her second Oscar.

A similar scenario unfolded four years later when another respected character actor took on a leading role in an independently produced comedy.

Following the success of *Topper*, Hal Roach hired several young executives to manage his growing slate of feature film productions. Among them was Frank Ross, the husband of Columbia star Jean Arthur, who had come to Hollywood on a short-term contract with Paramount in the early days of talking pictures after making his mark on the New York high society party circuit as a singer.[1] Although his career as an actor was unsuccessful, Ross developed skills behind the camera and by 1939 he had been promoted to vice-president of Roach Studios with a credit as associate producer on *Of Mice and Men* directed by Lewis Milestone.[2]

That year, his wife appeared in Frank Capra's *Mr Smith Goes to Washington* and consolidated her position as one of Hollywood's top comediennes. After a protracted legal battle with Columbia, Arthur was under a new three-year contract which required her to appear in two pictures for the studio while allowing her the option of making another film elsewhere.[3]

When Columbia cast her in two disappointing productions in 1940, *Too Many Husbands* and *Arizona*, a frustrated Ross decided to make use of the clause in his wife's contract allowing her to appear in a third film away from her studio. As biographer John Oller explained, the mediocrity of the two films "finally led Frank Ross to form an independent production company as a means of getting his wife better roles ... Ross and Broadway writer Norman Krasna decided to collaborate on a social comedy from a story Krasna had developed. Thus was born Frank Ross/Norman Krasna Productions."[4] The company's debut effort was *The Devil and Miss Jones*, a comedy made in partnership with RKO between December 1940 and February 1941 and released two months after principal photography wrapped.

The Devil and Miss Jones is a social comedy with a pro-union message about the richest man in the world, fictional retail tycoon John P. Merrick (the devil of the title), who poses as a shoe salesman in one of his department stores in order to investigate recent industrial relations disturbances among the employees. His harsh views, however, are softened by his encounters with Miss Jones, a kind-hearted sales clerk, and her union organiser boyfriend, and as he subsequently learns about his staff's job insecurity worries and their struggle to survive on inadequate pay.

Arthur played the role of Miss Jones, while the romantic lead was given to Robert Cummings, a young actor who had made an impact the year before in *Three Smart Girls Grow Up*, a Deanna Durbin vehicle. In the film's third lead role, the wealthy retail tycoon, Ross cast veteran character actor Charles Coburn. A respected Broadway actor, Coburn had moved to Hollywood in 1937 following the death of his wife and embarked on a film career aged sixty. Neither Cummings nor Coburn were under studio contract when cast in *The Devil and Miss Jones*.

While Arthur and Cummings took on the young romantic leads, it is Coburn who played the central character in *The Devil and Miss Jones*. The film is set in John P. Merrick's store and most of its characters are his employees. The plot begins with his decision to go undercover in his own store and in character development terms, the film is principally about his gradual reformation into a more compassionate man. Although not accorded above the title billing with Arthur, Coburn shared equal screen time with his famous co-star and played a lead role. As John Oller acknowledged in his biography of Arthur, "the picture really belonged to Coburn".[5]

Upon its release, the film garnered strong reviews for Arthur and Coburn, about whom *Variety* wrote "stands out in a fine characterization", but enjoyed only modest success at the box office making a profit of $117 000. When the Oscar nominations were announced the following February, *The Devil and Miss Jones* was nominated in two categories: Best Writing (Original Screenplay) for Norman Krasna and Best Supporting Actor for Charles Coburn.

The nomination of Coburn in the supporting category was a repeat of Roland Young's nomination for *Topper* four years earlier. He played the central character in an independent comedy and as an actor in a lead role enjoyed screen time equal to that of the top-billed star. But the Academy placed him in the supporting category because he was a renowned character actor rather than an established leading man. Like Young, he was working in Hollywood on a freelance basis and so had no major studio interested in promoting him for a Best Actor nomination in order to make him a more valuable commodity for their future productions.

Coburn lost the Oscar that year to Donald Crisp in *How Green Was My Valley*. Two years later, however, he took home the Best Supporting Actor award for Columbia's *The More the Merrier* in which he again played a millionaire opposite Jean Arthur.

As he had in *The Devil and Miss Jones*, Coburn played a character at the centre of the action in *The More the Merrier* and commands substantial screen time. Based on a short story by Garson Kanin, the plot revolves around Connie Milligan, a prim government employee who reluctantly sublets half of her apartment to Benjamin Dingle, an eccentric millionaire who is advising the government on the housing shortage. The fatherly Dingle decides that Milligan deserves better than her dull bureaucrat fiancé and so sublets half of his part of the apartment to a dashing Air Force Sergeant. While the film follows the unfolding romance between Milligan and the sergeant, it is Dingle who drives the narrative with his gentle manipulation of events. Film historian John Dileo described Dingle as "the catalyst ... [who] confidently pulls the story's strings."[6] Dingle's almost familial relationship with Milligan is given equal focus making *The More the Merrier* a genuine three-handed comedy.

Arthur played Connie Milligan and Joel McCrea took on the romantic lead as the sergeant. Drawing on his successful pairing with Arthur in the independently produced *The Devil and Miss Jones*, Columbia overlooked its own contract artists and cast Charles Coburn as Benjamin Dingle.

Deftly directed by George Stevens, *The More the Merrier* was a hit with both critics and audiences and endures as a classic of the Hollywood war years. *The New York Times* lauded it as "the year's outstanding comedy" while *Variety* called it "a sparkling and effervescing piece of entertainment" and said that Coburn "walks off with the honors". The film received six Academy Award nominations, including nods for Best Picture, Director and Actress. As he had been two years earlier, Coburn was placed in the supporting category despite playing a lead role because he didn't rank equally in the hierarchy of studio-era Hollywood with Arthur or McCrea. They were movie stars and he was merely a featured player. His victory was the only one enjoyed by *The More the Merrier* at Grauman's Chinese Theatre that evening.

Both of Coburn's nominations as Best Supporting Actor in 1941 and 1943 demonstrate the prevailing view in Hollywood during the early years of the Oscars that the lead categories were for film stars regardless of the size of their role while the newer supporting categories were for featured players regardless of the size of their role, their screen time or their billing.

> *Alternate Winner* – If Charles Coburn had instead been considered for the Best Actor category for *The More the Merrier*, who might have won the Oscar as Best Supporting Actor of 1943? The Academy Award would most likely have been presented to the Golden Globe winner Akim Tamiroff for his performance in *For Whom the Bell Tolls*.

> *Alternate Nominee* – If Charles Coburn had instead been considered for the Best Actor category for *The Devil and Miss Jones* and *The More the Merrier*, who might have been in the race for the Best Supporting Actor statuette? In 1941 the Academy would likely have shortlisted either Claude Rains for *Here Comes Mr Jordan* or Peter Lorre for *The Maltese Falcon*. Two years later, the Academy might have nonetheless chosen Charles Coburn, selecting him for *Heaven Can Wait*, while another likely nominee was Erich von Stroheim for *Five Graves to Cairo*.

After reading the script, Gary Cooper declined to appear in *The Westerner* because the film was clearly about Judge Roy Bean, the eccentric saloon-keeper who acted as a self-appointed judge in a remote part of Texas after the Civil War. Producer Samuel Goldwyn had assigned Cooper to play the part of a drifter who opposes the judge's persecution of homesteaders. Cooper was reluctant to play what he considered a secondary role even though he would have top-billing in the credits following the casting of featured actor Walter Brennan in the main part. "It looked like his picture," Cooper later explained. "A cowboy ultimately rode in and exchanged a few shots to the detriment of the judge, but that struck me as being incidental. I couldn't see that it needed Gary Cooper for the part."[7]

Even after the script was revised following assurances that Cooper's part would be expanded, the star refused to appear in the film. "After careful and reasonable consideration," Cooper wrote to Goldwyn, "I regret to advise you that the character, Cole Harden, is still inadequate and unsatisfactory for me."[8] Goldwyn had Cooper under a six-year contract, however, and insisted that the star fulfill his obligations. Eventually, Cooper relented and appeared under protest.

While Cooper was notionally the star of *The Westerner*, the film really belongs to Brennan as Judge Roy Bean. When it was released in October 1940, leading film critic Bosley Crowther declared in *The New York Times*, "Gary Cooper is an exceedingly modest fellow – too modest for his own good, perhaps. For in Samuel Goldwyn's *The Westerner*, which arrived yesterday at the Music Hall, he casually permits the most important role in the picture to be taken away from him and bestowed upon capable Walter Brennan. Too modest for his own good, did we say? Then too modest for the picture's good, too. For this strangely ambiguous situation, which finds Mr. Cooper as the star and Mr. Brennan as the leading player, seems to be the fatal weakness in this frequently fascinating picture." Crowther concluded that attempts to expand Cooper's role had fragmented the plot and created a "confusion in its fundamental purpose" that left the movie with "no core". He nonetheless lauded Brennan for "one of the finest exhibits of acting seen on the screen in some time".

Variety also regarded Brennan as the lead actor in *The Westerner*. "Although Gary Cooper is starred, Walter Brennan commands major attention with a slick characterization of Judge Roy Bean," the trade paper opined. "Supplied with a particularly meaty role, of which he takes fullest advantage, Brennan turns in a socko job that does much to hold together a not too impressive script."

When it came to the listing of performers on the annual Reminder List, however, Goldwyn placed Cooper in contention for Best Actor and promoted Brennan for the Best Supporting Actor prize because Cooper was a movie star and Brennan a featured player, as their billing in the film's opening credits demonstrated. Cooper's name appears alone above the title at the start of *The Westerner*. Brennan, meanwhile, is listed after the title along with contract artists Doris Davenport and Fred Stone, both of whom had supporting roles in the film and whose names appear in the same sized type. The billing ignores Brennan's screen time and his role as the film's antagonist and credits him in accordance with his status as a featured player. The Academy followed suit and nominated Brennan in the Best Supporting Actor category for the third time in five years.

A film extra during the silent era, Brennan became one of Hollywood's most respected and popular featured players during the 1930s and many believe he benefitted greatly from the expansion of the Academy Awards franchise to include the entire membership of the Screen Actors Guild which at the time included thousands of extras. In the first year of the two new supporting acting awards, when Spencer Tracy's acclaimed supporting turn in *San Francisco* had been nominated in the Best Actor category, Brennan triumphed in the Best Supporting Actor stakes as a Swedish lumberjack in *Come and Get It*. He won again two years later for his turn as a crotchety old horse-breeder in *Kentucky*. When he took home a third award for *The Westerner*, nominee Jack Oakie, who had been strongly favoured to win for Charlie Chaplin's *The Great Dictator*, "told friends that Brennan won because the extras always voted for him out of loyalty since he had come from their ranks."[9] He was not the first to reach that conclusion. When Warner Bros. actor John Garfield was defeated by Brennan for the 1938 prize, studio boss Jack Warner had bemoaned, "The extras, again!".[10]

Historians have reinforced Warner's assessment ever since. In his history of the awards, 'Behind the Oscar', Anthony Holden wrote that Chaplin's film was that year's "victim of the perennial aberration of the extras; their block vote ensured the Best Supporting Actor award for one of their own graduates, Walter Brennan."[11] Film critic Tom O'Neil, meanwhile, recently concluded, "[Brennan] owed his third career trophy to the large voting bloc of movie extras, who considered him one of their own."[12]

Despite playing the central character in *The Westerner*, Brennan was credited in line with his standing in the Hollywood community as a featured player and his lead performance was similarly recognised by the Academy in the Best Supporting Actor category. After all, the Academy had established the supporting categories to honour *supporting players* like Brennan and Coburn, regardless of the size of their role.

> *Alternate Winner* – If Walter Brennan had instead been considered for the Best Actor category for *The Westerner*, who might have won the Oscar as Best Supporting Actor of 1940? The frontrunner leading into the ceremony was thought to be Jack Oakie for *The*

Great Dictator and he should be regarded as the most likely to have collected the statuette.

Alternate Nominee – If Walter Brennan had instead been considered for the Best Actor category for *The Westerner*, who might have been in the race for the Best Supporting Actor statuette? George Sanders could well have been a nominee for *Rebecca*, the winner of the Best Picture Oscar, but the Academy might have recognised Sir Cedric Hardwicke for the otherwise unremarkable *The Howards of Virginia*.

When Barry Fitzgerald won the Best Supporting Actor Academy Award for *Going My Way*, it was the third time in five years that a character actor had received the award for a performance in a leading role, following on from wins by Walter Brennan for *The Westerner* and Charles Coburn for *The More the Merrier*. What forced the Academy to amend it rules, however, was the fact that Fitzgerald had also been nominated in the Best Actor category that year for the same performance.

From the following year, the rules stated that a "performance by an actor or actress in any supporting role may be nominated for either the General Best Performance or the Awards for Supporting Players". This meant that the tradition of including movie stars in the Best Actor and Best Actress category, even if they had appeared in a supporting role, could be continued.

The revised rules also stated, however, that a "performance by an actor or actress in any leading role shall be eligible for nomination only for the General Awards for acting achievement". This meant that featured players in leading roles, such as Stuart Erwin in *Pigskin Parade*, Roland Young in *Topper*, Walter Brennan in *The Westerner*, Charles Coburn in both *The Devil and Miss Jones* and *The More the Merrier* and Barry Fitzgerald in *Going My Way*, could no longer be considered for the Awards for Supporting Players on the basis that they were mere character actors. Under the new rules, such performances in leading roles would only be eligible in the Best Actor or Best Actress categories regardless of the rank in the studio hierarchy of the particular performer.

Interestingly, the impact of the rule change is evident in the nomination of Clifton Webb in the Best Actor category for the comedy *Sitting Pretty* just four years later.

By the late 1940s, Webb was an established featured player under contract at Twentieth Century-Fox. He had previously received Oscar nominations in the Best Supporting Actor category for his performances in *Laura* and *The Razor's Edge*. In *Sitting Pretty*, Webb played one of three central characters but was not equal in status with his famous movie star colleagues Robert Young and Maureen O'Hara. In this respect, Webb was in a similar situation to featured player Roland Young opposite stars Cary Grant and Constance Bennett in *Topper* and character actor Charles Coburn opposite stars Jean Arthur and Joel McCrea in *The More the Merrier*. And with his two previous nominations in the supporting category, his career situation had parallels to that of Walter Brennan when his work in *The Westerner* fell due for recognition. And yet, Twentieth Century-Fox put Webb's name forward for Oscar consideration in the Best Actor category for his performance in *Sitting Pretty* and Oscar voters followed their guidance and shortlisted him along with Lew Ayres, Montgomery Clift, Dan Dailey and Laurence Olivier.

What had changed? Despite their continued nomenclature as "Awards for Supporting Players" in the rulebook, the supporting categories were no longer for *supporting players* in any role as they had been when they were created. Following the post-*Going My Way* rule changes, in practice the supporting categories had become for performances by *supporting players in supporting roles*. As the revised rules stated, "A performance by an actor or actress in any leading role shall be eligible for nomination only for the General Awards for acting achievement". That included those performances in leading roles given by actors like Clifton Webb who the studios had under contract as featured players.

There was one other group of actors, however, whose performances in lead roles were accorded special treatment by the Academy during the studio era: juveniles.

Two years before the Academy introduced the categories for supporting players, six-year-old Shirley Temple was the box office sensation of the year. She starred in three vehicles for Twentieth Century-Fox and many historians argue that she "single-handedly kept the studio from going under."[13] When the Oscar nominations for 1934 were revealed, however, none of Temple's films were in contention for Best Picture and the little girl herself was absent from the Best Actress list. Three and a half years earlier, nine-year-old Jackie Cooper had received a Best Actor nomination for Paramount's *Skippy* and Fox had harboured hopes that the Academy would similarly honour the extraordinarily popular Temple.

On the day of the Academy Awards ceremony, *The Hollywood Reporter* revealed that the Board of Governors had decided to bestow a special award on Temple "in grateful recognition of her outstanding contribution to screen entertainment during the year 1934". At the end of the evening, she received a miniature Oscar statuette, about seven inches tall or approximately half the height of the usual trophy. It remains unclear whether or not the Academy intended the prize to be a one-off novelty, but when fourteen-year-old Bonita Granville was named among the Best Supporting Actress contenders when the category was introduced two years later, it turned out to be the start of a quarter century of parallel paths at the Oscars for juveniles in lead roles and juveniles in supporting parts.

Twelve young actors and actresses received special awards from the Academy between 1934 and 1961. The miniature statuette was presented intermittently and became known as the Academy Juvenile Award or Juvenile Oscar. The Academy's official historian Robert Osborne has said the idea was to acknowledge young performers' contributions to cinema in a way that did not make them compete against adults who had been trained in the art of acting and had years of experience.[14] Eight of the dozen recipients were honoured for their body of work in a particular year, although in each instance they had played a lead role in a commercial hit or a high-profile release and the accolade was widely seen as recognition for that particular film (Mickey Rooney for *Boys' Town*, Judy Garland for *The Wizard of Oz*, Peggy Ann Garner for *A Tree Grows In Brooklyn* and Claude Jarman Jr for *The Yearling*, for example). The citation for the other four honourees referred to a specific feature film in which they had played a starring role (most notably Ivan Jandl for *The Search* and Hayley Mills for *Pollyanna*).

During the same period, six performers under the age of eighteen were nominated for Oscars in the Best Supporting Actor or Best Supporting Actress categories: Bonita Granville in *These Three*, Ann Blyth in *Mildred Pierce*, Brandon de Wilde in *Shane*, both Sal Mineo and Natalie Wood in *Rebel Without a Cause*, and Patty McCormack in *The Bad Seed*. Unlike the recipients of the Academy Juvenile Award, all were recognised for performances in supporting roles. All lost to adult actors.

While it was not by design, a consistent pattern evolved. Significant performances by juveniles in leading roles were overlooked for competitive Oscar consideration and instead received special awards. Acclaimed performances by juveniles in supporting roles were included on the shortlist for the Best Supporting Actor or Best Supporting Actress statuettes. Jackie Cooper remained the only performer under the age of eighteen to receive a nomination in the two lead categories at the Oscars for over seventy years, until the nomination of thirteen-year-old Keisha Castle-Hughes for *Whale Rider* in 2003.

As the Hollywood studio system disintegrated in the early 1960s, this fascinating situation concerning juvenile performers at the Oscars unravelled. The year after Hayley Mills collected a Juvenile Oscar for *Pollyanna*, two young actresses were nominated in the Best Supporting Actress category for performances that some considered to be lead (or co-lead) roles: ten-year-old Mary Badham in *To Kill a Mockingbird* and sixteen-year-old Patty Duke in *The Miracle Worker*. While their classification as leading roles is questionable, the outcome in that category set a new course for juvenile performances, one that has become a significant part of the category fraud phenomenon.

Some commentators argue that Mary Badham played the main character in *To Kill a Mockingbird* and was considered for the Best Supporting Actress prize only because she was a child. David Sims, for example, recently argued in *The Atlantic* that "Mary Badham, who played Scout ... is in almost every scene of the film, but because she was 10 years old at the time of filming, she was nominated as a supporting actress."[15]

Sims exaggerates Badham's presence throughout the film, however, and himself acknowledges that screen time is not the only metric by which a role ought to be determined as a lead or a supporting one. The character of Scout is central to the first half of the film, although she is only a passive observer of events involving her father or her brother in many sequences and is not involved at all in others. Often Scout is merely a device to enable Atticus Finch to appear fatherly and wise: he speaks while she sits quietly and listens. In the second half of the film, which is dominated by the courtroom sequences, she appears in only a handful of shots observing events from the gallery. While she is a significant character, it is difficult to sustain the argument that Scout is a protagonist in *To Kill a Mockingbird* and that Badham played a lead role.

The Miracle Worker, meanwhile, is sometimes described as a two-hander. Since the roles of Annie Sullivan and Helen Keller as protagonist and antagonist are so tightly intertwined and because the journey of self-discovery they take together is the story's emotional arc, many consider them co-leads. As historian Danny Peary has commented, "Because one character is a child, many viewers overlook the fact that this is one of the first films about one female helping another to achieve something. At first there is a battle of wills between these stubborn females, later to be replaced by a partnership based on love, understanding and mutual respect."[16] And because Anne Bancroft and Patty Duke had played the roles together on Broadway before taking them on again in the film adaptation, critics often wrote about them as a pair. *Variety*, for example, wrote "Anne Bancroft and Patty Duke tackle the juicy roles with great artistry and conviction. It is very likely that re-enacting these roles on film posed the greatest challenge of all to their thespic resources." Bosley Crowther, meanwhile, opened his review of the film in *The New York Times* by stating, "The absolutely tremendous and unforgettable display of physically powerful acting that Anne Bancroft and Patty Duke put on in William Gibson's stage play 'The Miracle Worker' is repeated by them in the film made from it by the same producer, Fred Coe, and the same director, Arthur Penn.".

But the original television production and the subsequent Broadway play and Hollywood film, are all entitled *The Miracle Worker* rather than *The Miracle*. Ultimately, while the story is ostensibly about Helen learning to communicate, it is really Annie's story. Annie arrives at the Keller farm determined to prove that she can successfully forge an independent life as a teacher. "Refusing to be handicapped by her own near-blindness or her sex, Sullivan strives to reach her own potential in her profession," explains Peary. "This is a film about liberation, how Helen's breakthrough also frees Annie from her self-doubts and guilt." *The Miracle Worker* is about Annie Sullivan's determination to thwart her demons and defy her limitations. It is about how she achieves the goals she has set for herself. The case of Helen Keller is the crucible for Anne Sullivan's own breakthrough. It is appropriate, therefore, that Bancroft was regarded as the star and the leading player in *The Miracle Worker* while Duke was classified as a supporting artist.

For their performances on Broadway, Bancroft and Duke both won prestigious awards: Bancroft collected her second Tony Award as Best Actress while Duke received a Theatre World Award. Reprising their roles in the film version garnered both of them Academy Awards. Bancroft won the Best Actress statuette and Duke was named Best Supporting Actress in a what was widely regarded as a surprise result (in the lead up to the evening, Angela

Lansbury, winner of the Golden Globe for *The Manchurian Candidate*, had been the strong favourite).

With Duke's victory, the notion that it was necessary to bestow special awards on child performers because they couldn't compete successfully against adults was emphatically dispelled. Duke was the first person under the age of eighteen to win an Oscar in a competitive category. The Academy never handed out another special Academy Juvenile Award.

A decade later, the Academy made a curious category placement that proved to be a turning point in the history of category fraud. Producers and distributors subsequently felt encouraged to promote all juvenile performances for the supporting awards, regardless of whether or not they had a lead role. Drawing on the early tradition that the top prizes were for stars and the supporting prizes were for all other performers, an unwritten and unspoken rationale emerged in which child actors couldn't be regarded as leading players because they weren't stars and must be 'supporting' their famous, adult colleagues even if they had more screen time and portrayed one of the protagonists in the film's narrative. This rationale has been the justification for some blatant examples of category fraud.

It was while selecting music that director Peter Bogdanovich settled on a title for his upcoming film, a drama about an orphaned girl travelling through Depression-era Kansas with a conman who might be her biological father. Inspired by the Ella Fitzgerald recording of 'It's Only a Paper Moon', he chose the title *Paper Moon* with the encouragement of his mentor Orson Welles. In order to justify his choice to the producers Bogdanovich revised the shooting script to include a scene in which the orphaned girl has her picture taken seated on a large, paper crescent moon and then had the photograph appear onscreen as part of the story's emotional climax.

Paper Moon was an adaptation of the fifth and final novel by Joe David Brown. It had been published two years earlier with the title 'Addie Pray', the name of the story's narrator and central character. Screenwriter Alvin Sargent made several changes when adapting the novel for the cinema, including reducing Addie's age from twelve to nine to accommodate the casting of eight-year-old Tatum O'Neal in what was originally the title role.

Bogdanovich had recently completed the comedy *What's Up, Doc?* starring Barbra Streisand and Ryan O'Neal and decided to cast Ryan O'Neal and his young daughter as the lead characters in *Paper Moon*. The roles had originally been earmarked for Paul Newman and his daughter, Nell Potts, but their association with the production ended when director John Huston left the project. Ryan O'Neal had become a major movie star on the back of the unexpected success of the melodrama *Love Story* in 1970 and would star in Stanley Kubrick period film *Barry Lyndon* as a follow up to *Paper Moon*.

His daughter, however, had no experience as an actress. Tatum O'Neal was eight when she was tested for the part of Addie and turned nine during production. At the time, Bogdanovich told reporters, "What makes her good is that she isn't professional. She's just being natural."[17] The *New York Daily News*, however, noted that the director was making as many as fifty takes of some scenes, which was five times his usual number. He apparently admitted to the journalist that Tatum O'Neal's acting was very much a "manipulated performance."[18]

When the film was released, critics heaped praise on the father and daughter duo. In *The New York Times*, Vincent Canby lauded the "two first-class performances by O'Neal and his 9-year-old daughter." *Variety* declared Tatum O'Neal to be "outstanding [in] a sensational screen debut" and in London *The Times* said she "played with devastating assurance, faultless skill and the reticence of great clowning." Canby also recognised Addie as the main character in *Paper Moon* and the two O'Neals as co-stars noting how Ryan O'Neal moved "easily between his roles as star and as straight-man for Tatum". Rather than his daughter acting as comic relief in his movie, he was the straight-man in her comedy.

In December, *Paper Moon* was listed by the National Board of Review as one of the ten best movies of the year, and on 9 January, 1974 the film received Golden Globe nominations in six categories, including Best Motion Picture (Comedy or Musical). Ryan O'Neal was shortlisted for the Best Actor in a Motion Picture (Comedy or Musical) prize, while Tatum O'Neal was included on the ballot in both the Best Actress in a Motion Picture (Comedy or Musical) and the Most Promising Newcomer (Female) categories. She took home the newcomer trophy, but lost the main prize to Glenda Jackson for her performance in *A Touch of Class*. In the Best Supporting Actress category, Madeline Kahn was among the unsuccessful nominees for her performance as a sassy carnival stripper in *Paper Moon*, losing out to fifteen-year-old Linda Blair for the horror film *The Exorcist*.

The day after the Golden Globes were presented, an article appeared in *The New York Times* under the headline "Will The Real Devil Speak Up? Yes!". In the piece that followed, journalist Charles Higham drew on an extensive interview with Mercedes McCambridge, winner of the 1949 Best Supporting Actress Oscar for her performance in *All the King's Men*. It had just been revealed in *Variety* that in the sequences in *The Exorcist* in which the character of twelve-year-old Regan MacNeil speaks with the voice of the Devil, McCambridge's voice had been lip-synched with Blair's performance and dubbed over the top. As McCambridge's contribution to some of the film's most electrifying sequences had not received an onscreen credit, *The New York Times* sensed an awards season scandal.

"Doing that sound track was a terrible experience," McCambridge revealed. "I didn't just do the voice, I did all of the demon's sounds. That wheezing, for instance. My chronic bronchitis helped with that. I did it on one microphone, then on another, elevating it a bit, then a third and fourth, two tones higher each time, and they combined them, as a chorus." She spent nine days in a sound studio recording dialogue, groans and screams for the film's soundtrack and was devastated when she received no recognition for what she considered "the most difficult performance of my life". Director William Friedkin "promised me special credit," she told Higham. "He broke his promise – it's heartbreaking when someone you thought was a friend does that."[19]

When it was reported that Warner Bros. had sought to downplay her involvement in order to preserve Blair's chances of winning an Academy Award, McCambridge was furious. "People will think the soundeffects people simply fixed her voice up – that it was her vocal performance," cried McCambridge. "It's not true that some of her words were blended with mine on the final track. All of the devilish vocality is mine – all of it. Every word." The ensuing controversy threw the awards campaign for Linda Blair into disarray. She remained eligible for nomination under the Academy's rules as only part of her performance had been dubbed, but hopes of her taking home the Best Supporting Actress statuette appeared to have been dashed.

It was in this context, with the early frontrunner seemingly out of serious contention, that members of the Academy's acting branch made a somewhat strange, collective choice as they voted for nominees for the 46th Academy Awards: they placed Tatum O'Neal's lead role performance in *Paper Moon* in the Best Supporting Actress category. Paramount, the distributor of *Paper Moon*, had promoted O'Neal for the Best Actress category, consistent with her nomination at the Golden Globe Awards.[20] Her selection as a candidate for the Best Supporting Actress award did not therefore result from a fraudulent campaign by the studio, but was rather a decision made individually by hundreds of Academy members.

As a result of the Academy's choice, O'Neal was in direct competition with a supporting cast member, much to the chagrin of Bogdanovich. "I don't understand how Madeline Kahn, who's onscreen for maybe eighteen minutes, can be up against Tatum, who's in 100 of the 103 minutes of the film," he complained.[21] Vincent Canby also weighed into the debate, writing in *The New York Times*, "How can Sylvia Sidney, also nominated for best supporting actress award for her work in *Summer Wishes, Winter Dreams* compete with the souped-up electronics and editing that went into Miss Blair's performance in *The Exorcist* and with the pre-conditioned responses that were elicited by Miss O'Neal's?".[22]

Did Academy members simply baulk at shortlisting a child performer for the Best Actress Oscar? It had been more than forty years since a child actor had been in contention for one of the main acting trophies, and that was in the days before the introduction of the supporting categories. For decades children had been awarded special miniature statuettes or competed in the secondary categories. Did they think children weren't eligible for the Best Actor and Best Actress categories? Were voters influenced by the precedent of Patty Duke's win for a substantial role? Some had considered Duke as a co-lead in *The Miracle Worker* and part of an acting partnership between two performers. Faced with another set of adult and child co-leads in an acting *pas de deux*, did Academy members feel they were taking a consistent approach by putting O'Neal's name forward in the Best Supporting Actress category?

It is perhaps telling that the journalists of the Hollywood Foreign Press Association nominated O'Neal for Best Actress at the Golden Globe Awards but the members of the Academy's acting branch placed her in the Best Supporting Actress category at the Oscars. The journalists were evidently content to consider the size and centrality of O'Neal's role and follow the lead actress classification proposed by Paramount. In a traditional assessment of the film's roles, however, the actors in the Academy, however, set aside such measures of O'Neal's role as screen time, agency and narrative importance and focused entirely on O'Neal's status as an actress. As an experienced actor, an established movie star and a thirty-three-year-old white male, Ryan O'Neal was obviously, in the thinking of many, the lead in *Paper Moon*. Whereas nine-year-old Tatum O'Neal, in her debut performance, was supporting her father's starring role. "In 1973, Tatum O'Neal was on screen in nearly every scene of *Paper Moon*," critic Guy Lodge recently explained in *Variety*, "[but] on the dim rationale that kids can't be leads, she cruised to a supporting win, trumping her co-star Madeline Kahn's 12-minute performance in the process."[23]

On Oscar night, ten-year-old Tatum O'Neal became the youngest person to win a statuette in a competitive category, a record she retains over four decades later. "All I really want is to thank my director Peter Bogdanovich and my father," she told the audience gathered at the Dorothy Chandler Pavilion in Los Angeles as she collected her prize dressed in a mini-tuxedo. The wisdom of the Academy's choice continues to be debated. Historian John Harkness, for example, has argued, "O'Neal's Oscar marks the most extreme ever of a lead performance winning a supporting Academy Award – she's in virtually every frame of the film."[24]

While O'Neal took away a statuette, studios and distributors took away a lesson. They noted the decision by the Academy membership to ignore the studio's campaign for O'Neal to be a Best Actress contender and to instead place her performance in the Best Supporting Actress category, apparently on the basis of her age. This decision, combined with the fact that O'Neal was subsequently awarded the statuette, encouraged producers to campaign for all performances by juveniles in the supporting categories, regardless of whether they had lead roles or how absurd the classification in terms of screen time or centrality to either the plot or the film's emotional arc.

Alternate Winner – If Tatum O'Neal had instead been considered for the Best Actress category for *Paper Moon*, who might have won the Oscar as Best Supporting Actress of 1973? While Linda Blair was the early frontrunner for *The Exorcist* and won the Golden Globe Award, the controversy about the dubbing of key parts of her performance by Mercedes McCambridge probably reduced her chances of winning to the extent that Madeline Kahn would have taken home the Academy Award that year for *Paper Moon*.

Alternate Nominee – If Tatum O'Neal had instead been considered for the Best Actress category for *Paper Moon*, who might have been in the race for the Best Supporting Actress statuette? Golden Globe nominee Kate Reid is the most likely candidate for her performance in *A Delicate Balance* although Cindy Williams might have made the list for *American Graffiti* for which she was a nominee for the British Academy Award the following year.

Christine Lahti and Judd Hirsch were the notional stars of the 1988 drama *Running On Empty*. They portrayed a married couple who had been on the run from the FBI since an act of student radicalism they perpetrated in the 1960s went awry and seriously injured an innocent bystander. Thirty-eight-year-old Lahti had been an Oscar nominee four years earlier for her supporting turn in *Swing Shift* and was following up the film *Housekeeping* for which she had been the runner-up for the New York Film Critics' Best Actress prize. Fifty-three-year-old Judd Hirsch, meanwhile, had been an Academy Award nominee for his supporting performance in the drama *Ordinary People*, winner of the Best Picture Oscar in 1980. Both were overshadowed, however, by seventeen-year-old River Phoenix in the role of the couple's musically-gifted eldest son, Danny; the film's largest role.

As the protagonist in *Running On Empty*, Danny is "the pivotal role" in the film.[25] It is Danny's desire to break free from his parent's underground life and his blossoming relationship with the daughter of his music teacher that provides the film with its principal storyline and emotional arc. Biographer and film historian Gavin Edwards summarized the film's theme as "a son's conflicted response to his parents' legacy".[26]

As critic Janet Maslin noted in *The New York Times*, "The catalyst for change is 17-year-old Danny ... Were it not for Danny (played outstandingly well by River Phoenix), *Running On Empty* ... would be as threadbare as the Popes themselves. The parents' story is much less affecting than their son's. ... The heart of *Running On Empty* is the slow-burning romance between Danny and the smart, tomboyish Lorna". In the *Chicago Sun-Times*, Roger Ebert concurred by saying, "there are great performances in the central roles. Phoenix essentially carries the story; it's about him."

Although he played the film's main character, carried the main plotline and had more time on screen than any other member of the cast, Hollywood did not consider Phoenix to be a leading man in *Running On Empty*. At seventeen, with no formal training as an actor and with limited screen credits, he was only beginning to make the transition from child actor (*Explorers* and *Stand By Me*) to more adult roles such as Danny in *Running On Empty*. Most of his recent experience had been playing adolescents in pulp films aimed at teenage audiences (*Little Nikita*, *A Night in the Life of Jimmy Reardon* and *Indiana Jones and the Last Crusade*). When it came to the annual awards season, Phoenix was classified as a supporting player on the basis of his youth and career status. The "dim rationale that kids can't be leads" that saw Tatum O'Neal placed in the supporting category for *Paper Moon* fifteen years earlier, resulted in Phoenix contesting the supporting categories for *Running On Empty*. As it had so many times before, Hollywood considered the actor rather than the role.

Phoenix was named Best Supporting Actor by the National Board of Review while Lahti received the Best Actress prize from the Los Angeles Film Critics. Both earned Golden Globe nominations from the Hollywood Foreign Press Association: Phoenix as Best Supporting Actor and Lahti as Best Actress (Drama). The film also garnered Globe nominations for Best Picture (Drama) and Best Director and won the Best Screenplay trophy for Naomi Foner (mother of future Oscar nominees Maggie and Jake Gyllenhaal). Subsequently, the Academy shortlisted Phoenix as Best Supporting Actor and Foner for Best Original Screenplay.

Phoenix was only the fifth male actor to receive an Academy Award nomination by the age of eighteen. Many commentators at the time said that recognition at such a young age and so early in his career meant that "it was only a matter of time before [he] would win the golden statuette … and it wouldn't be for a supporting role, either, but as Best Actor."[27] As if in support of their predictions, the Best Actress Oscar that year was won by Jodie Foster who had been a nominee as a teenager for a supporting role in *Taxi Driver* and had won acclaim and a statuette as an adult in a lead role in *The Accused*.

The other four nominees for the Best Supporting Actor Academy Award were more than twice Phoenix's age. Kevin Kline was forty-one. Both Martin Landau and Dean Stockwell were in their fifties. Sir Alec Guinness was seventy-four. Few expected Phoenix to emerge as the winner against such an experienced field. Landau had won the Golden Globe Award for *Tucker: The Man and His Dream*, but the Academy chose to honour Kline for the hit comedy *A Fish Called Wanda* in something of a surprise result (Kline hadn't even been a nominee at the Golden Globes).

Phoenix was typically philosophical about his nomination and the impact it would have on his career. "I think that in a way I'm being challenged," he said. "I feel that there are great minds up there who would like to see what I can do with an Oscar nomination. I guess many people would change after a nomination in the way they see things. In my case it's really irrelevant in terms of what I do. Still, it was an incredible experience which I will put in my memories, like everything else."[28]

Just three years later, Phoenix was named Best Actor by the National Society of Film Critics and finished as runner-up in the voting for the New York Film Critics Circle's Best Actor prize for his performance as a narcoleptic gay hustler in *My Own Private Idaho*. He missed out on Golden Globe and Academy Award nominations, however, and he died eighteen months later, aged just twenty-three.

> *Alternate Nominee* – If River Phoenix had instead been considered for the Best Actor category for *Running On Empty*, who might have been in the race for the Best Supporting Actor statuette? Lou Diamond Phillips would seem the most likely for his performance in *Stand and Deliver* given he was a Golden Globe nominee and the Academy nominated Edward James Olmos as Best Actor for the same film.

The second-highest grossing film at the box office in 1999 was *The Sixth Sense*, a surprise hit about Cole Sear, a troubled boy who can see the ghosts of the dead, and Dr Malcolm Crowe, the unhappy psychologist who tries to help him. Director M. Night Shyamalan cast ten-year-old Haley Joel Osment in the lead role of Cole. The young actor had previously appeared in small roles in *Forrest Gump*, *Bogus* and *For Better or Worse* and various television productions.

Although dismissed by some leading film critics, most notably Stephen Holden in *The New York Times*, the film received multiple nominations for awards including six Oscar nominations and four British Academy Award nominations. Osment was shortlisted for the Best Supporting Actor awards at the Golden Globe Awards and the Academy Awards where he became the second youngest male actor in Oscar history to receive nomination in a competitive category.

Like *Paper Moon* a quarter of a century earlier, *The Sixth Sense* is a two-character drama featuring a child as the principal protagonist and an adult as the secondary lead. Cole is the plot's central character – he, and only he, has relationships with all the other characters: his psychologist, his mother, his teachers and classmates, and the ghosts of the dead whom only he can see.

Osment has more screen time than the film's star, Bruce Willis, in the role of Dr Crowe. And Osment's character drives the film's emotional arcs, particularly those experienced by Cole and his mother. In terms of screen time, narrative agency and centrality to the film's theme, Osment unquestionably has a lead role in *The Sixth Sense*.

When the movie was released, film critic Roger Ebert commented in the *Chicago Sun-Times*, Osment "is a very good actor in a film where his character possibly has more lines than anyone else. He's in most of the scenes, and he has to act in them – this isn't a role for a cute kid who can stand there and look solemn in reaction shots. There are fairly involved dialogue passages between Willis and Osment that require good timing, reactions and the ability to listen. Osment is more than equal to them ... Those scenes give the movie its weight and make it as convincing as, under the circumstances, it can possibly be." In the *Philadelphia Inquirer*, critic Carrie Rickey observed, "*The Sixth Sense* sits squarely on Osment's hunched little shoulders. He carries the movie, a lyrical and eerie meditation upon loss and hurt and healing."

Given his role was clearly a leading part, the placement of Osment in the supporting category can only be explained on the basis of his status as a young actor. Although he had a leading role, Hollywood's "dim rationale" about child actors evidently insisted that, as an inexperienced child, he must be providing support to Willis, the film's big-name star. It was a scenario that drew heavily on the precedent of Tatum O'Neal's nomination in 1973.

Many historians and film commentators cite Osment's nomination as one of the worst cases of category fraud. Joe Reid recently included Osment on a list of fourteen nominations in the supporting categories that were actually leads. He wrote, "Sure, he was just a kid. Sure, Bruce Willis got his name above the title. But Osment's character is in every way the focal point of *The Sixth Sense* ... This is the award campaign way, however. The kid stays out of the picture when it comes to the Lead Actor/Actress category."[29]

In the lead up to the ceremony, *The Wall Street Journal* set out to survey as many Academy members as possible about their choices in the Best Picture, Director and four acting categories and their reasons for voting the way they did. While journalist Lisa Gubernick and her team succeeded in obtaining responses from only about six percent of the membership, the results correctly predicted all six winners and yielded some fascinating comments, including about the Best Supporting Actor race. While one voter said the Academy should give the statuette to Tom Cruise because he was "due" after so many years as a box office star, the survey revealed the contest to be between Osment and sixty-seven-year-old Michael Caine for *The Cider House Rules*. But it was not a close contest. According to Gubernick, "Ultimately, 121 of them chose Mr Caine, nearly double the 66 who preferred Mr Osment."[30]

When *The Wall Street Journal* published the results of its survey, a handful of Academy members went on the record, including comedian Buddy Hackett. Best known for performances in *It's a Mad, Mad, Mad, Mad World* and *The Love Bug*, Hackett had told the journalists that he planned to vote for Caine rather than Osment because, "In another five years, he'll have pimples, and no one will want to talk about him." The article revealed that Hackett was far from the only Academy member to determine his vote on factors other than an assessment of the merits of each performance. Many of the interviewed members explained their voting choice in terms of the personality of the nominee and the point at which they were in their career. In the case of ten-year-old Osment, Gubernick revealed "many members told us they were leery of voting for a child."[31]

There is a widespread reluctance in the industry to reward child performers. Actors in particular seem uncomfortable with the idea, perhaps wary of suggestions that acting is so simple that even an untrained child can do it, and very successfully! The previously mentioned notion that children can't be leads is not unconnected to this attitude. Hollywood's strange way of regarding child performers is at the heart of why Osment was included in the supporting category for his lead performance in *The Sixth Sense* and was a key factor in why Michael Caine won his second Best Supporting Actor Academy Award that year.

> *Alternate Nominee* – If Haley Joel Osment had instead been considered for the Best Actor category for *The Sixth Sense*, who might have been in the race for the Best Supporting Actor statuette? There were an extraordinary number of strong contenders that year, and yet the same five were nominated for both the Golden Globe and the Oscar. The three most likely candidates are New York Film Critics winner John Malkovich for *Being John Malkovich*, Los Angeles Film Critics winner Christopher Plummer for *The Insider* and National Board of Review winner Philip Seymour Hoffman for *Magnolia*.

On 30 September 2003, the Motion Picture Association of America announced a ban on studios and distributors sending 'for your consideration' copies of movies to awards season voters. Nearly 40 000 such videotapes and DVDs, known as 'screeners', had been distributed the previous season and MPAA President Jack Valenti argued the ban was necessary to combat digital piracy.

A week later, Patrick Goldstein reported in the *Los Angeles Times*, "it's an open secret in Hollywood that the Oscar screener ban was instigated by Warner Bros. Chief Executive Barry Meyer."[32] With its blockbuster releases as prime targets for piracy, he argued, Meyer's company "has money on its mind, not Oscars." Warner Bros. did not receive a single nomination from the Academy the previous year, he noted.

Other commentators were more cynical, however. The MPAA is essentially a trade association for the nine major Hollywood studios which stood to benefit from a screener ban since their releases, backed by well-funded publicity campaigns, had much greater visibility than small, art cinema releases handled by independent companies. The latter relied on screeners to get their contenders seen by critics and awards season voters. Lou Lumenick in the *New York Post* said "the screener ban isn't about piracy – but is a blatant attempt by the old-line Hollywood studios to take back control of the Oscars which have been increasingly dominated by the indies, almost all of which are based in New York." He particularly noted that Warner Bros. had initiated the ban just when it had "its first serious Oscar contender in years in *Mystic River*."[33] The film was expected to be in strong contention for the Best Picture, Director and Actor awards.

In addition to the major studios, the ban also applied to their art cinema divisions and subsidiary companies, such as Fox Searchlight, Fine Line and Miramax. Among the companies not captured by the MPAA's edict, however, was Newmarket Films. With a sudden advantage over its rivals, the independent distribution company moved quickly to aggressively promote the releases on its slate, among them the New Zealand film *Whale Rider*.

Directed by Niki Caro, *Whale Rider* is the story of a twelve-year-old Maori girl who dreams of becoming the chief of her tribe, a position customarily reserved for men. For the lead role, Caro cast Keisha Castle-Hughes, a young girl first spotted by Diana Rowan, the New Zealand-based casting director who had previously discovered Anna Paquin for *The Piano*. Like Tatum O'Neal thirty years earlier, Castle-Hughes came into her first feature film with no prior acting experience. "I'd done no acting at all, not even in school productions," she subsequently told the media. "I've always wanted to act, but it was only because I'd see these beautiful stars, and they would all be wearing beautiful dresses."[34]

The film screened at the Toronto Film Festival in September 2002, more than a year before the MPAA screener ban and Newmarket's Oscar campaign were launched. It received a standing ovation and won the People's Choice Award for best picture at the festival. The film also won praise for the mature and empathetic performance of its young leading lady. *Whale Rider* proved to be a crowd-pleaser as it progressively opened in cinemas around the world over the months that followed and Castle-Hughes amassed an impressive array of reviews. When the screener ban effectively left the studios' art cinema divisions hamstrung, Newmarket Films decided to promote the teenager for an Oscar nomination.

Although she was the film's lead performer, the independent distributor chose to campaign for Castle-Hughes to be recognised in the Best Supporting Actress category. The film's producers were mindful of the success that juvenile performers had enjoyed in the supporting categories, including those in lead roles such as O'Neal. They also knew how difficult it was for foreign films to break into the major categories at the Academy Awards. As producer John Barnett explained, "You don't think for a moment that you're going to finish up getting a Best Actress nomination because that had always seemed to be the preserve of big pictures and Hollywood pictures."[35] Noting the examples of O'Neal, Phoenix and Osment, the team behind *Whale Rider* promoted thirteen-year-old Castle-Hughes for the secondary prize.

The age and inexperience of Castle-Hughes were not, however, the only factors behind Newmarket Films' decision. It was also a strategic move. The favourite for the Best Actress statuette that season was Charlize Theron. The South African actress had shaken off a reputation as a mere screen beauty with an acclaimed portrayal of serial killer Aileen Wuornos in *Monster*. The film debuted at the AFI Film Festival in mid-November 2003 and was distributed across the North American market by Newmarket Films. By promoting Castle-Hughes for a Best Supporting Actress nomination, Newmarket was deliberately keeping her out of the way of Theron's bid for a place in the Best Actress category. The independent distributor didn't dare dream of securing two of the five nominations in the Best Actress category, so used Castle-Hughes' age as the rationale for an audacious bid for her to be shortlisted for the Best Supporting Actress award.

It was an extraordinary example of category fraud. Unlike Tatum O'Neal, River Phoenix and Haley Joel Osment in their Oscar-nominated roles, Castle-Hughes played the only main character in *Whale Rider*. There was no adult lead role, no movie star in a secondary lead part with top billing in the credits. If Castle-Hughes was a supporting actress, who exactly was she supporting?

Within days of the MPAA's announcement, the screener ban was under attack from across the industry. Leading directors and actors published open letters in the media and studio executives pushed behind closed doors for a reversal of the policy.

A compromise was announced just three weeks later. Under the deal, the ban would be lifted for members of the Academy, who would receive videotapes encoded with identifying marks so any pirated copies could be tracked to an Oscar voter. The leading critics' groups and other awards and industry organizations were furious. "The implication of your action is that you regard Screen Actors Guild members as less trustworthy than Academy members," said two senior guild executives in a letter to Valenti. "We suggest that this discrimination is arbitrary and born of expediency rather than reason."[36] The Los Angeles Film Critics Association, meanwhile, announced that it was cancelling its annual awards in protest.

In early December, a New York federal judge quashed the ban and the MPAA backed down. The studios and their specialty art wings immediately rushed out screeners, but Newmarket Films' two lead actresses were already firmly established in the minds of awards season voters by then. Required to abide by the classifications made by the film distributors, the Screen Actors Guild nominated Castle-Hughes as Best Supporting Actress, but other groups, free to place talent in whichever category they deemed appropriate, took a different view. In the voting for the annual Chicago Film Critics Association Awards, Castle-Hughes finished as the runner-up to Theron for the Best Actress accolade. In mid-January, a week prior to the announcement of the Oscar nominees, Castle-Hughes was shortlisted for the Best Actress prize at the NAACP Image Awards.

When the Academy Award contenders were revealed in late January 2004, both Castle-Hughes and Theron were included among the candidates for the Best Actress statuette. Thirteen-year-old Castle-Hughes set a record as the youngest nominee in the category's history and, over seventy years after the nomination of Jackie Cooper as Best Actor for *Skippy*, became only the second juvenile performer shortlisted for one of the main acting prizes.

Castle-Hughes' nomination was also historic in that the Academy membership had voted for her contrary to the campaign mounted on her behalf by Newmarket Films. The key to the Academy's defiance, observers declared, was the fact that she played the only leading role in *Whale Rider*. Crucially, this was something she shared with nine-year-old Quvenzhané Wallis who was subsequently nominated as Best Actress for *Beasts of the Southern Wild*.

The Academy's rejection of category fraud in the case of Keisha Castle-Hughes did not, however, prove to be a turning point. Within a decade, another teenager in a lead role was nominated for an Oscar, as Best Supporting Actress.

Regarded by some as one of the greatest American novels of the twentieth century, Charles Portis' 'True Grit' was published in 1968. Like 'Addie Pray', which appeared in bookstores three years later, it is a novel about a young girl who embarks on a journey with a complete stranger. The young female protagonists serve as narrator in both novels.

Set in the Oklahoma Territory a decade after the end of the Civil War, 'True Grit' tells the story of Mattie Ross, a fourteen-year-old girl determined to track down the man who murdered her father. She hires a drunken U.S. Marshal to assist her, and the unlikely pair are accompanied on the revenge mission by a Texan Ranger hunting the same quarry for a previous murder. Throughout the novel Mattie is the instigator of events and a key driver of what subsequently unfolds, playing a crucial part in the climatic shoot-out.

A year after it was published, the novel was adapted into a film starring Kim Darby as Mattie. For his performance as 'Rooster' Cogburn, the U.S. Marshal hired by Mattie to track down the murderer, John Wayne won the Best Actor Academy Award.

Four decades later, the brothers Ethan and Joel Coen announced plans to adapt the novel for the big screen for a second time. In interviews with the media, they expressed a desire to make a film that was much closer to the original source material. "It's partly a question of point-of-view," Ethan explained. "The book is entirely in the voice of the 14-year-old girl. That sort of tips the feeling of it over a certain way ... I think it's much funnier than the [1969] movie was so I think, unfortunately, they lost a lot of humour in both the situations and in her voice. It also ends differently than the movie did. You see the main character – the little girl – 25 years later when she's an adult."[37]

The interview makes clear that the Coen brothers recognised Mattie Ross as the story's main character and wanted her voice to be at the heart of the film. The reviews that eventually greeted the movie suggest that they were successful. In *The New York Times*, Manohla Dargis described Mattie as "a richly conceived and written eccentric, as memorable on the page as she is now on screen. Softened for the first film … she has been toughed up again by the Coens so that she resembles the seemingly humorless if often unintentionally humorous Scripture-quoting martinet of Mr Portis's imagination."

For the lead role of Mattie, the Coen brothers chose Hailee Steinfeld, a thirteen-year-old from California with limited acting experience. While she had made some short films and commercials and had appeared in half a dozen television episodes, she had never appeared in a feature film prior to *True Grit*. She nonetheless made what Dargis called "a terrific film debut" and found herself mentioned as a possible awards contender.

Steinfeld was not, however, the only lead performer in *True Grit* in the way that Keisha Castle-Hughes had been in *Whale Rider*. Just as Tatum O'Neal and Haley Joel Osment had done in their Oscar-nominated performances, Steinfeld shared the screen with adult co-leads who were bona fide movie stars. A year after winning the Best Actor Academy Award for *Crazy Heart*, Jeff Bridges took on the role of 'Rooster' Cogburn. Matt Damon, meanwhile, played the Texan Ranger.

While Bridges understandably received top-billing and was the focus of the film's publicity, the Coen brothers kept Steinfeld's character at the centre of the film. In her review, Dargis noted that "Despite Mr Bridges's showy turn, the movie opens and closes with Mattie's voice-over, which shifts the story away from Rooster and back to her." She concluded that in Mattie, the filmmaking brothers "have created a character whose single-minded pursuit of vengeance has unmistakable resonance."

Paramount decided that Steinfeld would have a better chance of winning an Oscar in the Best Supporting Actress category. Like O'Neal, Phoenix and Osment before her, she was "demoted" and the various critics and awards organizations followed the studio's cue. [38] Steinfeld duly received Best Supporting Actress nominations from both the Screen Actors Guild and the Academy. During the entire season, it was only at the British Academy Awards in London that Steinfeld was placed in the Best Actress in a Leading Role category.

The blatant category fraud did not pass unmentioned. Following Steinfeld's Screen Actors Guild Award nomination, the *Los Angeles Times* questioned Lea Yardum, Paramount's award consultant, about the studio's classification of Steinfeld's role as supporting. "Her character is in almost every scene of the film. So why is she a *supporting* actress?" asked the paper's Nicole Sperling.[39] With the consent of her parents, Yardum explained, Paramount had decided to submit Steinfeld for consideration in the supporting category because of her age and inexperience. "This is the standard place where you put a kid who's never done a movie before," she explained. When confronted with the precedent of Keisha Castle-Hughes' Best Actress nomination for her acting debut in *Whale Rider*, Yardum responded, "Keisha was playing opposite a whale. Hailee is part of an ensemble cast. *True Grit* is also Jeff Bridges' movie and he's carrying it as a lead actor does."

It was another case of the industry and Academy voters considering the performer rather than the role. Because she was a juvenile making her feature film debut Steinfeld was nominated in the secondary category. She was treated as a *supporting player*, not as an actress in a *supporting role*. As Yardum's remarks also made clear, the situation was compounded by the fact that Steinfeld was appearing opposite a famous white male actor. In such a scenario, was the industry's attitude, the adult white male star must be the lead and the juvenile female newcomer must be a supporting player, regardless of their relative screen time, narrative agency or importance to the film's central themes and emotional arc. Nearly forty years after the release of *Paper Moon*, the previously discussed "dim rationale that kids can't be leads" was, shockingly, still in evidence. Also frustrating was that category fraud in the cases of child and juvenile performers was widely accepted as "standard".

While Paramount succeeded in securing a Best Supporting Actress nomination for Hailee Steinfeld, she didn't take home the golden statuette. The winner that year was Melissa Leo for her work in *The Fighter*.

Leading film commentator Steve Katz has since decried Steinfeld's nomination in the supporting category as one of the most "egregious" cases of category fraud in the history of the Oscars. "She was nominated for Supporting Actress at the 2011 ceremony," he recently wrote, "despite being absolutely and incontrovertibly *the* lead part of *True Grit*, being in nearly every scene and acting as the central figure and prime mover of the plot."[40]

Alternate Nominee – If Hailee Steinfeld had instead been considered for the Best Actress category for *True Grit*, who might have been in the race for the Best Supporting Actress statuette? Almost certainly, Mila Kunis would have received a nomination for *Black Swan*, the film that won Natalie Portman the Best Actress Oscar that year. Kunis was nominated for both the Golden Globe Award and the Screen Actors Guild Award.

The arguments made by Paramount about Hailee Steinfeld and *True Grit* were repeated five years later by A24 with regard to nine-year-old Jacob Tremblay and *Room*. The independent studio was the distributor of the film in North America and heavily promoted Tremblay for consideration in the Best Supporting Actor category even though he had one of the film's two lead roles.

"By minutes spent on screen, Jacob Tremblay is the real star of *Room*," wrote David Sims in *The Atlantic*. "Though the movie is about a woman (Brie Larson) who's been held captive for years, the story is mostly told from the perspective of her son, played by Tremblay."[41]

Reviewing the movie for *The New York Times*, Manohla Dargis agreed that Tremblay rather than Larson was the heart and centre of *Room*. "Mr. Abrahamson, by following the book's lead and embracing Jack's point of view so strongly, specifically in his Expressionistic translation of the novelistic first-person to the screen, has managed the difficult task of externalizing the inner life of another person," she wrote. "In the process, however, he leaves Ma behind. Ms. Larson, her bright face dimmed and eyes ringed, works hard to bring Ma to persuasive life, digging into grief in her corner of the room between hopeless smiles, but Mr. Abrahamson's lack of attention turns her into an overly muted supporting player."

In the first half of the movie, Larson and Tremblay share equal screen time as the audience witnesses the life of enforced confinement experienced by Joy and Jack, the characters the pair portray. In the second part, however, it is actually Tremblay who receives more attention than Larson as the film chronicles the struggles Joy and Jack have with adjusting to life in the outside world and renew or forge relationships with other people. At first Jack refuses to engage with anyone other than his mother. After Joy is hospitalized following a suicide attempt, however, Jack bonds with his grandmother and makes friends with a boy his own age for the first time. Throughout this section of the film, Jack is the film's principal protagonist and the driver of his emotional arc. At the end of the movie, it is Jack who instigates the final, cathartic visit to the place of their captivity, not Joy.

In *Room*, Larson and Tremblay are an interdependent acting partnership akin to the pairing of Ryan O'Neal and Tatum O'Neal in *Paper Moon*. Together they dominate the narrative and drive the emotional arc. Yet at the very outset of the awards season, A24 announced that it was campaigning for Larson as Best Actress and promoting Tremblay as Best Supporting Actor. "Is A24's decision a cynical ploy to game the system?" asked Sims, "Or is it just good business? Because winning an Oscar is, of course, as much a matter of business as anything else."[42]

"Kids almost never land noms in the lead categories," asserted Scott Feinberg in *The Hollywood Reporter* in an article about category fraud.[43] Another nine-year-old, Quvenzhané Wallis, had been nominated in the Best Actress category only two years earlier for the independent drama *Beasts of the Southern Wild*. Like Keisha Castle-Hughes, however, she had played the only lead character in the film. Tremblay shared his movie with an adult co-lead. As a result, the distributor shifted him into the supporting category, heeding the lesson of the Academy's own placement of Tatum O'Neal in the secondary category for *Paper Moon* and following the example of the campaigns for Haley Joel Osment in *The Sixth Sense* and Hailee Steinfeld in *True Grit*.

Most commentators regarded the move as purely strategic. "A24 is pushing nine-year-old Jacob Tremblay for Best Supporting Actor ... [even] though the younger actor has more screen time than his co-star, which again seems a case of keeping an actor out of a more competitive field," wrote blogger Jason Bailey.[44] "Having a 9-year-old go up against the likes of Leonardo DiCaprio, [Eddie] Redmayne and Johnny Depp is a completely impossible win," agreed Erin Whitney in an article on the website ScreenCrush.[45]

Others like Feinberg, however, suggested that the classification could have some justification. "Tremblay's character generally is more passive than Larson's, who drives the action," he wrote.[46]

Screen Actors Guild members, who are required under the union's rules to follow the classifications made by studios and film distributors, nominated Tremblay as Best Supporting Actor for his performance in *Room*, but he was overlooked for nominations at the Golden Globes, British Academy Awards and the Oscars. While some groups considered him in the supporting category, several rejected A24's campaign.   The San Diego Film Critics' Society shortlisted him in the Best Actor category and he received a Best Actor in a Leading Role nomination at the Canadian Screen Awards.

While Brie Larson and screenwriter Emma Donoghoe had been widely expected to receive nominations from the Academy, many commentators were surprised that *Room* was also shortlisted for the Best Picture prize and secured a Best Director nomination for Lenny Abrahamson.   Given the film evidently attracted more support from Academy members during the nomination period that had been anticipated, it is interesting to speculate on why Tremblay did not receive a nomination as well for a performance that "had been called one of the greatest given by a child actor"[47] and which many felt had been the key to the film's success.   In *The New York Times*, for example, Dargis had written: "his presence in the movie has a crystalline purity, and while Jack makes life bearable for Ma, Mr. Tremblay makes the movie bearable for you. His essential child being, his fragility and buoyancy, his shrieks of happiness and complaint, air the room out."

The Academy's rules state that a performance "in any role shall be eligible for nomination either for the leading role or supporting role categories" and that the "leading role and supporting role categories will be tabulated simultaneously. If any performance should receive votes in both categories, the achievement shall be placed only on the ballot in that category in which, during the tabulation process, it first receives the required number of votes to be nominated." And therein, perhaps, lay the rub for Tremblay. What if Academy members, who the rules state shall themselves determine whether a role is leading or supporting, are equally divided in their opinion resulting in the vote for a particular performance being split between the two categories and falling short of the necessary threshold in both instances as a consequence?

While interviews with a sample of Academy members conducted by *The Wall Street Journal* in early 2000 revealed a reluctance to reward child performers, since then the Academy had nominated Keisha Castle-Hughes, Abigail Breslin, Saorise Ronan, Hailee Steinfeld and Quvenzhané Wallis.   Two of these youngsters were even shortlisted in the Best Actress category in a break with over seventy years of Oscar history.   Tellingly, since then the Academy's membership had also twice rejected a studio's push for a leading performance to be nominated in the supporting categories and instead placed the contenders in the Best Actress category: Newmarket's campaign for Keisha Castle-Hughes in *Whale Rider* and The Weinstein Company's bid for Kate Winslet in *The Reader*.

It could be that Tremblay simply succumbed to "the Oscars' historical bias against young male actors",[48] but it could also be that enough members defied A24's supporting actor classification that ballots were cast for him in both categories such that he missed out on a nomination entirely. Would the outcome have been different had A24 promoted him as Best Actor instead?

Contemporary films are dominated by protagonists in their thirties and forties which is the age when most movie stars are at the peak of their popularity and power. A key reason why child and adolescent performers have consistently been nominated in the supporting categories even when they have given a performance in a leading role has been their age relative to their adult co-lead. The view in the industry has been that children and young people can't be leads and must be providing support to the experienced and famous movie star with whom they are sharing the screen. The star is the box office draw and is therefore the one carrying the film. "Hailee is part of an ensemble cast," a Paramount spokesperson defensively responded when asked why the studio was mounting a Best Supporting Actress campaign for Hailee Steinfeld in *True Grit* when she was the film's protagonist and lead character. "*True Grit* is also Jeff Bridges' movie and he's carrying it as a lead actor does." It is a view of actors' roles through the prism of the movies as a business and one entirely removed from an assessment of films as texts in which a character's agency, connection to theme and emotional arc and amount of screen time are all key metrics.

This business-centric "dim rationale" has been the excuse studios and distributors have proffered when pursuing category fraud campaigns strategically aimed at securing nominations in the ostensibly less competitive secondary categories. It was perhaps only a matter of time, before similar arguments were proposed concerning older performers with famous, popular and middle-aged co-stars.

The black-and-white comedy *Nebraska* was well received by critics and audiences when it premiered in competition at the 2013 Cannes Film Festival. Directed by Alexander Payne from a script by Bob Nelson, the film tells the story of David Grant, an electronics salesman who agrees to drive his estranged father, Woody, from Montana to Nebraska so he can claim a lottery windfall. For his performance as the ornery old man, Bruce Dern collected the festival's prestigious Best Actor prize.

Several commentators quickly suggested that the veteran actor should be backed for the Best Supporting Actor Academy Award. Scott Feinberg of *The Hollywood Reporter* argued, "the performance is and should be pushed as a supporting performance with the Academy. ... As I see it, the film may open and close on images of Dern – walking down a highway and driving a pickup truck, respectively – but its lead is Will Forte, as a lost young man trying to be a good son to – and come to terms with – his elderly and declining father, who never seemed to care very much for him. I haven't clocked the exact screen time that the two have, but I am almost certain that Forte's outweighs Dern's. And I am certain that Forte has more dialogue than Dern, who hardly speaks throughout the entire film."[49] As far as Feinberg was concerned, it was forty-three-year old television personality Will Forte as David who had the role of protagonist and who drove the story's emotional arc.

Feinberg also pushed a familiar strategic argument. "If he goes lead he'll have an outside chance of getting nominated, but if he goes supporting he has an exponentially better chance of getting nominated – and he might even win," he wrote. "The best actor race is always jam-packed with viable contenders, whereas the best supporting actor race is not."

Many online commentators agreed that Dern would "have a better shot in the supporting actor category" and that "to maximize his chances to win an Oscar, he should position himself for a run at best supporting actor rather than the more competitive best actor prize." [50] Rumours soon spread that Paramount Vantage was preparing to campaign for Forte as Best Actor and Dern as Best Supporting Actor.

Dern, however, would have none of it. "My take is this," he told Tim Appelo of *The Hollywood Reporter*. "The story is about who Woody is and where he's going. It's probably 50-50 screen time with Will Forte, but Woody is a leading role. If I go supporting, I'm a whore!" Echoing the sentiments of Peter Finch over three decades earlier, he continued, "I never came to Hollywood to win an award. I came to do good movies. If I go supporting, it's embarrassing to the Academy ... I'd rather go the right way than backdoor my way into a supporting [Oscar] because of my age."[51]

When the film played at the Telluride Film Festival in August, Paramount Vantage announced that they would be pushing Dern for Best Actor. "He's the lead in the movie," a studio spokesperson said, "and we are campaigning him in the lead actor category." Rather than accept Forte and Dern as co-leads, however, the studio instead switched Forte into the supporting contest.

When the awards season got underway that December, Dern collected the Best Actor prizes from the Los Angeles Film Critics and the National Board of Review and the latter awarded their Best Supporting Actor accolade to Forte. When the Oscar nominations were announced a month later, Dern was included among the Best Actor candidates, but Forte was overlooked. On the big night, Matthew McConaughey won the golden statuette for his performance in *Dallas Buyers Club*.

While Paramount Vantage's rumoured plan to push the popular forty-something Forte for the main prize and promote the veteran Dern as a supporting player was evidently thwarted by Dern and his representatives, it is likely to be a sign of things to come in the Oscar race: older actors consigned to supporting categories along with juveniles on account of their age because, in the eyes of Hollywood, only adults in their prime can be a star and leading player!

Child and juvenile actors weren't the only performers in lead roles to be placed in the supporting categories at the Oscars and other awards ceremonies. Despite rules that leading performances could only be considered for the main acting prizes, numerous actors and actresses have been fraudulently nominated in the supporting categories for performances in lead roles because they weren't the star of their film. The mindset in which children and adolescents by definition must be supporting a famous adult star, also determined that newcomers and lesser names must likewise be supporting players. Regardless of the importance of their role to the plot or their overall screen time, these performers found themselves contending the secondary acting prizes because of their status as newcomers. It was, in many ways, a natural extension of the traditional thinking about the acting categories at the Oscars: Best Actor and Best Actress were for movie stars while Best Supporting Actor and Best Supporting Actress were for everyone else: children, newcomers and character actors; the screen's ordinary people.

When Orson Welles came to Hollywood on a contract to produce a series of films under his own Mercury Productions banner for distribution by the small studio RKO Radio Pictures, he brought with him from New York many of the talents he had assembled for his theatre and radio productions. Known as the Mercury Players, these experienced performers became the principal ensemble cast of both *Citizen Kane* and *The Magnificent Ambersons*. Among them was Agnes Moorehead, whom Welles considered one of the greatest actresses he had ever encountered.[52]

Moorehead was forty-years-old when she made her first appearance in a feature film as Mary Kane, the woman who gives up her young son so that he might have a better life, in *Citizen Kane*. She appears in only one scene, near the beginning of the picture. A year later, however, Welles cast her in *The Magnificent Ambersons*, his second production, in the female lead role. The film was based on Booth Tarkington's Pulitzer-Prize winning novel about the declining fortunes of a wealthy mid-Western family and the changing social mores at the onset of the automobile age. Moorehead played Fanny Minafer, a neurotic, spinster aunt.

In the original version of the film, as far as can be deduced from the shooting scripts and Welles' notes, Moorehead had a major role. Film scholar Brian Eugenio Herrera likens Aunt Fanny in the original version to a Lady Macbeth figure in relation to the main protagonist, Georgie Amberson Minafer, played by Tim Holt.[53] But RKO baulked at the one hundred and thirty-five minute running time of the first cut Welles submitted. Following the failure of *Citizen Kane* at the box office, the studio was also alarmed by poor responses to the film at two preview screenings. Exercising its rights under the contract with Welles, the studio seized the picture, ordered editor Robert Wise to cut forty minutes and instructed assistant director Fred Fleck to re-shoot key scenes, including a new happier ending. "The biggest loss it seems, among the storied tragedies of Welles' production is perhaps Agnes Moorehead's performance," says Herrera. "Hers is clearly a great performance edited to shreds."

The character of Fanny was central to many of the scenes removed from the film, including two long sequences on the porch of the family mansion in which Fanny laments the changes in the town and discusses the fateful investment that subsequently ruins the family's finances. "Where Robert Wise's edits retained as protagonist contract-player Tim Holt's constipated Georgie, the changes to Moorehead's performance effectively relegate her to third female," laments Herrera.

Moorehead was also asked to re-shoot sequences, most notably the scene in the boiler room in which Aunt Fanny breaks down in front of Georgie. Reports indicate that preview audiences had laughed at the original rendition of the scene because Moorehead's performance was over-wrought. She delivered a more subdued reading in the restaged scene, the version which now appears in the surviving prints of the movie. The sequence is considered by many to be Moorehead's signature scene in *The Magnificent Ambersons*. Herrera says, "this scene alone warrants the Oscar nod, even the prize perhaps". Crucially, however, the altered tone of her performance in this scene contributes to the sense that her performance overall is "nearly incoherent" in its inconsistency.

As RKO expected, the cut-down version of *The Magnificent Ambersons* was a box office flop when it was released on a double bill with the comedy *Mexican Spitfire* starring Lupe Velez. Although the film received favourable reviews, as the awards season approached the studio focussed its attention on its other prestige production, *The Pride of the Yankees* starring Gary Cooper.

The studio was caught by surprise when Moorehead's performance was one of thirty citations for the year's Best Acting made by the National Board of Review on Christmas Eve. And even leading film critics were stunned when Moorehead was named Best Actress by the New York Film Critics' Circle two days later, edging out Greer Garson's performance in *Mrs Miniver* by eleven votes to seven on the sixth ballot. "The failure of Miss Garson to clean up was probably the one big surprise in the awards, for certainly her *Mrs Miniver* had been the most-talked-of role of the year," wrote Bosley Crowther in *The New York Times*. "We won't even try to explain it."[54] Apparently, Garson had led after the first ballot with seven votes versus three each for Moorehead and Katharine Hepburn in *Woman of the Year*.

Despite the upset result in New York, Garson was considered an overwhelming favourite for the Best Actress Academy Award. Believing that Moorehead had no chance of winning the statuette and hoping to secure a place in the lead category for Teresa Wright in *The Pride of the Yankees*, RKO decided to list Moorehead as a supporting actress in *The Magnificent Ambersons*.[55] As a newcomer to Hollywood with a reputation from theatre and radio as an exemplary character actress, the studio felt she was a better fit in the secondary category that in the Best Actress field with famous movie stars like Bette Davis, Greer Garson, Katharine Hepburn and Rosalind Russell, or popular rising talents like Teresa Wright.

When the Oscar nominations were announced in early February, Moorehead received the first of her four Best Supporting Actress nominations. Wright was nominated both as Best Actress for *The Pride of the Yankees* and Best Supporting Actress for *Mrs Miniver* (she triumphed in the latter category).

Listed among the ten candidates for the Best Picture Academy Award was *The Magnificent Ambersons*.

In the early 1940s, the New York Film Critics did not present separate awards for leading and supporting performances. Their selection of Moorehead as Best Actress of 1942 should not be taken unreservedly as evidence that her subsequent nomination in the Best Supporting Actress category at the Oscars was a case of blatant category fraud. While the role of Aunt Fanny is significant and Moorehead has considerable screen time, the studio-mandated edits leave Georgie as the main protagonist of the surviving version of the film. It remains debatable as to whether Moorehead should have been included in the lead category for her work in *The Magnificent Ambersons*. Her case is significant, however, in foreshadowing a trend that would emerge in the following decade and upend the approach the studios had taken to the four acting prizes at the Oscars in the years before the Second World War: the nomination of rising stars in the supporting categories for leading performances because they were Hollywood newcomers.

When Daphne du Maurier's novel 'My Cousin Rachel' was published in 1951, Twentieth Century-Fox immediately bought the film rights. Hollywood was keenly aware that the new novel was in the same vein as her earlier work 'Rebecca', the source material for the 1940 Best Picture Academy Award winner. Both were historical mystery-romances set on an estate in Cornwall. Twentieth Century-Fox was hoping that lightning would strike twice.

Studio head Darryl F. Zanuck assigned some of the industry's most respected talents to the production, entrusting the adaptation of the screenplay to Nunnally Johnson and inviting George Cukor to direct. Johnson would also double as the film's producer. The pair quickly began considering options for the male and female lead roles: Philip Ashley, the young man who has inherited an estate from a beloved elder cousin, and Rachel Sangalletti Ashley, the widow of the cousin who Philip suspects is a murderess. The film was what studio-era Hollywood referred to as 'a women's picture' so Zanuck wanted a major star for the role of Rachel. Rather than paying a second large salary for a male star, he was interested in a promising newcomer whose casting could generate its own kind of publicity heat.

Zanuck wanted Vivien Leigh for the role of Rachel.[56] The English actress was riding high on the critical acclaim that greeted her portrayal of Blanche

DuBois in *A Streetcar Named Desire* and which would bring her a second Best Actress Academy Award in early 1952. Johnson, meanwhile, was taken with the idea of getting Greta Garbo to accept the part.[57] The legendary Swedish actress hadn't appeared in a movie for a decade and her casting would have been a sensational coup.

In the meantime, Humphrey Bogart and Lauren Bacall went to see Anthony Quayle in his adaptations of 'Henry IV, Part 1' and 'Henry IV, Part II' at the Shakespeare Memorial Theatre in Stratford-upon-Avon and were struck by the marvellous performance of a young actor named Richard Burton in the role of Prince Hal. They recommended him to Johnson, who went to see the plays himself and then immediately cabled Zanuck. When Cukor arrived in England a few months later to pursue Leigh at the behest of Zanuck, he went to see Burton play the title role in **Emmanuel Roblès** adventure 'Montserrat' at the Old Vic. He agreed with Johnson's assessment that the young Welshman would be perfect for the protagonist in *My Cousin Rachel*.[58]

Garbo had eventually declined to play Rachel. "I admire your directing," she told Cukor, "but I do not admire myself anymore in film ventures."[59] Leigh did agree, but only on the condition that production take place in England so she could remain close to her husband, Sir Laurence Olivier.[60] Zanuck, however, would not countenance inflating the cost of the production by filming in England and, without consulting Cukor, engaged Olivia de Havilland for the part.[61] *My Cousin Rachel* would be de Havilland's first film since winning her second Best Actress Oscar three years earlier for *The Heiress*. Both Cukor and du Maurier criticized the choice. When du Maurier expressed strong reservations about Johnson's rather free adaptation of her novel, Cukor left the production. He was replaced by Henry Koster, a contract director at Twentieth Century-Fox.

According to Burton, his co-star wanted him replaced too. Preferring to appear opposite an established name, she wanted the role to be given to Gregory Peck. Hoping that Burton would quit the film in protest, she used her clout to deny him a co-starring credit in the billing. The manoeuvre failed. "I didn't mind about the billing a bit," he explained in his memoir notebooks.[62]

When the film opened in December, studio publicity focussed on de Havilland, declaring she "adds another brilliant performance to her gallery of distinguished portrayals." The press, however, heaped praise on Burton. In *The New York Times*, Bosley Crowther wrote, "Olivia de Havilland does a dandy job of playing the soft and gracious Rachel with just a fain suggestion of the viper's tongue.   But it is really Richard Burton, an English actor new to Hollywood, who gives the most fetching performance as the young gentleman of the doubts and storms. Mr. Burton, lean and handsome, is the perfect hero of Miss du Maurier's tale. His outbursts of ecstasy and torment are in the grand romantic style." Twentieth Century-Fox launched a Best Actress campaign for de Havilland, but listed Burton for consideration in the Best Supporting Actor category.

Burton unquestionably plays the protagonist in *My Cousin Rachel*.   He narrates the film and has more screen time than his famous co-star; Olivia de Havilland's first proper scene doesn't take place until after a quarter of the film's running time has elapsed.   Philip is the object of the narrative, while Rachel is the subject of his view; she is the person Philip tries to comprehend and the mystery that he tries to solve.   Even the title confirms the relationship dynamic: Rachel exists in relation to Philip, the story's main character.   Both Twentieth Century-Fox and the Academy, however, ignored all these metrics concerning the role of Philip, and focussed instead on Burton, the newcomer actor.

Twentieth Century-Fox had other productions in contention for the Academy Awards that year and, as historians Damien Bona and Mason Wiley recounted, "Zanuck had high hopes for *Viva Zapata!*, a biography of Mexican revolutionary-turned-president Emiliano Zapata written by John Steinbeck, directed by Elia Kazan, and starring Marlon Brando."[63] In order to maximize his studio's chances at the Oscars, Zanuck had Burton listed as Best Supporting Actor "to keep him out of the way" of Brando whom he promoted for recognition in the Best Actor category.[64]

Zanuck would have been less likely to adopt this approach had Burton been under contract to Twentieth Century-Fox, but he wasn't.   The young Welshman had signed with producer Sir Alexander Korda and appeared in *My Cousin Rachel* under a loan-out arrangement. Had Twentieth Century-Fox held a vested interest in Burton as an asset with a future at the studio, Zanuck would almost certainly have lobbied for him to be nominated in the prestigious Best Actor category just as M-G-M had in the late 1930s for Spencer Tracy in *San Francisco*, Luise Rainer in *The Great Ziegfeld* and Greer Garson in *Goodbye, Mr Chips*.   Without a studio interested in his reputation and future, however, Burton was dropped into the supporting category in a manner akin to the nominations of freelance character actors Roland Young in *Topper* and Charles

Coburn in *The Devil and Miss Jones* and *The More the Merrier*, all of whom gave performances in lead roles.

And the Academy didn't baulk at Zanuck's strategic move because Burton was a newcomer. He was unknown to the public and not yet a movie star. Even though Burton played the main character in *My Cousin Rachel*, Academy members had no qualms about placing him on the ballot for Best Supporting Actor because, as an unknown actor, he was providing support to the film's only bona fide star, Olivia de Havilland.

Three weeks before the Oscars, Burton collected a Golden Globe as Most Promising Newcomer (Male) and *Variety* predicted that he would take home the Academy Award after creating "a strong impression in the role of a love-torn, suspicious man".[65] As historian Tom O'Neil has noted, however, the trade paper thought it would be a close contest with Anthony Quinn in *Viva Zapata!*. Quinn "may be one of the upset victors at the awards ceremony," it declared.[66] As it transpired, Quinn won the golden statuette and Burton went home empty-handed.

In the following years, the Hollywood studios followed Zanuck's example and repeatedly campaigned for newcomers in the supporting categories for performances in leading roles.

> *Alternate Nominee* – If Richard Burton had instead been considered for the Best Actor category for *My Cousin Rachel*, who might have been in the race for the Best Supporting Actor statuette? For his performance in *My Six Convicts*, Millard Mitchell was the first winner of the Golden Globe Award for Best Supporting Actor to be overlooked by the Academy and is a possible candidate, but the most likely is previous Oscar winner Barry Fitzgerald for his performance in *The Quiet Man*, a popular Best Picture nominee and winner of the Best Director Oscar for John Ford.

The Hollywood studio bosses took particular note of Richard Burton's nomination as Best Supporting Actor in 1952 for his leading role performance in *My Cousin Rachel* and of the victory in the same category the following year by A-list singer Frank Sinatra for his supporting turn in *From Here to Eternity*. In both cases, recognition by the Academy in the secondary category turned out to be a stepping stone to success as leading men and movie stars rather than as defining moments limiting their careers to supporting character parts. A year after his nomination for *My Cousin Rachel*, Burton was on the Academy's Best Actor shortlist for his starring role in the major box office hit *The Robe*, while Sinatra received a Best Actor nomination for his starring role in the drama *The Man with the Golden Arm* just two years after his Oscar win.

Established movie stars remained unwilling to have their name put forward for the supporting categories, especially actresses wary of being shifted from leading lady roles into featured actress parts. Rosalind Russell, for example, would not countenance suggestions by studio boss Harry Cohn that her supporting performance in *Picnic* be promoted for the Best Supporting Actress category in 1955, just three years after Burton's nomination for *My Cousin Rachel* and two years after Sinatra's win for *From Here to Eternity*. Newcomers to Hollywood, however, were more co-operative with studio strategies to earn fame and prestige for their newest talents through Oscar nominations in the supporting categories. While Cohn's proposal for Russell was blocked, his suggestion of a Best Supporting Actor bid that same year for Jack Lemmon's performance in *Mister Roberts* met with no such resistance.

'Mister Roberts' had been a major hit when it opened on Broadway in February 1948. It played more than one thousand performances over nearly three years before touring nationally for another year. For his performance in the title role, Henry Fonda won a Tony Award for Best Actor in a Play. Adapted from a collection of short stories by Thomas Heggen, the play recounts the experiences of a U.S. Navy cargo ship's crew in the last months of the Second World War and has three lead roles: protagonist Lieutenant Roberts, the executive officer who attempts to protect the crew from the petty cruelties of their commanding officer; antagonist Lieutenant Commander Morton, the ship's harsh and unpopular captain; and comic relief Ensign Pulver, who shares quarters with Lieutenant Roberts. Another character, the ship's doctor, was a significant featured part.

Warner Bros. acquired the rights for a film version initially as a vehicle for William Holden and then subsequently for Marlon Brando. When John Ford took over the production as director, however, he insisted that Fonda have the opportunity to reprise his stage success despite the studio's concerns that he was by then too old for the part and that his box office power had been diminished by a lengthy absence from the screen (his last film has been *Fort Apache* in 1948).[67] Ford cast Warner Bros. star James Cagney as the captain and it proved to be the last feature he made for the studio. For the role of Ensign

Pulver, which had been originated on Broadway by David Wayne, he obtained the services of Jack Lemmon under a loan-out agreement. After considerable success as a comedic actor on television, Lemmon had been signed by Columbia in 1953 and given leading roles in back-to-back Judy Holliday vehicles, *It Should Happen To You* and *Phffft!*.

Although the production was plagued with problems and was ultimately made by a series of three different directors, the film version of *Mister Roberts* was a huge success upon its release in July 1955. It was the second highest-grossing film of the year and finished as the runner-up for the New York Film Critics' Best Picture prize. In *The New York Times*, critic A. H. Weiler had declared the movie to be "strikingly superior entertainment".

As awards season approached Warner Bros. mounted a Best Actor campaign for Fonda whose performance in *Mister Roberts* had been lauded as one of the greatest of his career. *The New York Times*, for example, had praised him for "a beautifully lean and sensitive characterization, full of dignity and power". The studio was also promoting Cagney as Best Actor for his portrayal of a gangster in *Love Me or Leave Me*.

With both Fonda and Cagney in the race, Cohn decided to push Lemmon for the Best Supporting Actor despite the fact that, as historian Tom O'Neil has concluded, he "really had a lead role".[68] The fact that Columbia contract player Ernest Borgnine was a strong contender for the Best Actor award that year for his performance in the independently produced *Marty* was also a critical factor in Cohn's decision.

In adapting the play, screenwriter Frank Nugent and director John Ford had emphasized the comedic elements and created additional business for the character of Ensign Pulver.[69] "Because Ford liked me and he liked what I was doing," the actor later recalled, "he made up a whole bunch of stuff for when I bring the nurses aboard – leaning on a hot gun, drinking dirty dishwater for soup and telling them to put more salt in it, all kinds of crap."[70] Lemmon performed some of his best scenes under replacement director Mervyn LeRoy, however, including the reading of Roberts' letter to the crew towards the end of the film. "I did not like the scene the first time I did it, with Ford," he explained. "It was too indulgent, too big, too sentimental – you could see the acting too much. I did it again with Mervyn and he let me be a lot simpler. That's the one we used."[71] Lemmon was listed in the film's opening credits as one of the four stars of the production. Fonda and Cagney are listed together immediately after the title. William Powell, in the featured role of the ship's doctor, and Lemmon are listed on the second title card in the same sized type. The supporting cast are then credited in smaller type.

When the Academy Award nominations were announced in mid-February, *Mister Roberts* received only three nominations, including for Best Picture. In one of the biggest surprises in Oscar history, Fonda missed out on a nomination. "It was a blatant omission on the part of the Academy to leave Henry Fonda out of the running," nominee Spencer Tracy told reporters. "He was great in *Mister Roberts*."[72] Cagney was shortlisted for the Best Actor award for *Love Me or Leave Me* and Lemmon was included among the five candidates for the Best Supporting Actor prize despite having a lead role and significant screen time.

Academy members didn't flinch from Cohn's suggestion that Lemmon ought to be a candidate in the supporting category for *Mister Roberts* principally because he was a relative newcomer to Hollywood. While there was no question about his status as a leading man (he had already co-starred in two comedies for Columbia), *Mister Roberts* was only his fourth feature film. And opposite stars of the calibre of Fonda, Cagney and Powell, Hollywood was content to ignore such metrics as screen time and accept Lemmon as a supporting player. It was, once again, a case of the industry placing a performer in a particular category on the basis of their status in the studio hierarchy rather than on an assessment of the role's significance to the film.

As predicted by the annual poll of Academy voters by *Variety*, on Oscar night Lemmon won the Academy Award for Best Supporting Actor. He thanked the "highest professionals with whom I've had the good fortune of working ever since I got into this business."

While Cohn was delighted that his new contract actor was an Oscar winner, others were dismayed that leading players were using the supporting categories as an alternative way of getting their hands on a golden statuette. "What will become of the many wonderful supporting players who can hope only to qualify in the one category?" asked a letter to *The Hollywood Reporter*. "Like many lovable old spinsters, their chances could surely become fewer as the years go by for that highly coveted Academy Award nomination."[73] High-profile members of the Screen Actors Guild requested that the Academy amend the rules governing nominations in the acting categories to exclude stars and leading players from contesting the supporting categories.[74] The Academy refused.

Alternate Winner – If Jack Lemmon had instead been considered for the Best Actor category for *Mister Roberts*, who might have won the Oscar as Best Supporting Actor of 1955? Nominated for a third time, sentiment may have delivered the statuette to Arthur Kennedy for his performance in *Trial*, but many think the winner would have been Sal Mineo for *Rebel Without a Cause*.

Alternate Nominee – If Jack Lemmon had instead been considered for the Best Actor category for *Mister Roberts*, who might have been in the race for the Best Supporting Actor statuette? The most likely candidate is Charles Bickford, winner of the National Board of Review prize for *Not as a Stranger*. It would have been his fourth nomination in just seven years.

When Paddy Chayefsky's drama 'Marty' was telecast live on 24 May 1953 as part of the fifth season of the 'The Philco Television Playhouse' program, it ran for fifty-one minutes. Rod Steiger portrayed the title character, a hard-working Bronx butcher who meets a shy schoolteacher named Clara just when he has all but given up hope of ever finding someone to marry. When independent producers Burt Lancaster and Harold Hecht struck a deal with United Artists to distribute a feature film version of the teleplay the following year, they invited Steiger to reprise his role. Unwilling to commit to the contract terms offered by the producers, he declined. The role was offered to Ernest Borgnine instead.

In the original teleplay, the role of Clara had been portrayed by Nancy Marchand. While the producers considered Marchand for the feature film version, there were concerns over the fact that she had never appeared in a movie. The part had been considerably expanded by Chayefsky in his adaptation of the teleplay and Lancaster and Hecht decided to audition actresses with film experience. Among the candidates was Betsy Blair, the wife of movie star Gene Kelly, who had appeared in small roles in *A Double Life* and *The Snake Pit* before her career had been derailed by an investigation of her communist sympathies. Desperate to escape the blacklist and appear in what she believed would be "an important film, [that] was new and different [and] about ordinary people", Blair lobbied hard for the part.[75] In the end, it was her connections that enabled her to overcome the reservation of the industry's anti-communist watchdogs: Kelly threatened to stop shooting the musical *It's Always Fine Weather* if his wife wasn't cast as Clara.

Acknowledging that the drama was principally a two-hander, Borgnine and Blair were given equal billing in the opening credits of *Marty* with their names appearing on screen together immediately after the title. In *The New York Times*, Bosley Crowther wrote, "Ernest Borgnine as the fellow and Betsy Blair as the girl give performances that burn into the mind ... Mr. Borgnine's performance is a beautiful blend of the crude and the strangely gentle and sensitive in a monosyllabic man ... Miss Blair is wonderfully revealing of the unspoken nervousness and hope in the girl who will settle for sincerity. The two make an excellent team."

The acting partnership of Borgnine and Blair was also recognised when Hecht and Lancaster took *Marty* to the Cannes Film Festival in the hopes of generating some extra publicity. When the film became the first American production honoured with the Palme d'Or, the citation read "For the beautiful humanity of the film and for the performances of Betsy Blair and Ernest Borgnine".[76]

According to historian Tom O'Neil, the film's producers used the prestige of the Cannes prize as the lynchpin of a major awards season campaign in the United States. "Lancaster and Hecht invested heavily to get it further awards notice," he wrote in 'Movie Awards'. "They thus became the only producers in showbiz history to spend more on a film's awards campaign ($400,000) than they did on making the movie ($343,000)."[77]

While a Best Actor push for Borgnine was the centrepiece of the campaign, the decision was taken to promote Blair for the Best Supporting Actress accolades rather than as a candidate for the Best Actress awards. Blair has less screen time than Borgnine in *Marty*, but her character is central to the plot and to the movie's emotional arc. *Marty* is essentially a romance and Chayefsky's original title for the teleplay was 'Love Story'. Blair was placed in the supporting race, however, because she was a lesser name and had no studio backing. It had been four years since she she had last appeared in a movie and Clara was her first leading role. At the time, Blair was better known in Hollywood as Kelly's wife than as an actress. And while Columbia's Harry Cohn was eager to see contract player Borgnine succeed in the Best Actor stakes, Blair was a freelance artist who had never signed a contract for one of the studios. There was therefore no studio operation prepared to expend resources promoting her for the Best Actress Oscar on the basis that a nomination in the lead category would enhance her reputation and make her a more valuable and bankable asset. The Oscars were a business for Hollywood, and there wasn't much of a business case for backing Blair for Best Actress rather than for Best Supporting Actress where a nomination could ostensibly be more easily secured.

The placement of Blair in the race for a Best Supporting Actress nomination effectively doomed the chances of the film's supporting actresses being recognized by the Academy. In *The New York Times*, Crowther had said, "as the disquieted mother of the hero, Esther Minciotti is superb, and Augusta Ciolli is devastating as the grimly dependent aunt". Both women were reprising their roles from the original teleplay, as was Joe Mantell in the role of Marty's best friend. When the Academy Award nominations were announced, Mantell was shortlisted for the Best Supporting Actor statuette, but Minciotti and Ciolli were both overlooked. Instead, it was Betsy Blair who earned a nomination as Best Supporting Actress that year for *Marty*.

On Oscar night, *Marty* added a Best Picture statuette to its Palme d'Or and Columbia's Harry Cohn delightedly watched two of his contract players win awards for movies they had made under loan-out arrangements: Ernest Borgnine as Best Actor for *Marty* and Jack Lemmon as Best Supporting Actor for *Mister Roberts*. Jo Van Fleet outpolled Blair to take home the Best Supporting Actress Academy Award that year for *East of Eden*.

Despite her nomination, Blair found that her political beliefs remained a barrier to roles in America. "I may not have been employable in Hollywood, but in Europe for a few years after the success of *Marty*, I was bankable."[78] It would be eighteen years before she appeared in another American film, and even then it was the independently produced *A Delicate Balance* rather than a feature from a Hollywood studio.

> *Alternate Nominee* – If Betsy Blair had instead been considered for the Best Actress category for *Marty*, who might have been in the race for the Best Supporting Actress statuette? Esther Minciotti is a likely candidate for her performance as the title character's mother in *Marty*. Although the film is now admired, *The Night of the Hunter* was not well received at the time which is probably why the Academy ignored the performance of silent film legend Lillian Gish.

In the wake of the 1956 Academy Awards ceremony at which Betsy Blair had been a nominee for Best Supporting Actress and Jack Lemmon had collected the Oscar as Best Supporting Actor, high-profile members of the Screen Actors Guild requested a change to the rules under which performers were nominated. They wanted the Academy to prevent leading players from receiving nominations in the supporting categories and the move was supported by several in the industry who recalled that the supporting awards had been created to enable Hollywood to honour the contribution of featured and character players without having them to compete with famous movie stars in leading parts. When the Academy refused to embrace reform, it "prompted another undignified rush toward the Supporting category".[79]

A year after Lemmon's victory for *Mister Roberts*, three actors were nominated for the Best Supporting Actor Oscar for performances in leading roles: former movie star Mickey Rooney in *The Bold and the Brave*, rising movie star Robert Stack in *Written on the Wind* and newcomer Don Murray in *Bus Stop*. The traditional approach to the acting categories in which famous movie stars were nominated in the lead categories and featured players and unknowns were placed in the supporting categories informed the strategies behind the nominations of former star turned character actor Rooney and newcomer Murray, but the promotion of Stack for the supporting category was blatant category fraud and was controversial (see the beginning of the next chapter).

When he made *The Bold and the Brave*, Rooney hadn't been a box office draw for over a decade. Since returning from army service in Second World War, he had mainly been working in television since discovering he was too short to be a heroic or romantic Hollywood leading man and was too old to continue playing the comic teenager roles which had been the basis of his fame in the late 1930s and early 1940s. He had been offered a contract by M-G-M to make one film a year for a quarter of his previous asking price, but decided to retain his independence and work as a freelance artist.

In mid-1955, Rooney accepted one of the lead roles in a drama entitled *Battle Hell* about a trio of American soldiers (an idealist, a religious zealot and a gambler), serving in Italy during the Second World War. Rooney played the gambler, an entertaining character operating a floating crap game up and down the frontline. He also co-wrote the title song and reportedly directed at least one of his character's pivotal scenes. Directed by Lewis R. Foster, the movie was released in April 1956 by RKO under the title *The Bold and the Brave*.

Rooney's performance was singled out by critics with *The New York Times* declaring that he "walks off with the show".

Having successfully directed the film version of 'Picnic' for Columbia, Joshua Logan was invited by Twentieth Century-Fox to direct a big screen adaptation of 'Bus Stop', another play by William Inge. The production was as a vehicle for Marilyn Monroe who starred as Chérie, a singer in a roadside diner, a role originated on Broadway by Kim Stanley. In the other lead role of Beauregard Decker, the boorish and naïve young cowboy who is entranced by Chérie, Logan cast twenty-six-year-old Don Murray who he had seen on Broadway opposite Mary Martin in 'The Skin of Our Teeth'.

Bus Stop was Murray's feature film debut, having previously appeared only in theatre and television productions based in New York. He declined a standard, seven-year studio contract, but signed a six-year deal with Fox for two pictures a year and the opportunity to perform on Broadway every second year. [80] Today, his performance is seen as hopelessly over-the-top. Historians Sam Kashner and Jennifer MacNair recently wrote, "He talks in an unbelievable hayseed drawl and he can't seem to say a line – he must shout it."[81] At the time, however, his debut was met with praise from many leading critics. Calling him a "wondrous new actor", *The New York Times* said, "A great deal is owed to Mr. Murray. His tempestuous semi-idiocy exploding all around a juvenile softness sets up a mighty force to be curbed by Miss Monroe."

Twentieth Century-Fox saw an opportunity to garner prestigious publicity for their new contract player by promoting him for an Academy Award nomination. Ignoring the fact that Murray played one of the film's two principal, leading characters and has substantial screen time, Fox placed his name on the reminder list for the Best Supporting Actor award because he was an unknown newcomer and therefore was providing support to the film's famous movie star headliner, Marilyn Monroe. It was the same approach the studio had successfully pursued for Richard Burton in *My Cousin Rachel* four years earlier. And as had been the case then, the studio had an ulterior motive for classifying Murray as a supporting player in *Bus Stop*. That same year Fox's major Oscar contender was *The King and I* starring Yul Brynner and Deborah Kerr, a film version of the hit Broadway musical of the same name. Putting Murray in the secondary category would keep him out of the way the studio's major campaign for Brynner as Best Actor.

The Bold and the Brave was produced independently by the Filmmakers Production Organization and released by RKO Radio Pictures. With little studio machinery behind the film and absolutely none behind him personally as a freelance actor, Rooney's Oscar campaign was entirely his own initiative. The winner of an Academy Juvenile Award in 1938, ostensibly for his secondary lead performance opposite Spencer Tracy in *Boys Town*, Rooney saw an Academy Award as an opportunity to revitalize his flagging career. He was motivated less by Jack Lemmon's victory for *Mister Roberts* than Frank Sinatra's win two years earlier for *From Here to Eternity*. Sinatra's career, both as a singer and an actor, was in a slump when he appeared in a dramatic supporting part in the film version of the popular James Jones novel about military personnel on Hawaii at the time of the Pearl Harbor attack in 1941. Within two years of winning his Academy Award, Sinatra was a leading man in films and a Best Actor nominee. Rooney hoped an Oscar nomination, and hopefully a full-sized statuette, could turn around his own professional fortunes.

In mid-January 1956, two months before Lemmon's win for *Mister Roberts*, trade paper *The Hollywood Reporter* ran an article stating that "Mickey Rooney is so keen to gain an Academy Award for Best Supporting Actor that he has waived his star billing in *The Bold and the Brave*. He shares top-line with Wendell Corey. Rooney has had star-billing ever since *Ah, Wilderness!* in 1935."[82] In actual fact, Rooney had been forced to relinquish top-billing since returning from service in the army. He had been billed after Bob Hope in *Off Limits* and behind William Holden and Grace Kelly in *The Bridges at Toko-Ri*, for example. That he was keen to win an Oscar and was prepared to have his leading role performance placed in the supporting category, however, was quite true.

When the Academy Award nominations were announced on 18 February 1957, both Murray and Rooney were included among the finalists for the Best Supporting Actor statuette along with Robert Stack for his co-starring lead performance in *Written on the Wind*. None of them had been among the Hollywood Foreign Press Association's nominees for the Best Supporting Actor Golden Globe Award that year and so their inclusion was quite unexpected. "I was surprised that I was nominated," Murray said nearly half a century later in an interview with film historian Leo Verswijver. "I didn't have a private publicist, I did nothing about the Academy Awards: I didn't do any publicity before or after being nominated."[83]

The controversy that had followed Lemmon's win the previous year, quickly "engulfed Oscar's acting categories".[84] According the historian Tom O'Neil, many "Hollywood insiders howled over the lower contests." In addition to members of the Screen Actors Guild, media commentators soon joined the debate. "It started coming out in the newspaper that it was not fair for me to be nominated as a supporting actor while I played the leading role," recalled Murray. "I thought, 'Well, that's true.' I didn't know anything about the Academy, or about the rules, but such a big fuss was made out of it. There was a famous columnist who wrote an article, he called me one day and asked me to comment. I agreed with him: I was the leading man, and was nominated as a supporting actor, but it was all new to me. I expected him in his column to express that, and to remind the audience and the industry that I didn't do anything to get nominated and after being nominated still didn't [advertise] and ignored the whole process. And all he said in his column was, 'Scratch Don Murray from the Oscar consideration because he refuses to advertise'."[85]

The annual poll of Academy members by *Variety* suggested that Robert Stack would edge out Mickey Rooney for the Best Supporting Actor statuette. It was widely anticipated that their sizeable roles would give them an advantage over the only two candidates who had actually given performances in supporting roles: Anthony Perkins in *Friendly Persuasion* and Anthony Quinn in *Lust for Life*. The audience in attendance at the Oscar ceremony in the Pantages Theatre "gasped in surprise", therefore, when Jo Van Fleet revealed that in a major upset, Quinn was the winner. Four years earlier, Quinn had been the unexpected winner in the same category ahead of the highly favoured Richard Burton for his leading role performance in *My Cousin Rachel*. In 1956, he was the only performer nominated for both the Golden Globe Award and the Academy Award.

According to historians Damien Bona and Mason Wiley, when the result was announced Rooney turned to Stack in the row behind him and said, "We wuz robbed!".[86] Many in Hollywood, however, were delighted that the Oscar had been awarded to an actor in a genuinely supporting role. For his portrayal of artist Paul Gauguin in *Lust for Life*, Quinn had just nine minutes of screen time.

Having resisted calls for a rule change the year before, the Academy capitulated to the outcry that followed the triple nomination of Murray, Rooney and Stack and the win that year in the Best Supporting Actress category by Stack's co-star Dorothy Malone for *Written on the Wind* (see the beginning of the next chapter). While the studios continued to place performers on the annual reminder list for consideration in either the leading or supporting categories, the Academy established a new committee with the power to arbitrate any dispute of the appropriateness of a studio's listing decision. The reform did not last, however. The system was abolished after just seven years.

> *Alternate Nominee* – If Don Murray, Mickey Rooney and Robert Stack had instead been considered for the Best Actor category, who might have been in the race for the Best Supporting Actor statuette? Likely candidates include Golden Globe Award winner Earl Holliman for *The Rainmaker*, National Board of Review winner Richard Basehart for *Moby Dick*, Golden Globe Award nominee Eli Wallach for *Baby Doll* and Rod Steiger for *The Harder They Fall*.

In his biography of Elia Kazan, film critic Richard Schickel examines *Splendor in the Grass*, the director's last commercial hit, at considerable length. The film's screenplay was written by William Inge, whose award-winning hit Broadway plays 'Picnic' and 'Bus Stop' had been adapted into major films in the previous decade. According to Schickel, however, it was Kazan himself who was "the prime mover" behind the production and who made significant contributions to the screenplay for which Inge subsequently won an Oscar.[87]

Splendor in the Grass revolves around Bud Stamper, the scion of a wealthy family, and Wilma Loomis, the daughter of a shopkeeper, and its central theme of sexual repression is explored, says Schickel, through "an intense adolescent love story that the two principals try to keep secret from their prying parents".[88] For the lead roles, Kazan cast twenty-two-year-old newcomer Warren Beatty, the younger brother of movie star Shirley MacLaine, and former child star Natalie Wood, who would subsequently appear that same year in the musical *West Side Story*.

Schickel describes Beatty's character as "the starring role in *Splendor in the Grass*."[89] As a young man struggling to escape his father's ambitions for him and to navigate his first romantic relationship, Bud is at the centre of Inge's story and of the emotional arc in Kazan's film. Prior to making the movie, Beatty had appeared in only a handful of television programs and one play on Broadway, William Inge's 'A Loss of Roses' for which he received a Tony Award nomination as Best Featured Actor in a Play. He was widely credited, however, with the success that *Splendor in the Grass* enjoyed at the box office. "The authority and eloquence of the theme emerge in the honest, sensitive acting of Mr Beatty and Miss Wood," declared Bosley Crowther in *The New York Times*. "The former, a surprising newcomer, shapes an amiable decent, sturdy lad whose emotional exhaustion and defeat are the deep pathos in the film."

The Hollywood Foreign Press Association included both Beatty and Wood among the nominees for the annual Golden Globes. In the Motion Picture (Drama) categories they were nominated as Best Actor and Best Actress, while Beatty was also shortlisted for the Most Promising Newcomer (Male) award.

When the Academy issued ballots for the selection of Oscar nominees, however, Beatty's name appeared on the studio-issued Reminder List as a candidate for Best Supporting Actor.[90] It is not clear whether he was listed for *Splendor in the Grass* or for his subsequent film, *The Roman Spring of Mrs Stone* in which he appeared opposite Vivien Leigh. Most likely, Warner Bros. promoted him for both performances. Although Beatty was one of the two leads of *Splendor in the Grass*, played a protagonist and drove both the film's story and emotional arc, the studio focussed on his status as a newcomer. In placing him in the supporting category, Warner Bros. was following the approach it had used for Richard Burton in *My Cousin Rachel* nine years earlier and had subsequently been successfully copied by Columbia for Jack Lemmon in *Mister Roberts* and by Twentieth Century-Fox for Don Murray in *Bus Stop*. While it is difficult to argue that Beatty was providing support to headliner Wood in *Splendor in the Grass* since she had only previously been a child star and had never carried a production, it could be said that he was supporting famous movie star and two-time Oscar winner Leigh in *The Roman Spring of Mrs Stone*.

Warner Bros. was also motivated to campaign for Beatty in the supporting category by its broader strategy for the Academy Awards that year. Its main Oscar contender was *Fanny*, a non-musical film adaptation of the musical of the same name starring Leslie Caron, Maurice Chevalier and Charles Boyer. For his first non-singing role in an American film, Chevalier was "actively courting Oscar honours"[91] and was nominated alongside Beatty for the Best Actor in a Motion Picture (Drama) Golden Globe Award. Warner Bros. executives would have been eager to avoid having the two men similarly contest the Best Actor Oscar, and consequently dropped Beatty down to the supporting race.

"I think it is unfair for any actor who plays a lead role to compete, or attempt to compete, with other actors who did supporting roles," Beatty stated at the time. "My representative asked the Academy to cross my name off the list, and they said it was too late."[92] According to historians Damien Bona and

Mason Wiley, the young star publically declared that if he received a nomination, "he'd refuse the honor."[93]

As it transpired, neither Beatty nor Chevalier were nominated for an Oscar that year. The Academy shortlisted Charles Boyer in the Best Actor category for *Fanny* rather than his co-star and countryman. And Beatty did not make the list of Best Supporting Actor candidates. He presumably missed out either because he was in contention for two different films or because his opposition to receiving a nomination in the supporting category had become widely known.

Ironically, the Best Supporting Actor Oscar nominees did include George C. Scott for his performance in *The Hustler*. Dismissing acting awards as "a weird beauty or personality contest," he asked the Academy for his name to be dropped from consideration, just as Beatty had said he would have done in the event he had made the cut. The Academy declined, advising that it was the performance not the actor that received the nomination. It can only be imagined how this explanation was taken by the actors and actresses who had missed out on nominations for performances in genuine supporting roles because Academy members had accepted the studios' placement in the supporting categories of leading players on the basis of their status as a performer.[94]

In the biting comedy *The Fortune Cookie*, writer-director Billy Wilder explored one of his favourite themes: the repercussions of a man pulling off a scam. The plot centres on Harry Hinkle, a television cameraman injured when he collides with a player on the sidelines of a professional football match, and his brother-in-law Willie Gingrich, an unethical lawyer who convinces him to feign serious injury in order to secure a huge insurance payment.

Having previously worked with him on *Some Like It Hot*, *The Apartment* and *Irma La Douce*, Wilder cast Jack Lemmon in the role of Hinkle, while the part of Gingrich was written for Walter Matthau. "Before we put a word on paper we went to New York to see Mr Matthau," explained Wilder's co-screenwriter, I.A.L. Diamond. "We told him the story and got him committed to do it before we began to write. We thought he was ideal for the part of the shyster brother-in-law."[95] According to biographer Ed Sikov, "Matthau was integral to *The Fortune Cookie* from the beginning"[96] and asked Lemmon at the start of production why had agreed to play Hinkle when Gingrich was obviously the better part with all the funny lines. Lemmon replied that it was about time somebody fed Matthau some decent lines.[97]

Historian Emanuel Levy says, "the whole film was based on team acting" by the two lead actors and the centrality of their partnership was acknowledged in the opening credits in which they both receive top billing above the title.[98] When the film was released in October 1966, Vincent Canby in *The New York Times* praised "Walter Matthau [as] an ambulance-chasing legal eagle, and Jack Lemmon, his schnook brother-in-law, a television cameraman whom Matthau entices into an elaborate, $1-million insurance swindle". He concludes, "the superb performance of Mr. Matthau dominates the film [and] makes a fine figure of a comic villain".

At the Golden Globe Awards, Matthau received a nomination as Best Actor in a Motion Picture (Comedy or Musical), but his co-star was overlooked. When the annual Reminder List was issued along with the ballots for the Academy Award nominations, however, United Artists placed Matthau in consideration for the Best Supporting Actor category. According to Levy, the distributor calculated that "Matthau's chances to win were much better in the supporting classification because there were two extremely strong lead performances: Paul Scofield in *A Man for All Seasons* and Richard Burton in *Who's Afraid of Virginia Woolf?*." Levy argues that the promotion of Matthau for the secondary category for his work in *The Fortune Cookie* was a "quite clear" example of the designation of a performance being determined by "the chances to win" rather than an objective assessment of the role based on such metrics as screen time, importance to narrative, and billing.[99]

The rationale, as it had been for other co-lead roles played by Richard Burton in *My Cousin Rachel*, Jack Lemmon in *Mister Roberts*, Don Murray in *Bus Stop* and Warren Beatty in *Splendor in the Grass*, was that as a newcomer taking on a leading role in a feature film for the first time, Matthau was a lesser name and therefore providing support to Lemmon who, as a major film star and established leading man, was carrying the movie. But, as historians Damien Bona and Mason Wiley stated in their seminal work 'Inside Oscar', "Walter Matthau was no new face.[100] Originally a stage actor, he had been in movies for a decade, usually playing villains. He went back to Broadway in the early 1960s, and won two Tony Awards for comedy." Only three years earlier, Matthau had made a memorable appearance in a secondary lead role as the villain in the high-profile romantic comedy caper *Charade* starring Audrey Hepburn and Cary Grant.

The arbitration committee that the Academy had established in the late 1950s following a string of highly controversial category fraud placements had been abandoned two years earlier when the rules governing nominations in the acting categories were amended to include the statement, "the determination as to whether a role is a leading or supporting role shall be made individually by members of the branch at the time of balloting." It is wording that remains part of the rules today.

With no mechanism through which United Artists' strategy could be challenged, when the Oscar nominations were announced in mid-February, Matthau was among the candidates for the Best Supporting Actor statuette. Many protested his inclusion saying that it gave him an unfair advantage. Historian Tom O'Neil believes his subsequent victory was marred by the controversy. "Far less popular was the Best Supporting Actor champ, who was accused of competing out of category," wrote O'Neil in 'Movie Awards'.[101]

Following the abolition of the arbitration committee and Matthau's victory for *The Fortune Cookie*, category fraud became an increasing issue at the Academy Awards. As Levy has argued, "politicking through ad campaigns and other irrelevant factors have continued to operate" ever since.[102]

Alternate Winner – If Walter Matthau had instead been considered for the Best Actor category for *The Fortune Cookie*, who might have won the Oscar as Best Supporting Actor of 1966? Given the success on the big night for *A Man for All Seasons*, which won six Oscars including Best Picture and Best Actor, it seems likely that Robert Shaw would have been rewarded for his portrayal of King Henry VIII ahead of George Segal for *Who's Afraid of Virginia Woolf?*. Shaw had been the National Board of Review champion and a Golden Globe Award nominee.

Alternate Nominee – If Walter Matthau had instead been considered for the Best Actor category for *The Fortune Cookie*, who might have been in the race for the Best Supporting Actor statuette? The Academy may have nominated Golden Globe Award winner Richard Attenborough for *The Sand Pebbles* or Brian Keith for the comedy *The Russians Are Coming, The Russians Are Coming*.

Each year, numerous Oscar campaigns are, of course, unsuccessful. Nonetheless they can be revealing and one fascinating case was the campaign mounted by Twentieth Century-Fox in 1979 for Sigourney Weaver for her performance in the science fiction horror film *Alien*.

Originally, the seven human characters in the script by Dan O'Bannon and Ronald Shusett were written as generic parts for men but with a note in the script explicitly stating "The crew is unisex and all parts are interchangeable for men or women".[103] The film's producers sought to surprise the audience by having a woman play the lone surviving character. After an audition process in both the United States and the United Kingdom, twenty-nine-year-old Sigourney Weaver was cast as Lt Ripley, a character often cited as "the first female superhero." Film historian Rachel Abramowitz argues that director Ridley Scott "ensured that the character, while imperilled, showed grit and mettle."[104] The casting of a woman in the lead role also deftly underscored the script's exploration of basic male fears such as penetration, pregnancy and fatal birth.[105]

At the time of her casting, Weaver had appeared in only one feature film: a small part in Woody Allen's *Annie Hall*, released the previous year. Consequently, she was billed second, behind the film's notional star Tom Skerritt, but ahead of the high-profile supporting cast which included John Hurt, Ian Holm and Veronica Cartwright. Despite her inexperience, Weaver was singled out for praise by critics upon the film's release. In *The New York Times*, Vincent Canby wrote, "Sigourney Weaver is impressive and funny as ... a young woman who manages to act tough, efficient and sexy all at the same time."

The film was a significant commercial hit on both sides of the Atlantic and although reviews had been mixed, the studio launched an awards campaign focussed on the film's art direction and visual effects and the performances of Weaver and Hurt. Although she had portrayed the film's protagonist and had significantly more screen time than any other cast member, the studio promoted Weaver for the Best Supporting Actress category on the basis of her status as a newcomer. As critic Tim Gray recently wrote in *Variety*, "As for star power, Weaver was an unknown in *Alien*, while Tom Skerritt and John Hurt were established names, so she was considered supporting."[106] It was a classification which seemed absurd to many at the time, not just in retrospect.

The Academy did not nominate Weaver that year and some historians point to a reluctance by Academy members to honour work in the science fiction and horror genres beyond categories such as art direction, make-up and visual effects as a reason. It should be remembered however, that Twentieth Century-Fox's campaign for Weaver came at the end of decade in which Ellen Burstyn, Jason Miller, Linda Blair, Alec Guinness, Sissy Spacek, Piper Laurie and Melinda Dillon had all received Oscar nominations for performances in horror or science fiction movies such *The Exorcist, Star Wars, Carrie* and *Close Encounters of the Third Kind*. Although overlooked by the Academy, Weaver did receive a nomination from the British Academy in its Most Promising Newcomer to Leading Film Roles category. At the Saturn Awards, annual honours for achievements in science fiction, fantasy and horror films, she was shortlisted for the Best Actress prize while Veronica Cartwright was named the winner in the Best Supporting Actress category.

When Weaver reprised the role of Lt Ripley seven years later as the star of James Cameron's sequel, *Aliens*, her performance was rewarded with Best Actress nominations at both the Golden Globe Awards and the Academy Awards.

For most observers the nomenclature 'Best Performance by an Actor in a Supporting Role' suggests an objective determination of the whether a role is leading or supporting based on metrics such as screen time, narrative agency and centrality to the theme and emotional arc of the film. The name implies that the *role* is inherently a supporting part regardless of the actor performing it. As this chapter demonstrates, however, for publicists and executives in the film industry and for many members of the Academy, the classification of a role is all about the relative fame of the actor playing the part, regardless of other metrics. At the time that the supporting categories were introduced and through the decades that have followed, studios have been guided by the notion that the lead categories were for the famous stars carrying a movie regardless of the size or importance of their role, while the supporting categories were for featured players, character actors, juveniles and newcomers regardless of the size or importance of their role. This traditional approach focussed on the performer rather than the part is evident in the awards campaign mounted by Paramount for *Ordinary People*, the directorial debut of Robert Redford that won four Academy Awards, including Best Picture.

In the mid-1970s, Redford was at the peak of his Hollywood stardom following *Butch Cassidy and the Sundance Kid, The Candidate, The Way We Were* and

The Sting. Already a producer, he was seeking a new challenge and when he read the galley proof of Judith Guest's novel 'Ordinary People', he knew he had found the source material for his feature film directorial debut.

Guest's novel, published in 1976, is about a family struggling to cope in the aftermath of a family tragedy: the drowning of the eldest son in a boating accident. The chapters of the novel alternate between the perspectives of Calvin Jarrett, the grieving father, and Conrad Jarrett, the guilt-ridden younger son who survived the accident. The novel is driven by dialogue and stream of consciousness internal monologues with little description of character or setting.

In his adapted screenplay, Alvin Sargent made the teenage Conrad the principal protagonist. The story recounts his interactions with his parents, school friends, girlfriend and psychiatrist. The film's emotional arc is driven by Conrad's sessions with his psychiatrist, Dr Berger. It is in these sequences that his character gains insight and understanding and experiences the movie's cathartic emotional climax. When casting the film, Redford considered Conrad to be the lead character but regarded Dr Berger as the starring role.

Redford originally wanted Richard Dreyfuss for the part of the psychiatrist.[107] After starring in *Jaws*, *Close Encounters of the Third Kind* and *The Goodbye Girl*, for which he had won the Academy Award as Best Actor, Dreyfuss was one of Hollywood's hottest talents. For the secondary roles of Conrad's parents, Redford was considering Angie Dickinson and Anthony Franciosa, both of whom were lesser names primarily known for their television work. When Dreyfuss was unable to consider the project due to a nervous breakdown, Redford discussed the part with Gene Hackman and Donald Sutherland.

"I went into his office – he was seeing me to kind of audition for the part of the psychiatrist," Sutherland recalled more than three decades later. "But I wanted to play the father. The marriage reminded me of one that I was familiar with. So he thought about it, and then cast me." To balance the high-profile casting of Sutherland, Redford interviewed Lee Remick and Ann-Margret for the part of Conrad's emotionally repressed mother, before settling on Mary Tyler Moore. The casting of Moore, who had just ended her successful run on the television sitcom 'The Mary Tyler Moore Show', was dramatically against her image, as was the casting of Sutherland as the mild-mannered father.

Hackman accepted the role of Dr Berger, but just before production began he was forced to withdraw due to a schedule conflict with the reshooting of *Superman II*. Paramount executives pressured Redford to himself take on the role, but the director instead made another brave casting decision by giving the role to Judd Hirsch, one of the stars of the hit television comedy 'Taxi'. Historian Tom O'Neil described the choice as "an atypical male lead".[108] All the scenes involving the psychiatrist had to be shot in just nine days to enable Hirsch to take the part without interrupting production on 'Taxi'.

Nineteen-year-old Timothy Hutton was cast as the film's main character, Conrad. "I guess the casting director had seen a TV movie I had done called 'Friendly Fire' with Carol Burnett and Ned Beatty. They had cast a pretty wide net for [Conrad]. There was a total of five or six auditions; the fifth one was with Redford." *Ordinary People* was Hutton's feature film debut and it proved to be a huge challenge.

When filming began, Redford instructed the rest of the cast not to interact with the teenaged newcomer. "I wanted him to feel isolated," explained Redford in an interview decades later with *Entertainment Weekly*. "It would be up to him what to do with it, but I didn't want him to feel like he had a lot of support because the character didn't. He was wonderful ... he was raw and totally open." Hutton remembers that the experience was tough. "I didn't know what was going on," he has said. "If I had been aware of the strategy, it would have been easier for me, but it would have defeated the brilliant purpose Redford had in mind, which was to keep me off balance."

When the film was released, *Variety* declared that Hutton was "up to the considerable demands of the central role" and in *The New York Times*, Vincent Canby said he was "excellent in the difficult role of the deeply troubled boy". On the back of strong reviews, Paramount mounted a Best Supporting Actor campaign for Hutton. The studio set aside the fact that he played the film's central character and had considerably more screen time than any other member of the cast. His status as an inexperienced newcomer alongside established stars was the determining factor in his placement in the supporting category. As one website commented, "Hutton is the clear protagonist of *Ordinary People*, with his character's suicide attempt setting off the film's plot and his character development serving as it emotional crux. Because he was a young unknown, however, he was relegated to Supporting Actor at the Oscars." [109] In a recent online article on category fraud, critic Joe Reid described the placement of Hutton in the supporting category as "particularly galling."[110]

The categorisation of the film's other significant roles was also impacted by the eventual casting. Originally, the part of the psychiatrist was envisioned as the starring role, with Conrad's parents as secondary roles to be filled with lesser names. Had either Dreyfuss or Hackman played Dr Berger, Paramount would have promoted him for Best Actor. Instead the studio backed Donald Sutherland and Mary Tyler Moore for the lead categories, since they were the movie's top-billed stars, and placed Judd Hirsch in the supporting category alongside Hutton. Narratively, Dr Berger is a supporting character: he has no backstory, subplot or character development and exists purely as a device for the emotional progress of Conrad and, to a lesser extent, his father. In contrast, Conrad's parents carry their own subplot in the final version of the script and the emotional lives of both are explored by the film.

All four received nominations for the Golden Globe Awards. At the Oscars, however, Sutherland was a surprise omission from the final ballot. Moore was named in the Best Actress category, while Hirsch and Hutton both received nominations in the Best Supporting Actor category. On the big night, Hutton was a surprise winner. Even though he had collected the Golden Globe Award in the lead up to the Oscars, at twenty years of age, he was the youngest male performer to ever win a golden statuette in a competitive category.

> *Alternate Winner* – If Timothy Hutton had instead been considered for the Best Actor category for *Ordinary People*, who might have won the Oscar as Best Supporting Actor of 1980? The favourite for the statuette that year was Joe Pesci who had won prizes from the New York Film Critics' Circle, the National Board of Review and the National Society of Film Critics for his work in *Raging Bull* and it's difficult to imagine any other winner.

> *Alternate Nominee* – If Timothy Hutton had instead been considered for the Best Actor category for *Ordinary People*, who might have been in the race for the Best Supporting Actor statuette? With the same five actors having contested the Golden Globe Award and the Oscar, a deserving candidate is Jack Thompson who won a Best Supporting Actor prize at the Cannes Film Festival for *Breaker Morant*.

A year after Timothy Hutton's victory at the Academy Awards, Paramount attempted to replicate its successful strategy by promoting another relative newcomer for supporting category honours for a lead role performance in an Oscar contender: twenty-four-year-old Susan Sarandon in Louis Malle's *Atlantic City*.

In the five years prior to making *Atlantic City*, Sarandon had appeared in eleven features films. Whereas contemporaries such as Meryl Streep and Jessica Lange quickly established themselves as film stars with leading parts in prestigious productions, Sarandon's career stalled despite appearing in a variety of roles under the direction of some notable film-makers. "Her varied roles included among others, a cinema organist, a magazine writer, a gypsy fortune teller, a prostitute, a cinema attendant," explains film historian Alan Lovell. "The one constant in this patchwork was that she maintained the status of a featured actress, placed between the stars and the supporting actors." [111] Sarandon was still relatively unknown to the general public and as well as many in the industry when, in 1979, she was cast in *Atlantic City* as a twenty-two-year old.

Sarandon played Sally Matthews, one of the two protagonists in *Atlantic City*. A waitress in a casino, Sally plans to escape her dreary circumstances, including her estranged husband, by attaining accreditation as a croupier and moving to Monte Carlo. In the first half of the film, she is the main character in one of two parallel plots that are brought together by the murder of a supporting character at the film's mid-point. In the second half of the film, Sally is part of an unusual romance with her neighbour, a one-time gangster named Lou Pascal, played by Burt Lancaster. Sarandon shares almost equal screen time with Lancaster and plays a character with backstory, depth and agency and whose development is central to the film's emotional arc.

Released in Europe in late 1980 and in the United States the following April, *Atlantic City* brought Sarandon "recognition as a serious actress, which her campy earlier work in *The Rocky Horror Picture Show* had cause some critics to doubt," says biographer Betty Jo Tucker.[112] In *The New York Times*, Vincent Canby said she was "excellent" while film critic Pauline Kael wrote, "she keeps you tuned in to her feelings all the time."

Paramount's major Oscar contender that year was Warren Beatty's historical drama *Reds*. The studio promoted it heavily for Best Picture and mounted campaigns in the Best Director and Best Actor categories for Beatty, in the Best Actress category for Diane Keaton and in the Best Supporting Actress category for Maureen Stapleton. While *Reds* won Best Picture awards from the New York Film Critics and the National Board of Review, collected Best Director awards from the Los Angeles Film Critics and the National Board of Review and received Best Supporting Actress accolades from the Los Angeles Film Critics and the National Society of Film Critics, the film was not presented with any honours in the Best Actor or Best Actress races. As the major critics groups announced their winners, the studio was surprised to see *Reds* forced to divide the spoils with another of its own releases: *Atlantic City*, a film which Paramount had held over from the previous year and released quietly months before most awards contenders opened. *Atlantic City* emerged as a serious Oscar contender with Best Picture prizes from the Los Angeles Film Critics and the National Society of Film Critics, a Best Director award from the National Society of Film Critics and three of the four major critics' trophies for Best Actor. Named Best Actor by both the New York and Los Angeles Film Critics as well as the National Society of Film Critics, Lancaster became an early frontrunner for the Best Actor Academy Award.

As the Oscars approached, Paramount gave more attention to *Atlantic City* and ran advertisements promoting Sarandon's performance for the Best Supporting Actress category. [113]   Although she had a leading role with significant screen time, the category placement was determined by a combination of factors. Principally, the studio regarded her as supporting Lancaster, the film's headline talent, who had been a major movie star in the 1950s and '60s and was a previous Best Actor Academy Award winner. Sarandon had been a featured actress for years and the studio did not regard her as a star or a leading lady of equal status to Lancaster. Additionally, Paramount placed Sarandon in the supporting contest for strategic reasons. The studio did not want her compromising Keaton's chances in the Best Actress category for *Reds*. The prospect of her contesting the Best Supporting Actress statuette against Stapleton for *Reds* was less concerning because it was the lead categories that were regarded as prestigious and that meant the most from a business perspective in terms of publicity.

When the nominations were announced in mid-February 1982, *Reds* led the field with twelve nominations (the most for any film in fifteen years) and *Atlantic City* earned five nods. Both were shortlisted for Best Picture, Director and Actor. Unexpectedly, the films also squared off against each other in the Best Actress category where Keaton and Sarandon were both nominated. In *The New York Times*, Hollywood correspondent Aljean Harmetz wrote, "The biggest surprise in the acting categories was the nomination of Susan Sarandon, as a waitress with her eye on better things, for best actress for *Atlantic City*. The nomination was particularly surprising since Paramount, the studio that released *Atlantic City*, had been pushing Miss Sarandon for supporting actress. A flabbergasted Miss Sarandon said today that even she had voted for herself in the supporting-actress category."[114]

Sarandon's nomination in the Best Actress category is one of the very few occasions that the Academy's membership rejected a studio's fraudulent category placement and shortlisted a performer in the other category. Why it happened can only be a matter of speculation. Quite possibly, Sarandon had been around for too long to be accepted as a newcomer, especially given her role in *The Rocky Horror Picture Show* was quite high-profile even if not mainstream. It may also be that so many Academy members actually watched *Atlantic City* because of the buzz surrounding Lancaster's performance and thus realized that Sarandon had a lead role, that Paramount's proposed placement simply became untenable.

Interestingly, the beneficiary of the Academy membership's decision to include Sarandon among the Best Actress nominees was an actress in yet another film distributed by Paramount. Elizabeth McGovern, who had made her debut the year before in *Ordinary People*, had finished fourth in the Best Supporting Actress voting by the New York Film Critics' Circle for her portrayal of former chorus girl Evelyn Nesbit in *Ragtime*, but had been overlooked for a Golden Globe nomination. Her nomination by the Academy was a complete surprise, especially since, as Harmetz explained in *The New York Times* at the time, "Paramount did not take out a single advertisement for her."[115]

Thirty minutes of the Coen brothers' black comedy *Fargo* elapse before Frances McDormand first appears as Marge Gunderson, a heavily pregnant police chief investigating a homicide. On screen time alone, her role could be regarded a supporting one, but McDormand's top-billing is merited when other metrics are considered.[116] Despite her belated entry into the narrative, Marge is the film's protagonist; she drives the narrative and is crucial to the audience's connection with the dark story. As Janet Maslin explained in *The New York Times*, the film "has as its centerpiece the gloriously unhip Marge Gunderson … [she] is this film's ace detective as well as its closest thing to a moral center. The film adores her."

While Marge is the protagonist in *Fargo*'s crime investigation plot, the antagonist is Jerry Lundegaard, a fraudulent car salesman who arranges for his wife to be kidnapped in order to pay off a massive debt with the ransom money from his father-in-law. Maslin declared that "Jerry makes a milquetoast of a villain, what with the golf toys and matching pencils adorning his office or the galoshes and grocery bags that accompany him to a crime scene." Played by William H. Macy, it is Jerry who sets the plot in motion when he hires the kidnappers in a local bar at the start of the film and he is the one left to deal with the situation when the kidnapping plot goes horribly wrong. Listed second after McDormand in the film's opening credits, Macy has more screen time than any other member of the cast and plays the movie's leading role in terms of agency, character development and emotional arc. As critic Joe Reid recently commented, "The movie is about a crime and an investigation, and Macy shoulders the crime half of it."[117]

McDormand and Macy were recognised as the two leads in film reviews when *Fargo* was released and most summaries of the movie's plot recognize them as the protagonist and antagonist. When the nominations for the Independent Spirit Awards were announced in early January 1997, they were shortlisted as Best Actress and Best Actor. They subsequently took home those accolades and the Coen brothers collected the prize for Best Screenplay. *Fargo* was named Best Picture and Joel Coen won as Best Director.

At the Academy Awards, however, distributors Working Title and Gramercy placed Macy in the Best Supporting Actor category, presumably to avoid competing with Australian actor Geoffrey Rush who by then was emerging as a strong favourite for the Oscar. McDormand was promoted for the Best Actress statuette. "Even considering that McDormand owns the movie with one of the most memorable characters in film history," says Reid, "it's still puzzling that Macy wouldn't be listed as a lead."[118]

One website argues that "male lead William H. Macy was nominated as Best Supporting Actor for *Fargo*, probably because he plays the lead antagonist."[119] That seems unlikely, however, given Anthony Hopkins' victory in the Best Actor category only five years earlier for playing a villain in *The Silence of the Lambs*. An article in the *Chicago Tribune* a few years later reported that Macy "wanted to be positioned in support" in order to give him better chances of receiving a nomination.[120] The distributors could get away with the placement because he was unknown to the general public. Despite nearly twenty years of credits, he was a newcomer as far as the general public was concerned.

Historian Damien Bona says that when *Fargo* was released Macy was "a stage actor noted for his work with David Mamet and, onscreen, one of those character actors whose face everybody recognized without – until now – knowing his name."[121] As Reid succinctly wrote recently, "Nobody knew who William H. Macy was in 1996."[122]

Of course, Geoffrey Rush was a complete unknown to audiences when he portrayed pianist David Helfgott in *Shine*, but that didn't stop Fine Line successfully campaigning for him to be rewarded in the Best Actor category throughout that same awards season. Interestingly, because he portrayed Helfgott only in the sections of the film concerned with the pianist's adult life, Rush has less screen time in *Shine* than Macy does in *Fargo*. As a child and an adolescent, Helfgott was played by Alex Rafalowicz and Noah Taylor, respectively.

And then, as Reid correctly points out, "nobody knew who Frances McDormand was either".[123] It was the role of police chief Marge Gunderson in *Fargo* that made her famous. McDormand, at least, had a previous Oscar nomination to her name prior to her appearance in *Fargo* (as Best Supporting Actress for *Mississippi Burning*) which, in combination with her top-billing, helped give some credence to the distributors' listing of Macy as a supporting player in *Fargo*, relative to leading lady McDormand, despite his significantly greater screen time and the central importance of the character of Jerry to the movie's storyline.

Academy members accepted the classification of Macy and nominated him in the Best Supporting Actor category for his performance as the hapless Jerry in *Fargo*. On the big night, the Academy Award was presented to Cuba Gooding Jr. for his scene-stealing turn as an athlete in the comedy *Jerry Maguire*. McDormand, meanwhile, triumphed in the Best Actress category.

> *Alternate Nominee* – If William H. Macy had instead been considered for the Best Actor category for *Fargo*, who might have been in the race for the Best Supporting Actor statuette? It is likely that the Academy would have nominated either British Academy Award winner and Golden Globe Award nominee Paul Scofield for *The Crucible* or Screen Actors Guild Award nominee Noah Taylor for *Shine*.

In the last months of 2001, executives at Universal found themselves pondering how to handle the awards season prospects of two experienced young actresses with acclaimed performances in releases that were receiving considerable awards attention.

Five years after the release of *Twin Peaks: Fire Walk With Me*, a return to the characters and plot of his earlier acclaimed television series 'Twin Peaks', director David Lynch began development of another 90-minute pilot with Touchstone Television with a view to selling it to the US network ABC as an on-going television series. The pilot was shot in six weeks from February 1999 and starred thirty-year-old Australian actress Naomi Watts alongside Justin Theroux and Laura Elena Harring. Executives at ABC, however, declined to take up the pilot or the option of a series.

Over the twelve months that followed, Lynch reworked the screenplay, adapting the material in order to enable it be released as a feature film. Additional scenes were shot in October 2000 and edited together with the television pilot material. The final result premiered at the 2001 Cannes Film Festival under the title *Mulholland Dr.* and focused on characters portrayed by Watts and Harring. The festival's jury gave Lynch the Best Director prize.

The film was well received by critics when Universal opened it in North American cinemas in October. Many reviewers praised Watts' lead performance in dual roles as a perky, aspiring actress trying to solve the mystery of an amnesiac and a failed actress depressed about an unrequited love. The *New York Daily News* singled out her "jaw-dropping performance" while *Variety* described her work as a "stunning starring debut". The *San Francisco Examiner*, meanwhile, declared that "If there were any justice in the film world, Naomi Watts would receive an Oscar nomination – and win – for her performance." The *Guardian* agreed when the film opened in the United Kingdom a few months later, praising her "top-notch, all-stops-out, bells-ringing, light-flashing star performance ... [for which] she must surely be a favourite for the best actress Academy award."

Despite such endorsements from leading film critics, Universal promoted Watts for recognition in the Best Supporting Actress category.[124] As would be the case two years later when Newmarket Films mounted a Best Supporting Actress campaign for Keisha Castle-Hughes in *Whale Rider*, the audacious category classification bemused observers and commentators throughout the industry. Who exactly in *Mulholland Dr.* was Watts supporting?

Despite over a decade of television and film credits in Australia and the United States, Watts was unknown to the general public when *Mulholland Dr.* was released. She had appeared in small roles and supporting parts, but had never previously taken on a lead role. Universal evidently wanted to avoid having her contest the Best Actress category with famous stars such as Halle Berry, Judi Dench, Nicole Kidman and Sissy Spacek. Following numerous precedents, the studio used Watts' status as a relative unknown in her first major role as a rationale for placing her in the supporting category even though she played one of the film's lead roles, a character who drives the narrative and has more screen time than any other. It also seems that Universal wanted to avoid Watts competing with an actress in the studio's principal Oscar contender that season: *A Beautiful Mind.*

From a very early stage, *A Beautiful Mind* was identified by Universal as a prestige production with significant potential for the annual awards season. It was a showcase vehicle for Russell Crowe, winner of the 2000 Best Actor Academy Award for *Gladiator*, in the role of John Nash, a mathematics genius and winner of the Nobel Prize for Economics whose career and marriage were impacted by his struggle with schizophrenia. The film was directed by Ron Howard, whose historical drama *Apollo 13* had been a major Oscar contender six years earlier.

While the film is an exploration of mental illness, it is also a portrait of a marriage. John Nash's schizophrenia is the theme of the film's narrative, but it is the relationship between John Nash and his wife, Alicia, portrayed by thirty-year-old Jennifer Connelly, which drives the film's emotional arc as well as providing a framework for the narrative. It was the view of several leading critics and commentators that Connelly "did most of the grunt work in *A Beautiful Mind*"[125] in a role that was "inherently less showy than Crowe's" and that "it was so obvious that [she] really had a lead role".

Although Connelly is only on screen for about forty-five minutes in *A Beautiful Mind*, which is approximately one third of the running time, her character is an active force in the narrative and carries the film's emotional story. And as *The Wall Street Journal* pointed out, she has exactly the same amount of screen time (total minutes and percentage) as Sissy Spacek has in the drama *In the Bedroom* for which Spacek was a Best Actress nominee.

Universal adopted a strategy for *A Beautiful Mind* predicated on releasing the film relatively late in the awards season. The film premiered in mid-December, opened in limited release just prior to Christmas and finally opened in wide release in early January 2002. It was the studio's main Oscar contender with executives eyeing the Best Picture, Director and Actor statuettes. Initially, it appears that the strategy involved promoting Connelly for Best Actress. When executives submitted category lists to the Screen Actors Guild, Connelly was entered in the Best Actress category. The studio listed Watts in *Mulholland Dr.* for Best Supporting Actress honours.

Universal's plans, however, began to go amiss when the major critics' groups began to announce their annual accolades. Ignoring the studio's suggestion that Watts be considered for the supporting awards, both the New York and Los Angeles Film Critics featured her in the voting for the Best Actress prizes at their meetings. In both cases, Watts finished as the runner-up to Spacek. She subsequently turned the tables on the Hollywood veteran to win the National Society of Film Critics plaudit. The studio quickly reversed course as a result. "Universal was initially pushing Watts in the Supporting Actress category only to revamp their campaign after Watts took several runners-up citations for lead actress at several critics' circles," explained Ed Gonzalez at *Slant* magazine. "Will it hurt her chances? Let's hope not."

With the campaign for Watts in *Mulholland Dr.* switching to Best Actress, the studio's campaign for Connelly in *A Beautiful Mind* was switched to Best Supporting Actress just as the film was opening and garnering attention. Claiming the previous classification of Connelly as a lead actress for the Screen Actors Guild Award was a clerical error, a studio spokeswoman declared, "We knew from the day we saw the movie that she was a supporting actress."[126] As Tom King explained in *The Wall Street Journal*, the same spokeswoman, however, didn't deny that "one of the factors for campaigning for her in the supporting category was simply that [the studio] thought she'd have a better chance of winning there, instead of duking it out against Ms Spacek and Ms Berry in the best actress category."[127]

Given the importance of the character of Alicia Nash to the plot and arc of *A Beautiful Mind* and the fact that Connelly's screen time was comparable to that of Spacek in *In the Bedroom*, King put Universal's revised campaign down to "growing Oscar hunger."[128] He reported, "While this kind of award deflation has happened before, people in Hollywood say it's happening more now because of overheated jockeying for the awards ... Studios are expected to spend a record $50million campaigning for Oscars, including, some now say, on trying make sure some of their actors get bumped down."

The by now all too familiar rationale was that Connelly, a little known actress was providing support to Crowe, who as the film's star and famous leading man was carrying the movie at the box office. While it was certainly true that Watts had struggled through minor parts in obscure films for the decade prior to her casting in *Mulholland Dr.*, Connelly's career prior to her appearance in *A Beautiful Mind* could not be portrayed in the same light. The former child model had made her feature film debut as a fourteen-year-old in Sergio Leone's *Once Upon a Time in America* and gained a degree of stardom two years later when she played the lead role in Jim Henson's fantasy film *Labyrinth*. She had significant roles in both *The Rocketeer* and *Dark City* and had been promoted for Best Supporting Actress consideration for her work in *Requiem for a Dream* just one year before her 'break-through' appearance in *A Beautiful Mind*. For her performance in *Requiem for a Dream*, for which Ellen Burstyn was a Best Actress Academy Award nominee, Connelly had received Best Supporting Actress nominations for both the Independent Spirit Awards and the Online Film Critics Society Awards. While not a star, it was something of a stretch to contend that Connelly was either an unknown or a newcomer.

The Screen Actors Guild shortlisted Connelly in the Best Actress category following the alleged clerical error in the studio listing. At the inaugural American Film Institute Awards, the Golden Globe Awards, the British Academy Awards and the Academy Awards, Connelly was nominated in the Best Supporting Actress category and was victorious on each occasion. "The whole Oscar campaign was a sort of deer in the headlights kind of experience," she later confessed.[129] While Crowe missed out on back-to-back Best Actor wins at the Oscars, *A Beautiful Mind* received the Academy's top prizes for Best Picture and Best Director. Connelly's inclusion in the secondary category is perhaps the definitive example of the Academy's alleged propensity to equate being an actress in the role of a *supportive* girlfriend/wife with being an actress in a *supporting role*.

The awards season did not unfold as successfully for Watts. Included on the ballot for Best Actress by the American Film Institute, she was overlooked for the Golden Globe Awards, the British Academy Awards and the Oscars. While the divisive and controversial nature of *Mulholland Dr.* probably played a factor with awards voters (who often tend to be more conservative than critics and less willing to embrace avant-garde works), the confusion over Universal's switching category placements almost certainly played a factor in her omission from the field of Oscar nominees.

Alternate Winner – If Jennifer Connelly had instead been considered for the Best Actress category for *A Beautiful Mind*, who might have won the Oscar as Best Supporting Actress of 2001? The winner would almost certainly have been Helen Mirren for *Gosford Park*. A well-respected actress, whose Oscar-winning performance in *The Queen* was still a few years away at that time, Mirren had been the winner of the Screen Actors Guild Award and had won the prizes from the New York Film Critics and the National Society of Film Critics.

Alternate Nominee – If Jennifer Connelly had instead been considered for the Best Actress category for *A Beautiful Mind*, who might have been in the race for the Best Supporting Actress statuette? The most likely candidate appears to be Cameron Diaz, a nominee at the Golden Globe Awards, the American Film Institute Awards and the Screen Actors Guild Awards for her performance in *Vanilla Sky*.

Studio bids for Naomi Watts in *Mulholland Dr.* and Keisha Castle-Hughes in *Whale Rider* to be nominated in the supporting categories were both rejected. Critics groups dismissed Universal's classification of Watts and recognized her as a leading actress, forcing the studio to hastily amend its campaign. In the end, Watts did not receive an Oscar nomination for her widely acclaimed performance and the studio's initial category fraud push was likely to have been a contributing factor. In the case of Castle-Hughes, it was the Academy members themselves who ignored the suggested category placement by Newmarket Films and placed the teenager on the ballot in the Best Actress category. Despite these precedents, Fox Searchlight mounted a controversial Best Supporting Actor campaign in late 2008 for the performance of eighteen-year-old Dev Patel in the lead role of Jamal Malik in *Slumdog Millionaire*.

Based on the acclaimed novel 'Q&A' by diplomat Vikas Swarup and adapted for the screen by Simon Beaufoy, *Slumdog Millionaire* focuses on the story of Jamal Malik, a penniless orphan from the slums of Mumbai who is arrested on suspicion of cheating just when he is on the verge of winning a fortune on a television quiz show. Over the course of one night, Jamal recounts his extraordinary life to a cynical police inspector, each story revealing how he knows the answer to one of the show's difficult questions.

Casting directors considered hundreds of young Bollywood actors for the role of Jamal and gave director Danny Boyle a shortlist headed by Ruslaan Mumtaz. Boyle, however, felt that Mumtaz was too good-looking for the part and, according to *The Hollywood Reporter*, he dismissed the field of experienced Bollywood candidates as "strong, handsome hero-types" lacking the sensitivity and innocence he wanted for the film's protagonist. [130] Instead, Boyle cast British actor Dev Patel, then a seventeen-year-old appearing on the television series 'Skins', his only professional screen credit.

Most of the financing for *Slumdog Millionaire* came from Warner Independent Pictures, a specialty division of Warner Bros. which was shut down in early 2008 amid accusations of mismanagement and declining output. North American distribution rights for the film reverted to Warner Bros. which initially slated the production for a direct-to-DVD release before striking a last-minute deal with Fox Searchlight Pictures in August. Fox Searchlight, which already had a small financial stake in the production, agreed to purchase half of Warner Bros.' interest in the film and handle the cinematic release in the United States and Canada. [131] *Slumdog Millionaire* premiered at the Telluride Film Festival and, just a month after the distribution deal was struck, subsequently won the People's Choice Award at the Toronto International Film Festival. Fox Searchlight suddenly found itself with an Academy Awards contender on its hands; a film both acclaimed by critics and popular with audiences.

Fox Searchlight swiftly launched an awards season campaign for *Slumdog Millionaire* which went into limited release in mid-November and opened wide in late January after strong reviews, enthusiastic word-of-mouth and some major accolades had generated considerable interest. Controversially, one aspect of the distributor's strategy was promoting Patel for the Best Supporting Actor accolades.

Jamal is unquestionably the protagonist in *Slumdog Millionaire* and is the film's only leading character. While he is played in several flashback sequences by two younger actors, as the eighteen-year-old 'present day' Jamal, Patel has the vast bulk of the film's screen time. The movie starts and ends with him and he is at the heart of both the narrative and the emotional arc. And unlike Timothy Hutton in *Ordinary People* and River Phoenix in *Running On Empty*, Patel does not appear opposite any famous stars who it could be argued he was supporting while they carried the movie. Patel has top-billing and was the focus of the film's publicity material. Like the earlier campaigns for Watts and Castle-Hughes, the push for Patel to be recognised as supporting performer begged the question, 'who is he supposed to be supporting?!'.

Decades of category fraud, however, had ingrained the belief in Hollywood that an unknown, eighteen-year-old foreign actor making his feature film debut simply could not (and indeed should not) compete with established leading men and famous movie stars in the Best Actor contest. As a newcomer, Patel was one of the industry's 'ordinary people' and belonged in the secondary category. After eighty years, Best Actor was still the preserve of movie stars. In accordance with numerous precedents over many years, Fox Searchlight listed Patel as a supporting player. The members of the Screen Actors Guild, who are not free to disregard studio classifications of performances as lead or support, duly shortlisted him for their annual Best Supporting Actor award.

Executives at Fox Searchlight, of course, had little reason to believe that they could secure a Best Actor nomination for Patel. The nomination of Castle-Hughes as Best Actress for *Whale Rider* five years earlier had been considered something of a fluke amidst the controversial attempt that season to ban the distribution of screeners to awards voters. She was only the third performer to earn an Oscar nomination in a lead category before the age of twenty. In the Best Actor category, the Academy hadn't nominated anyone under the age of twenty since shortlisting Mickey Rooney for *Babes in Arms* as a nineteen-year-old in 1939. But then it must be remembered that no young actor had been promoted for the category in decades. Acclaimed lead performances by young actors such as Hutton, Phoenix and Haley Joel Osment in *The Sixth Sense* had all been pushed for Best Supporting Actor honours. The apparent weight of Academy Awards history was, therefore, something of a self-fulfilling prophecy.

Slumdog Millionaire ended up receiving ten Academy Awards nominations in nine categories. Patel was not among those shortlisted. He was nominated, however, at both the British Academy Awards and the European Film Awards, in the Best Actor category. On Oscar night, *Slumdog Millionaire* collected eight golden statuettes. It went on to become the highest-grossing film ever released by Fox Searchlight Pictures.

One year earlier, Warner Bros. succeeded in garnering Best Supporting Actor nominations at the Golden Globe Awards, Screen Actors Guild Awards and Academy Awards for Casey Affleck's lead role performance in *The Assassination of Jesse James by the Coward Robert Ford*. The studio's campaign appeared to be predicated on Affleck's relative lack of fame compared to his world-famous co-star, Brad Pitt.

Affleck was thirty-two-years-old when he appeared in his first two feature film lead roles in 2007. In the historical drama *The Assassination of Jesse James by the Coward Robert Ford* he portrayed Robert Ford, the man who shot outlaw Jesse James, and in *Gone Baby Gone*, a crime thriller directed by his elder brother, Ben Affleck, he appeared as a tough private detective investigating the disappearance of a child. Released just one month apart, the films were the first productions, after a dozen years in Hollywood, in which Affleck played the protagonist at the centre of the narrative. Together they were regarded as a career breakthrough for him. In *Entertainment Weekly*, Lisa Schwarzbaum said his portrayal of Ford was "revelatory", a sentiment echoed by Claudia Puig in *USA Today*. In her review of *Gone Baby Gone*, meanwhile, Manohla Dargis in *The New York Times* declared, "I'm not sure exactly when Casey Affleck became such a good actor".

The films appeared in cinemas at the same time because of considerable post-production delays on *The Assassination of Jesse James by the Coward Robert Ford* which opened almost two years after principal photography was completed and, following a major re-edit, twelve months after it had originally been slated for release. Brad Pitt is the top-billed star and appears front-and-centre on the movie's theatrical poster. But ultimately, it's not his movie. In exploring the story of Jesse James' death, the film tells the story of the infamous outlaw's relationship with the man who killed him and its focus is squarely on the assassin rather than the train robber. Dargis described Pitt's performance as "curious ... at once central and indistinct, but then, so too is the character." In contrast, she praised Affleck's portrayal "which manages to make the character seem dumb and the actor wily and smart". Throughout the film, James is a distant figure, the object of Ford's obsession and his gaze. He remains, as Dargis correctly says, "indistinct". In contrast, the audience develops a quite distinct understanding of Ford, his yearnings and motivations. The narrative starts and ends with Ford and with his portrayal Affleck carries the plot with the bulk of the screen time. He also drives the film's entire emotional arc. It is Ford that takes the audience on a journey, whose psychology is explored and for whom the viewer has empathy. While Pitt was top-billed, it is Affleck who plays the story's main character. He appears on the poster behind and to the side of Pitt, but he is billed alongside the star, above the title.

"Casey Affleck was the protagonist .... but was nominated in a supporting category because Brad Pitt was the film's top-billed star," David Sims recently explained in *The Atlantic*.[132] For many, this rationale makes little sense. Leading film commentator Joe Reid, for example, recently described it as "a puzzler". In an article about category fraud he wrote, "Maybe the idea was that Brad Pitt was a much bigger star and thus would more easily be able to campaign against the Clooneys and the Depps in the lead category. But a) Pitt's role is *really* small in this movie, b) Affleck got all the best reviews and c) no one was rushing to nominate Pitt in either category anyway."[133]

Affleck's fame relative to Pitt was the justification for his placement in the secondary category. Largely unknown to the general public and a newcomer to lead roles, Affleck was considered by the industry's business hardheads to be supporting Pitt. It was Pitt who attracted audiences to the film, which is why he was featured prominently in the publicity material even though Affleck had the more significant role. Fox Searchlight calculated that Affleck's chances of a nomination for *The Assassination of Jesse James by the Coward Robert Ford* were better in the supporting category than in the Best Actor race where George Clooney, Daniel Day-Lewis, Johnny Depp and Viggo Mortensen were among the frontrunners. And then there was the matter of Affleck's other film.

While Miramax's awards season campaigns were focussed on *No Country For Old Men* and *There Will Be Blood*, the distributor also mounted a push for *Gone Baby Gone* which included promoting Affleck as Best Actor. With Miramax backing him for Best Actor for *Gone Baby Gone* it made little sense for Fox Searchlight to be pressing for him to be recognised in the same category for *The Assassination of Jesse James by the Coward Robert Ford*. By asserting that Pitt was the movie's star and leading man, Fox Searchlight were able to position Affleck as a supporting player despite playing the protagonist, having far more screen time, driving the narrative and being the focus of the emotional arc. The Weinstein Company pursued a similar strategy a year later in order to avoid Kate Winslet's performance in *The Reader* competing in the Best Actress category with her performance in *Revolutionary Road*, a film distributed by rival DreamWorks.

Unsurprisingly, the various awards bodies accepted the classification of Affleck. For his first lead role in a feature film, he received Best Supporting Actor nominations from the Hollywood Foreign Press Association, the Screen Actors Guild and the Academy. In *Variety*, film critic Guy Lodge recently said

Affleck's nomination and that of Hailee Steinfeld for *True Grit* a few years later, were "the most glaring examples in recent years ... [of actors] playing active protagonists who were nonetheless demoted in favor of senior co-stars."[134]

> *Alternate Nominee* – If Casey Affleck had instead been considered for the Best Actor category for *The Assassination of Jesse James by the Coward Robert Ford*, who might have been in the race for the Best Supporting Actor statuette? The most likely candidate appears to be Tommy Lee Jones, a nominee at the Screen Actors Guild Awards and British Academy Awards for his performance in *No Country For Old Men*, the winner of the Best Picture Oscar. It is possible, however, Academy voters might have nominated Paul Dano for his work in *There Will Be Blood* for which Daniel Day-Lewis won a second Best Actor statuette.

The assertion that studio executives and publicists cynically promote actors for awards recognition in one category or the other based on a calculated assessment of their best chances of securing a nomination or reaping a statuette with no regard for such metrics as screen time, narrative agency or character agency and, increasingly, little consideration of star status or billing, is most clearly evident in seasons in which a distributor hastily changes tack mid-campaign once the season is already under way.

As previously mentioned, Universal initially pushed Jennifer Connelly's performance in *A Beautiful Mind* for Best Actress honours and Naomi Watts' performance in *Mulholland Dr.* that same season for Best Supporting Actress recognition, but abruptly swapped their category placements when Watts received runner-up citations from major critics' groups. Obviously, nothing about their performances had changed. Objective metrics by which their performances could be deemed leading or supporting such as screen time, narrative agency, character development and relative billing in the credits were unaltered. The only thing that had changed was the studio's assessment of their chances at the Oscars. And with that, a lead performance was suddenly a supporting one and a supporting performance was suddenly a leading one. A decade later, The Weinstein Company very publically made an equally cynical change in the strategic direction of its awards season campaign for the revisionist Western *Django Unchained*.

Written and directed by Quentin Tarantino, *Django Unchained* is notionally the story of Django, a freed slave, who sets out to rescue his wife from a brutal plantation owner in pre-Civil War era Mississippi. The character of Django is overshadowed, however, by Dr Schultz, a German dentist-turned-bounty hunter who frees Django from slavery, trains him to be a vigilante and then aids him in his quest. When Tarantino offered the title role to Will Smith, the Oscar nominated star turned the part down. He later explained in an interview with Adam Markovitz at *Entertainment Weekly* that he didn't want to be second fiddle to the actor playing Schultz. "Django wasn't the lead, so it was like, I need to be the lead. The other character was the lead!". Smith says he begged Tarantino to rewrite the script to give Django a more central role in the action. Specifically, he felt that Django rather than Schultz should be the one to kill the villainous plantation owner, Calvin J. Candie. "I was like, 'No, Quentin, please, *I* need to kill the bad guy!'" said Smith.[135] The role went to Academy Award winner Jamie Foxx. Tarantino had written the co-lead part of Dr Schultz specifically for Christoph Waltz after the Austrian-born actor had appeared in his earlier film *Inglourious Basterds* and taken home numerous accolades, including a Best Supporting Actor Academy Award. Leonardo DiCaprio was cast in the supporting role of Calvin J. Candie.

In early November, a Weinstein Company spokesperson confirmed to awards blogger Tom O'Neil that the studio would be promoting both Foxx and Waltz for Best Actor honours and campaigning for DiCaprio in the Best Supporting Actor contest. The company was confident that they could secure a nomination for Waltz in the lead category alongside frontrunners Joaquin Phoenix in *The Master*, another film being handled by The Weinstein Company, and Daniel Day-Lewis in *Lincoln*. "Christopher Waltz's performance is so amazing in *Django Unchained* that it towers over the whole movie," the unnamed publicist was quoted as declaring.[136] Responding to speculation that the actor would be pushed for the supporting accolades, the spokesperson said, "We're moving him up to the lead Oscar race."

When critics finally reviewed the movie in December, they confirmed that it was a two-hander for Foxx and Waltz. In *The New York Times*, A. O. Scott wrote, "Waltz, who played the charming, sadistic SS officer Hans Landa in *Inglourious Basterds*, here plays Dr King Schultz, a charming, sadistic German bounty hunter whose distaste for slavery makes him the hero's ally and mentor. That hero, first glimpsed in shackles and rags on a cold Texas night in 1858, is Django (Jamie Foxx), who becomes Schultz's sidekick and business partner. ...

Over time the traditional roles of white gunslinger and non-white sidekick are reversed, as the duo's mission shifts from Schultz's work to the rescue of Django's wife."

The studio's awards season campaign went awry, however, within two days of the first preview screenings for critics. While the National Board of Review honoured DiCaprio as Best Supporting Actor on 5 December, two days earlier Waltz finished as the runner-up in the New York Film Critics' Circle voting for Best Supporting Actor. That result was repeated when the Los Angeles Film Critics met on 9 December. Members of the Screen Actors Guild, who are not free to disregard studio classifications of performances as lead or support, could have put the campaign back on track by endorsing the studio's category placements but when the Guild's annual awards nominations were announced on 12 December, *Django Unchained* was entirely overlooked. Company boss Harvey Weinstein later admitted that his decision to delay sending out DVD screeners until five days after the announcement of the Screen Actors Guild nominations had backfired. "I wanted people to see it on the big screen," he explained in an interview with blogger Mike Fleming Jr. "I told Quentin we'd probably pay the price at the Oscars, but it was the right way to see an epic period movie about a man who does not give up. Eventually, we gave out the DVDs but we paid the price for being late." [137] A Weinstein Company representative quickly confirmed to O'Neil that "Christoph Waltz's role in *Django Unchained* will be campaigned as a Supporting role for the rest of the awards season."[138]

Nothing about Waltz's performance had changed. Critics, however, had decided that Foxx was the film's star and Waltz, who had already been labelled as a supporting actor with his numerous awards for *Inglourious Basterds*, was providing him with support. This impression had likely been aided by the absence of Waltz's character from most of the film's long, bloody climatic sequence. In the years since his Oscar win, Waltz's career in Hollywood had been dominated by showy supporting roles in films such as *The Green Hornet* and *Water for Elephants*. His only lead role had been in *Carnage*, Roman Polanski's film version of the award-winning play 'God of Carnage' by Yasmina Reza, and even then he had shared the screen equally with three co-stars. As blogger Daniel Boneschansker later wrote, the shift in strategy was simply because the studio realized "that Waltz had a much better chance of Oscar success in the supporting race".[139]

At the Golden Globes, DiCaprio and Waltz were shortlisted alongside each other in the Best Supporting Actor category while Foxx was overlooked in the Best Actor (Drama) category. In the end, Waltz took home his second Globe in just four years. When the Academy Award nominations were announced, Waltz was the only member of the cast to receive a nomination. All five nominees in the category were previous Oscar winners and three were in films distributed in North America by The Weinstein Company. On the big night, it was Waltz who collected the statuette.

Film commentator Erin Whitney cites the Oscar wins of Jennifer Connelly in *A Beautiful Mind* and Christoph Waltz in *Django Unchained* as the most prominent recent examples of actors who have "won Supporting Oscars for lead roles." [140] At the website, The Film Experience, meanwhile, blogger Nathaniel Rogers has said of Waltz, "he's like the Poster Boy for Category Fraud." [141]

> *Alternate Winner* – If Christoph Waltz had instead been considered for the Best Actor category for *Django Unchained*, who might have won the Oscar as Best Supporting Actor of 2012? Of the other nominees that year, the winner is most likely to have been Tommy Lee Jones for *Lincoln*. But if Waltz had been in the lead category, Leonardo DiCaprio may well have been nominated for *Django Unchained* and could possibly have won his first statuette.

> *Alternate Nominee* – If Christoph Waltz had instead been considered for the Best Actor category for *Django Unchained*, who might have been in the race for the Best Supporting Actor statuette? The most likely candidate appears to be Leonardo DiCaprio, a nominee at the Golden Globe Awards and the winner of the National Board of Review prize for *Django Unchained*.

For his performance as a young man from East Berlin who goes to elaborate lengths to prevent his dying mother from discovering that the Berlin Wall has fallen in *Goodbye, Lenin!*, twenty-five-year-old Daniel Brühl won the 2003 European Film Award as Best Actor and came to the attention of casting directors around the world. Within a year he had made his English-language feature film debut in *Ladies in Lavender* opposite Judi Dench and Maggie Smith.

While his first appearance in an American production was in a small role in *The Bourne Ultimatum* in 2007, within two years he had a significant role as a war hero in Quentin Tarantino's *Inglourious Basterds* and was soon regularly co-starring opposite American and British actors in productions on both sides of the Atlantic.

In the space of a few years, Brühl established himself as a leading man with the historical dramas *The Countess* and *In Transit*, opposite Julie Delpy and John Malkovich respectively, the horror film *Intruders* opposite Clive Owen and the biopic *The Fifth Estate* opposite Benedict Cumberbatch. In 2013, he co-starred in Ron Howard's racing car drama *Rush* opposite Chris Hemsworth. The Australian actor and rising star played British driver James Hunt while Brühl portrayed Austrian champion Niki Lauda.

Based on a screenplay by Peter Morgan, *Rush* centres on the rivalry between Hunt and Lauda in the late 1970s and the strange bond of respect and friendship that eventually develops between them. The screenplay divides its focus equally between the two men, exploring their backgrounds, personal lives and the psychological forces driving them to be champion drivers. Each narrates sections of the film and both characters drive the action forward. Initially, the Hunt-Lauda rivalry is portrayed in a binary protagonist-antagonist dynamic, but as the film progresses, the sympathy of the audience is increasingly drawn to Lauda, especially after the sequences recounting his disfiguring accident at the German Grand Prix, until both are protagonist heroes, albeit with very different styles. In her review in the *New York Times*, Manohla Dargis praised Morgan's screenplay for distilling "the thrill of racing into a clash of personalities, one nail-biting face-off, a catastrophic accident and a wild comeback."

While *Rush* is a two-handed drama about the rivalry between two men and the clash of their very different personalities, the events dramatized in the movie inherently give the spotlight more to Lauda. While Hunt, good-looking and charming, is the traditional idea of a hero, his character is unchanging throughout the story. It is Lauda, portrayed as an unlikeable workaholic, who experiences character development and carries the film's emotional arc. It is Lauda rather than Hunt who experiences the "catastrophic accident" and "wild comeback" to which Dargis referred and it is his journey from success through the depths of injury and back to the heights of victory in an extraordinary comeback that makes *Rush* an emotionally-engaging human drama as well as a visually-impressive and exciting spectacle of motor sport.

Produced independently, *Rush* was picked up for distribution by Universal which quickly promoted the film as a Hemsworth vehicle with appeal for fans of the *Fast & Furious* film franchise. As reviewer Dina Gachman commented, "To judge by the marketing campaign, you'd think *Rush* is the story of the handsome, blonde James Hunt. His face is plastered all over billboards, and when Lauda does appear, he's standing behind him, like an afterthought."[142] Ignoring the fact that the film was a drama about two men, the publicity material quickly positioned Hemsworth as the attractive movie star carrying the film's marquee appeal with Brühl, as the lesser known foreign actor, giving him support. Setting aside his numerous co-starring roles in American and British films over several years, the young German actor was presented as newcomer to mainstream American moviegoers. For the studio, his lack of fame and name recognition compared to Hemsworth justified his classification as a supporting actor.

When the film previewed to an enthusiastic response at the Toronto International Film Festival in September 2013, many observers pegged *Rush* as a contender for Academy Award honours. Critic Pete Hammond, for example, declared, "I also think it has Academy potential with no-brainer nominations for Anthony Dod Mantle's superb cinematography, the editing, sound, Hans Zimmer's score and **Daniel** Brühl's stunning supporting turn as Lauda ... That's all in addition to possible directing, writing and picture considerations." Hammond was quick to pick up Universal's classification of Brühl's co-starring lead performance as a supporting one for the purposes of awards season. Brühl "will be a supporting actor nominee if there is any justice at all," he wrote.[143]

When the film disappointed at the North American box office, however, the studio's interest waned. "But then the film failed to crack $30 million at the domestic box office and it was written off of the awards circuit," explained commentator Kris Tapley. "Even **Daniel** Brühl's acclaimed and clearly inspired performance as Niki Lauda began to slip down prediction charts."[144]

Even though Universal promoted the film for awards recognition less heavily than initially anticipated, Brühl nonetheless received Best Supporting Actor nominations at the Golden Globe Awards, the Screen Actors Guild Awards and the British Academy Awards. "I could tell that people really responded to the film in a good way, but all these strong movies were coming out and you wonder if people will forget," the actor told the media. "So I'm absolutely surprised and overwhelmed".

When the Academy Award nominations were announced, however, Brühl did not make the shortlist. In fact, *Rush* did not receive a single mention from the Academy. In the end the golden statuette in the Best Supporting Actor category was awarded to Jared Leto for his genuinely supporting performance as an HIV-positive transsexual in *Dallas Buyers Club*, an acclaimed independent drama released by Focus Features, the art house division of Universal which had entered the awards season just when *Rush* was disappointing studio executives with its box office grosses.

There is a moment in *The Danish Girl* when the supporting character of art dealer Hans Axgil, played by Matthias Schoenaerts, is interrupted during a phone call by his secretary knocking on the door to his office. "Look, I have to go," he says to the person on the other end of the line. "I have some Danish girl waiting to see me." The girl in question is not Lili Elbe, the female identity of painter Einar Wegener, portrayed by Oscar winner Eddie Redmayne, but rather it is Gerda Wegener, played by twenty-seven-year-old Swedish actress Alicia Vikander. It is the only time that the title of the film is alluded to in Lucinda Coxon's screenplay and the reference is significant because *The Danish Girl* is as much about Gerda as it is about Einar/Lili. In many ways it is her film.

Almost as soon as *The Danish Girl* went into production speculation was rampant among bloggers and industry pundits as to whether portraying the physical transformation of Einar Wegener into Lili Elbe would put Eddie Redmayne in contention for the Best Actor Oscar. It seemed to be exactly the kind of acting showcase Academy members admire and came with a period setting under the auspices of a director riding high from a recent Oscar triumph: Tom Hooper, director of *The King's Speech*. Interest in the film as an awards contender only increased when Redmayne collected a golden statuette for his portrayal of physicist Stephen Hawking in *The Theory of Everything*, another role requiring a physical transformation. In all the speculation it was assumed that the part of Gerda was secondary: just another in the long line of cinematic supportive spouses.

All that changed, however, when the film was finally screened. As Guy Lodge explained in *Variety*, "The surprise of *The Danish Girl* ... is that it's as much Vikander's showcase as it is Redmayne's. As told in Lucinda Coxon's screenplay, Gerda's story is as emotionally compelling as Lili's, as she has to override her own desires and reservations in order to set her husband free. The film is fashioned very much as the story of a marriage in crisis, forced to end despite deep reserves of love on either side."[145]

While Redmayne's Einar/Lili drives the narrative in *The Danish Girl*, it is Vikander's Gerda who is at the heart of the movie's emotional arc. Einar transforms physically into Lili, but it is Gerda's emotional journey to acceptance and understanding that ultimately delivers the audience's empathy and support. Coxon's screenplay and Hooper's direction make *The Danish Girl* a partnership between Redmayne and Vikander. Both their characters have backstory and depth, both exercise narrative agency and interact with supporting characters. Across the film as a whole, their screen time is equitable and if anything the movie focusses more on Gerda as it progresses.

With the awards season approaching Focus Features announced that it would promote Vikander for Best Supporting Actress honours. Coupled with The Weinstein Company's rival campaign in the same category for Rooney Mara's co-lead performance in *Carol*, the decision drew more sustained and widespread criticism from observers and commentators than has been thrown at any other examples of category fraud in recent years. Online, numerous bloggers voiced objections to the category placement including Nathaniel Rogers at The Film Experience, Marlow Stern at The Daily Beast, Ben Zauzmer at The Huffington Post, Joey Magidson at HollywoodNews.com, Jason Bailey at FlavorWire and Eric Henderson at Slant magazine.[146] At ScreenCrush, Erin Whitney wrote, "The beauty of [*The Danish Girl*] is how the title refers to both characters, establishing just how essential both Gerda and Lili are to the love story at the film's center. Vikander is in the film as much as, if not more than, Redmayne and gives a performance that is far from supporting. She should be honoured as a lead".[147] The bloggers' opinions were soon echoed by high-profile commentators in traditional media such as Guy Lodge in *Variety*, David Sims in *The Atlantic* and Scott Feinberg in *The Hollywood Reporter*.[148]

Such metrics as screen time, narrative agency and character development, however, had been repeatedly dismissed by distributors who pointed to the relative fame of the actors playing the protagonists in any given film. As Whitney explained, "when it comes to the studios' opinion, the actor with the bigger name tends to get campaigned as lead despite a co-star's equal-if-not-greater-than prominence in the film."[149] As far as Focus Features was concerned, Redmayne, the previous year's Best Actor Oscar winner, was the star carrying the film at the box office. Vikander, despite her break-through performance earlier in the year in *Ex Machina* and attention-grabbing turns in *Testament of Youth* and *The Man From U.N.C.L.E.*, was a newcomer who was still largely unknown to the general public.

The obvious comparison, as was often made during the course of the awards season, was with the performance of Jennifer Connelly in *A Beautiful Mind* opposite Russell Crowe. Both women had numerous screen credits to their names but were not famous movie stars when cast in their award-winning roles. Both portrayed the supportive wife of a troubled male protagonist played by the previous year's Best Actor Academy Award winner. Universal had put Connelly forward as a candidate in the Best Supporting Actress category and she had collected several of the major industry prizes, including the Oscar. And like Vikander, many observers contended at the time that she ought to have been considered for the Best Actress rather than the Best Supporting Actress prizes. As has been previously noted, Connelly had the same amount of screen time as that year's Best Actress frontrunner Sissy Spacek in *In the Bedroom*, and was the driver of her film's emotional arc.

A far more revealing comparison can be drawn between Vikander in *The Danish Girl* and Felicity Jones, Redmayne's co-star in *The Theory of Everything* the previous year. Thirty-one-year-old Jones was as much of an unknown newcomer to mainstream filmgoers when *The Theory of Everything* was released as Vikander was at the time *The Danish Girl* opened. She certainly did not have the public profile of her co-star who had appeared as Marius in the Oscar-nominated film adaptation of the musical *Les Miserables* two years earlier and had played a lead role opposite Michelle Williams' Oscar-nominated portrayal of Marilyn Monroe in *My Week With Marilyn*. While ostensibly a biopic about Stephen Hawking and the physical impact of motor neurone disease, *The Theory of Everything* is very much a portrait of a marriage in crisis, just like *The Danish Girl*. It is a two-handed drama that devotes as much time to exploring the impact Hawking's illness has on his wife and their relationship as it does depicting its effects on him and his career. Like Gerda in *The Danish Girl*, Jane Hawking is a fully rounded character in Anthony McCarten's script of *The Theory of Everything*. She is a protagonist with a backstory and narrative agency who is at the heart of the film's emotional arc. She occupies her own subplot, interacting independently with supporting characters. And yet, there was no assertion that Jones was providing support to Redmayne. Focus Features promoted Jones for Best Actress consideration for *The Theory of Everything* and secured an Oscar nomination for her in the lead category. Despite the striking parallels between their careers and characters, just twelve months later, the very same distributor ignored its own successful handling of Jones and pushed Vikander for Best Supporting Actress accolades. Why?

Vikander's status as an unknown newcomer relative to the fame of her Oscar-winner co-star was not the reason Focus Features listed her performance in *The Danish Girl* in the supporting category. Her lack of fame was merely the justification for the studio's category placement. It was all about strategy and maximising the chances of winning an Academy Award. "Their reasoning is pretty transparent," commented Lodge mid-way through the campaign. "The festival circuit has already turned up a surfeit of formidable best actress players. The supporting field, by comparison, has a little more breathing room, with no prohibitive frontrunners yet appointed even by the least patient pundits. Vikander wouldn't just have an easier time landing a nomination in this more fluid field – on the strength of her own career momentum, the presumed prestige of her vehicle and a beefier role than most of her competitors, she could well win."[150]

In the early part of the season, however, the strategy failed to yield dividends. In mid-November, the Hollywood Foreign Press Association announced that Focus Features' listing (along with The Weinstein Company's placement of Mara for *Carol*) had been rejected and that Vikander's performance in *The Danish Girl* would be considered in the lead actress category at the Golden Globe Awards. Soon after, several of the leading film critics groups endorsed the HFPA's decision. The Los Angeles Film Critics named Vikander as Best Supporting Actress for her supporting performance in the independent science fiction drama *Ex Machina* and she finished as runner-up for the National Society of Film Critics' Best Supporting Actress prize for the same film. Even though the critics groups often handed out citations for more than one film, Vikander's turn in *The Danish Girl* was not mentioned in either instance.

The rejection of Focus Features' category placement by the HFPA and major critics' groups was not surprising. An objective assessment of film through the prisms of screen time, narrative agency and importance to theme and emotional arc concludes that Redmayne and Vikander have co-lead roles. And at the time that the HFPA and the critics were making their own assessments, the material Focus Features was using to publicise the film was only reinforcing the perception that Vikander was a lead actress. In the main theatrical poster for *The Danish Girl*, Redmayne and Vikander appear in intimate close-up as Gerda and Lili. Redmayne appears in profile on the right, Vikander on the left, her face partly obscured by that of her co-star. At first glance, Redmayne attracts attention because he is positioned slightly in front of Vikander, but the observer's gaze is quickly captured and held by Vikander because while Redmayne is looking off to the side, Vikander is looking directly at the camera. The image captures the dynamic of *The Danish Girl*: an intimate, two-handed drama that is ostensibly about Einar/Lili, but which focusses more and more on Gerda. Looking at the poster for any length of time leaves the viewer with the strong impression that *The Danish Girl* is actually Vikander's movie, and it undermines the notion that Redmayne was carrying the movie as the star and that the relatively unknown Vikander was merely supporting him.

In mid-December 2015, just three weeks after the film had been released in the United States, Vikander received two Golden Globe Award nominations. She was shortlisted for the Best Supporting Actress prize for *Ex Machina* and was named among the candidates for the Best Actress in a Motion Picture (Drama) trophy for *The Danish Girl*. There was, however, no change in strategy from Focus Features the way there had been in previous years by Universal for Connelly in *A Beautiful Mind* and Naomi Watts in *Mulholland Dr.*, by New Line for Ian McKellen in *The Lord of the Rings: The Fellowship of the Ring* and by The Weinstein Company for Christoph Waltz in *Django Unchained*. Such a switch was considered an unacceptable risk by most studio executives. "The danger is confusion leading to votes being divided between the categories, allowing for other contenders to slide through," explained Kris Tapley at *Variety*. Such confusion and vote-splitting may well have been the reason why Watts had been overlooked for an Oscar nomination for *Mulholland Dr.*.

Focus Features remained convinced that Vikander's chances of claiming a golden statuette for *The Danish Girl* were strongest in the secondary category. Brie Larson was emerging as a strong favourite for the Best Actress Oscar for her performance in *Room*, but the contest for the Best Supporting Actress Academy Award remained open. In one article about the awards season race, Lodge explained that with strong reviews for her performances in *Ex Machina* and *Testament of Youth*, Vikander was "ideally primed for one of those unofficial body-of-work nominations the Academy sometimes gives to over-achieving actors, pinned on her vivacious, affecting turn as [Gerda] Wegener".[151] Even without the context of her other acclaimed performances, the size of her role in *The Danish Girl* gave her a significant advantage. As Feinberg noted in *The*

Hollywood Reporter, when it comes to the Oscars, "the supporting nominee with the most substantial part usually wins".[152]

Vikander left the Golden Globe Awards empty-handed. She lost to Larson in the lead category and to Kate Winslet in the supporting category for her performance in *Steve Jobs*. The outcome was the same at the British Academy Awards in London a month later. Like the HFPA, the British Academy had deemed Vikander's portrayal of Gerda Wegener to be a leading role in *The Danish Girl*. In fact, the only major instance in the lead-up to the Oscars where Focus Features' designation was accepted was at the Screen Actors Guild Awards. As has been previously noted, Guild members are not at liberty to nominate performers contrary to the studios' edicts on category classification. The Guild had nominated Vikander in the Best Supporting Actress category for her work in *The Danish Girl* and she duly emerged as the winner.

Even though the notion that Vikander was a supporting actress in *The Danish Girl* had been almost universally rejected during the awards season, both by critics and by their peers in the British Academy, the members of the Academy in Hollywood accepted Focus Features' campaign. When the nominations were announced in mid-January, Vikander was nominated in the Best Supporting Actress category for *The Danish Girl*. Alongside her on the ballot was Mara for *Carol*. They "absolutely deserved their nominations," wrote film critic Matt Brunson in *Connect Savannah*, "but in the Best Actress category. Instead of refusing to take the bait, the Academy mindlessly went along with the studio's efforts at category fraud ... The Academy's blunder will continue to allow the studios to get away with such nonsense."[153]

With performances in leading roles taking two of the five spots, there was little opportunity for the work of actresses in genuinely supporting roles to be recognised. Golden Globe and British Academy Award winner Winslet was included for her performance in *Steve Jobs* along with Jennifer Jason Leigh for *The Hateful Eight* and Rachel McAdams for *Spotlight*. Among those snubbed in favour of Mara and Vikander were Joan Allen in *Room*, Rose Byrne in *Spy*, Jane Fonda in *Youth*, Helen Mirren in *Trumbo*, Cynthia Nixon in *James White* and Kristen Stewart in *Clouds of Sils Maria*. Also pushed out of contention, of course, was Vikander's own performance in *Ex Machina*.

Although she had collected only one significant precursor, Vikander went into the Academy Awards as a firm favourite for the statuette. While Mara had a substantial role as well, for which she had won the Best Actress certificate at the 2015 Cannes Film Festival, Vikander had all the buzz and media attention of a new discovery. Appearing on the cover of the January edition of *Vogue* magazine, she was the season's glamorous 'It' girl. On the big night, it was Alicia Vikander who collected an Oscar statuette.

By playing the newcomer card once again, a distributing company's publicists had got away with category fraud.

> *Alternate Winner* – If Alicia Vikander had instead been considered for the Best Actress category for *The Danish Girl*, who might have won the Oscar as Best Supporting Actress of 2015? If the Academy had put Vikander in Best Actress for *The Danish Girl* but left Rooney Mara in Best Supporting Actress for *Carol* then Mara stands out as the most likely winner. In the event that neither were in contention, Golden Globe and British Academy Award winner Kate Winslet may have collected a second Oscar for *Steve Jobs*. The Academy may have given the statuette to Vikander anyway, however, if she'd been instead nominated for *Ex Machina*.

> *Alternate Nominee* – If Alicia Vikander had instead been considered for the Best Actress category for *The Danish Girl*, who might have been in the race for the Best Supporting Actress statuette? Vikander may have nonetheless been a nominee for *Ex Machina* as she was at the Golden Globe Awards where her performance in *The Danish Girl* was shortlisted in the lead category. Other possibilities are Kristen Stewart in *Clouds of Sils Maria* for which she was the first American actress to win a Cesar, or Jane Fonda in *Youth* for which she was a Golden Globe Award nominee.

When the Academy introduced the awards for Best Supporting Actor and Best Supporting Actress the intention was to recognise the contribution of featured players and character actors who could not successfully contest the main acting categories against famous movie stars and established leading performers. The notion that the lead awards were for stars regardless of whether they were in a leading or supporting role and that the supporting awards were for everybody else, again regardless of the size or importance of their role, has influenced the category of placement of numerous actors and actresses over the years. Metrics such as a screen time, narrative agency, character development and importance to plot and emotional arc have been repeatedly set aside in favour of factors such as billing and relative fame when studios have listed candidates for awards consideration. As a result, lead performances by established character actors, by children and juveniles and by relative newcomers have received Oscar nominations in the supporting categories for decades. Such category fraud has often occurred when these performers have appeared opposite a famous actor or actress.

There are many who argue that screen time and the significance of the role should be taken into account when deciding whether a role is deemed to be leading or supporting. They contend that a role is inherently leading or supporting in the script before it is cast and that a supporting role doesn't become a lead just because it is played by a famous actor and that, similarly, a leading role doesn't become a supporting one simply because it is given to a juvenile or newcomer. After all, in the case of the Academy Awards, the category is actually called Best Performance by an Actor in a Supporting Role and not, as it is usually more casually referred to, Best Performance by a Supporting Actor. Opponents of category fraud argue that the long title of the category points to objective assessments of a role's metrics whereas the practice in Hollywood is for the business-oriented approach suggested by the common short-hand in which the relative status of the performer is the main determining factor.

Most cases of category fraud at the Academy Awards remain debatable because of the contested interpretation of how a role is classified. Studio executives and publicists concerned with whether a performer is carrying the release at the box office with their name on the marquee contend that the category placements examined in this chapter are all entirely legitimate and justifiable. Those who believe metrics such as screen time, agency and significance count more cite these same examples as category fraud resulting in both the exclusion from Oscar contention of other worthy performances in smaller roles and the undermining of the integrity of the Academy Awards themselves.

There is one final set of cases, however, about which there is less argument. With studios and publicists discovering that they could secure the attention and acclaim of an Oscar nomination in a supporting category for newcomers and lesser known performers, it wasn't long before they began testing the limits of the practice by promoting stars for performances in secondary lead roles and then, in more recent years, campaigning for stars in co-lead roles simply to avoid having two stars of the same gender contest the lead category for performances in the same film. With these campaigns, the practice of category fraud went to a new level and the traditional rationale that the main categories were for stars and the secondary prizes were for the film industry's ordinary people was forever broken and forgotten. With these campaigns, Oscar nominations and victories were pursued shamelessly. It was calculated studio strategy pure and simple without the veneer of a justifying rationale. It was outright fraud.

Act Three

Carol

Frank Sinatra's victory in the Best Supporting Actor category at the 1954 Academy Awards ceremony is often cited as a turning point in the history of category fraud because it removed the stigma associated with the 'lesser' categories. As Scott Feinberg recently explained in *The Hollywood Reporter*, with Sinatra's Oscar win studio executives, publicists, agents and performers "realized that practically nobody remembers which Oscar someone won, only *that* they won an Oscar – which, regardless of category, can boost a film's gross and an actor's asking price."[1] Sinatra's role in *From Here to Eternity* was a genuinely supporting one, however, and Rosalind Russell's refusal to allow Columbia to promote her for Best Supporting Actress honours for her performance in a featured role in *Picnic* two years later demonstrated that the stigma had not been entirely washed away.

The real watershed moment was Jack Lemmon's victory in the Best Supporting Actor category for *Mister Roberts* at the 1956 Academy Awards ceremony. Columbia's placement of Lemmon in the supporting category was significant for two reasons. Firstly, unlike Sinatra two years earlier, Lemmon had a lead role but was pushed for recognition in the secondary category under the rationale that he was a relative newcomer. And secondly, while his newcomer status was the justification, the category placement was motivated by studio politics. *Mister Roberts* was a Warner Bros. release and the studio did not want their Best Actor campaign for Henry Fonda's performance in the title role undermined by competition from Lemmon, a Columbia contract player who had been cast under a loan-out agreement. Columbia boss Harry Cohn, meanwhile, wanted Lemmon in the Best Supporting Actor contest so that he would not compete with Ernest Borgnine, another Columbia contract player, who was seen as a strong contender for the Best Actor award that year for his performance in the independently produced *Marty*.

Lemmon's subsequent win was controversial. Among those voicing criticism was Charlton Heston who publicly declared, "That's not the purpose of that Academy Award category". [2] High-profile members of the Screen Actors Guild requested a change to the rules under which performers were nominated. [3] They wanted the Academy to prevent leading players from receiving nominations in the supporting categories. Their suggestion was in the spirit of the creation of the supporting awards two decades earlier for the purpose of honouring the contribution of featured and character players without them having to compete with famous artists in leading or substantial parts. When the Academy refused to embrace the proposal reform, explained historian Anthony Holden, it "prompted another undignified rush toward the Supporting category" the following year.[4]

A year after Lemmon's victory for *Mister Roberts*, three actors were nominated for the Best Supporting Actor Oscar for performances in leading roles: newcomer Don Murray in *Bus Stop*, former movie star Mickey Rooney in *The Bold and the Brave*, and rising movie star Robert Stack in *Written on the Wind*. Over in the Best Supporting Actress category, Stack's co-star Dorothy Malone also received a nomination for her co-lead role performance. The traditional rationale in which famous movie stars were nominated in the lead categories and featured players and unknown actors were placed in the supporting categories informed the strategies behind the nominations of both Rooney and Murray (refer to the previous chapter), but the placement of Stack and Malone in the supporting categories was blatant and ground-breaking category fraud.

A Universal release directed by Douglas Sirk, *Written on the Wind* was an adaptation of a best-selling novel by Robert Wilder about the spoiled children of a wealthy businessman and their romantic interests. The screenplay departed from the source material in terms of background and setting (for the film, the family's tobacco fortune became an oil fortune and the locale shifts from North Carolina to Texas), but left the fundamentals of the four central characters unchanged, although they have different names. At the centre of the narrative is Kyle Hadley, the insecure, alcoholic son of a Texas oil tycoon. His story is told through his relationships with his self-destructive, nymphomaniac sister Marylee, his childhood friend Mitch Wayne, and his wife Lucy, a former secretary from New York whom he married impulsively.

Having worked together on six previous films, including *Magnificent Obsession* and *All That Heaven Allows*, Sirk cast Rock Hudson as the solid, reliable Mitch and gave the unglamorous part of Lucy to Lauren Bacall. As the self-loathing Kyle, the director cast Robert Stack on a loan-out agreement with Twentieth Century-Fox. Stack had recently appeared opposite John Wayne in *The High and the Mighty*, while supporting player Dorothy Malone was cast against her 'nice girl' image as Marylee. The actress was apparently the director's only choice for the role. "An agent kept calling me [saying] that there is a director from Europe who wants you and only you," she later recalled in an interview for a Canadian newspaper.[5]

Over half a century later, it is easy to identify Hudson and Bacall as the film's stars and Stack and Malone as secondary leads or supporting players. Hudson and Bacall remain famous movie stars and in *Written on the Wind* they play the protagonists, even though they are rather dull, conventional characters. Meanwhile, Stack is only really remembered for the television serial 'The Untouchables' and Malone has been largely forgotten. They have the flashy, interesting roles in *Written on the Wind*, but are essentially the antagonists in the plot, roles which often equate to secondary lead or supporting status.

At the time of the casting of *Written on the Wind*, however, Hudson was yet to reach the heights of major movie stardom that would follow the release of *Giant* and his subsequent series of romantic comedies with Doris Day. And Bacall's career had stalled in the seven years since she had last appeared opposite her husband Humphrey Bogart in *Key Largo* and the comedy *How To Marry a Millionaire* had been her only box office success during the interim. With significant roles in *Bullfighter and the Lady*, *Bwana Devil* and *The High and the Mighty*, Stack had established himself as a dependable leading man and one of the industry's hottest rising stars. In 1955 he was dubbed Hollywood's most eligible bachelor. Similarly, there was such buzz about Malone following attention-grabbing appearances in the musical *Young At Heart* and the Western *Battle Cry* that Universal had just signed her to a contract with a view to establishing her as a new star.

The four leads received co-star billing above the title and their names appeared on publicity posters in the same-sized print. "Rock Hudson, Lauren Bacall, Robert Stack and Dorothy Malone, aptly cast in the star roles, add a zing to the characters that pays off in audience interest," opined *Variety* in its review. The trade paper went on to declare that Stack "in one of his best performances, draws a compelling portrait of a psychotic man ruined by wealth and character weakness" and that Malone "hits a career high as the completely immoral sister."

The response to the film was not universally positive. In *The New York Times*, Bosley Crowther wrote, "The trouble with this romantic picture – among other minor things, including Mr Stack's absurd performance and another even more so by Miss Malone – is that nothing really happens, the complications within the characters are never clear and the sloppy, self-pitying fellow at the center of the whole thing is a bore."

Although it was scheduled to open in early 1957, Universal screened *Written on the Wind* in selected cities in late December in order to qualify for the Academy Awards. Under the spurious pretext that Hudson and Bacall were the film's principal box office draws and therefore the main stars, the studio proposed awards season campaigns for Stack and Malone in the supporting categories where executives deemed they would have a better chance of securing nominations. As with the campaign for Lemmon the previous year, the decision was strategic and defied both their co-star billing and the size and importance of their roles. Universal was building up Malone to be a star and knew that the prestige of an Oscar nomination would help establish her as a respected actress as well as raise her profile with the public. Twentieth Century-Fox, meanwhile, eagerly consented to the plan to ensure that Stack was not in competition for the Best Actor statuette with Yul Brynner for *The King and I*, one of two prestige productions that Twentieth Century-Fox was pushing for the Academy Awards that year.

When the Academy Award nominations were announced on 18 February 1957, both Stack and Malone were included in the supporting category. Shortlisted alongside Stack were both Mickey Rooney and Don Murray. The controversy that had followed Lemmon's win the previous year, quickly "engulfed Oscar's acting categories," according the historian Tom O'Neil.[6] Many "Hollywood insiders howled over the lower contests." Despite the outcry in some sectors, the annual poll of Academy members by *Variety* suggested that Stack would edge out Rooney for the Best Supporting Actor statuette and that Malone would triumph ahead of Golden Globe Award winner Eileen Heckart. It was widely anticipated that their sizeable roles would give them an advantage over candidates who had given performances with significantly less screen time.

The audience in attendance at the Oscar ceremony in the Pantages Theatre "gasped in surprise",[7] therefore, when Jo Van Fleet revealed that Anthony Quinn was the Best Supporting Actor winner. According to historians Damien Bona and Mason Wiley, when the result was announced Rooney turned to Stack in the row behind him and said, "We wuz robbed!"[8] Many in Hollywood, however, were delighted that the Oscar had been awarded to an actor in a genuinely supporting role. For his portrayal of artist Paul Gauguin in *Lust for Life*, Quinn had just nine minutes of screen time. Decades later in his ghost written autobiography, Stack claimed that Twentieth Century-Fox had sabotaged his chances. "Tony [Quinn] had a movie coming up soon at Fox while my picture had been made at Universal," he wrote. "In addition, I was on suspension at a studio with the largest block of Academy votes. Their publicist had knowingly predicted that I would never win ... I felt that I had been robbed of the Oscar".[9] Stack's claim, however, does not ring true. An Oscar increased a performer's value to a studio and it didn't matter whether the award was won for a film made in-house or on a loan-out. The victory of Lemmon, a Columbia contract player, for a performance in a Warner Bros. film the previous year was a perfect example. Stack was most likely reaching for some explanation for a result that is still regarded as a "jaw-dropper" and "a major upset" in Oscar history.[10]

There was no such surprise in the Best Supporting Actress category. Although she had lost at the Golden Globe Awards a month earlier, Malone was the favourite heading into the Academy Awards. Upon opening the envelope, Lemmon announced that Malone was the winner of the golden statuette. *Variety* reported that she was "a popular choice"[11] but her selection soon caused such an uproar that the Academy amended its rules.

"Oscar Loophole Causes Criticism" read a headline in *The New York Times* on 29 March 1957, two days after the Academy had presented statuettes at its annual ceremony in Hollywood. In the article that followed, correspondent Thomas M. Pryor reported criticism of "a so-called 'loophole' in the academy's regulations that enabled Dorothy Malone to win the Oscar for the best supporting performance by an actress in *Written on the Wind*. Miss Malone got co-star billing in the Universal picture but volunteered to lower her standing in order to qualify in the supporting performance category." Among the Hollywood heavyweights voicing criticism of the category fraud was Mervyn LeRoy. The respected director was quoted as saying that such switches in classification from lead to support were "grossly unjust" to performers who genuinely deserved recognition as supporting players and that the rules ought to be tightened.[12] LeRoy had been the director of *The Bad Seed*, the film for which Heckart had triumphed at the Golden Globe Awards as Best Supporting Actress that year, only to then lose to Malone at the Oscars. Ironically, he was one of the directors of *Mister Roberts* the year before for which Lemmon had won the Best Supporting Actor statuette.

Having resisted calls from Screen Actors Guild members for a rule change the previous year, the Academy's Board of Governors capitulated to the outcry that followed Malone's win and the nominations of Murray, Rooney and Stack. Seven months later, it was announced that while the studios would continue to place performers on the annual reminder list for consideration in either the leading or supporting categories, a new special committee would ultimately determine the appropriate classification of any screen role, albeit only if the studio designation was questioned.

The campaigns for Stack and Malone were unlike any that had gone before because neither performer was a character player, juvenile or newcomer. Stack was an established leading man and Malone was a rising talent who was transitioning from substantial supporting roles to co-leading parts under a new studio contract. Both had been working in Hollywood movies for years. And not only did they play major characters in *Written on the Wind* and have substantial screen time, both had been billed above the title as co-stars equal to Hudson and Bacall. There was simply no justification for their inclusion in the supporting categories either on the basis of the metrics of their roles or on their status within the Hollywood studio hierarchy.

As a result of the outcry that followed the supporting category campaigns for Lemmon, Stack and Malone, the Academy took action to combat the rising tide of category fraud for the first time. Unfortunately, the reforms introduced in October 1957 were abandoned seven years later. In the decades since then, distributors and publicists have seized on the Stack-Malone precedent and pushed ever bolder campaigns for famous stars to be nominated in the supporting categories for performances in co-leading roles.

> *Alternate Winner* – If Dorothy Malone had instead been considered for the Best Actress category for *Written on the Wind*, who might have won the Oscar as Best Supporting Actress of 1956? The winner would almost certainly have been Golden Globe Award winner Eileen Heckart for *The Bad Seed*.

Alternate Nominee – If Dorothy Malone had instead been considered for the Best Actress category for *Written on the Wind*, who might have been in the race for the Best Supporting Actress statuette? The most likely candidates are Golden Globe Award nominee Marjorie Main in *Friendly Persuasion* and National Board of Review winner Debbie Reynolds in *A Catered Affair*.

For the role of Michael Corleone, the intellectual son of an ageing gangster, in *The Godfather*, Paramount executives wanted an established movie star and box office draw. Following the success of *Bonnie and Clyde*, the studio wanted Warren Beatty, but he declined.[13] Dustin Hoffman, Martin Sheen and James Caan auditioned for the role but as the start of filming drew near the role remained unfilled. Paramount production executive Robert Evans pushed for either Jack Nicholson or Ryan O'Neal, the star of the 1970 box office hit *Love Story*. Director Francis Ford Coppola, however, wanted Al Pacino, a New York theatre actor who had recently starred as a drug addict in the film *The Panic in Needle Park*. The studio was hesitant as Pacino "did not carry the marquee clout" they wanted. "Francis knew I could to the part and so did I," Pacino later recalled, "but he kept asking me to test again and again."[14] Eventually, the studio agreed and Pacino was cast.

That Paramount pursued movie stars like Beatty and Nicholson indicates that the studio considered the part of Michael Corleone to be a leading role. As discussed previously, while the film's lengthy opening sequence focusses on Don Vito Corleone, played by Marlon Brando, *The Godfather* is really about Michael and his ascendancy to the head of the criminal family organization. With Brando absent from the middle third of the film and making only brief appearances in the final third, it is Pacino who has the lion's share of the screen time. He portrays the central character, drives the narrative and carries the film's emotional arc. As biographer Peter Cowie has noted, it is Michael Corleone who "steadily envelops" the movie as he is transformed from soldier to mafia boss.[15]

Even after filming started, however, Paramount continued to harbour doubts. "They looked at the dailies, and they wanted to recast the part," Pacino recalled in an interview nearly twenty years later, "but Francis hung in there for me." The director and star were vindicated when the film was released in

March 1972. In *The New York Times*, Vincent Canby wrote that in addition to Brando many in the young cast "must be cited, especially Al Pacino, as the college-educated son who takes over the family business and becomes, in the process, an actor worthy to have Brando as his father". In *Variety*, A. D. Murphy singled out Pacino for making "a smash impression" with "an outstanding performance".

In addition to bringing him critical acclaim, *The Godfather* made Pacino a star. The film amassed over $85 million by the end of the year to not only top the box office but also eclipse *Gone with the Wind* to become the most successful cinematic release of all time. The phenomenal success of the movie made Pacino a household name, a sex symbol and a box office heavyweight. "Though Marlon Brando is great in *The Godfather*, Al Pacino is the one who has the girls and women panting," gushed Hearst Corporation columnist Dorothy Manners. "He has enough animal magnetism to get himself locked up in a zoo!"

When the various critics' groups met to vote for their annual awards, however, there was confusion about where to place Hollywood's newest star in relation to one of its enduring greats. In December, Pacino shared the National Board of Review's Best Supporting Actor prize with Joel Grey for his performance in the musical *Cabaret*, but then received the Best Actor award from the National Society of Film Critics. When Brando finished as the runner-up for the New York Film Critic's Best Actor accolade behind Laurence Olivier in *Sleuth* in early January, and the Hollywood Foreign Press Association then nominated both Brando and Pacino in the Best Actor (Drama) category at the Golden Globe Awards, there was growing concern among Paramount executives about the film's chances at the Academy Awards.

The studio was especially worried about the Best Actor contest where it had expected Brando to emerge as a frontrunner with early laurels from the critics. With Pacino receiving a trophy instead and appearing alongside Brando on the Golden Globe list, the studio made a strategic decision to list only Brando for recognition in the Best Actor category on the annual Reminder List issued to Academy members along with their nominating ballots. Controversially, Pacino was listed for consideration in the Best Supporting Actor category along with James Caan and Robert Duvall. Paramount executives feared Pacino would spoil Brando's chances, perhaps conscious of the fact that three years earlier *Midnight Cowboy* had won the Best Picture statuette but the film's stars, Dustin Hoffman and Jon Voight, had gone home empty-handed after both had been nominated for Best Actor. It is interesting to speculate whether their decision may also have been influenced by the publication in late 1972 of *More About All About Eve* in which director Joseph L. Mankiewicz voiced his belief that the nomination of Anne Baxter alongside Bette Davis in the Best Actress category for their performances in *All About Eve* had cost the Hollywood legend the third statuette she so desperately coveted. Ironically, the studio's move may have been unnecessary. When the Golden Globe Awards winners were announced at the end of January, Brando triumphed over Pacino and the three other nominees in the Best Actor (Drama) category, firmly establishing him as the Oscar favourite.

Even though Pacino played the film's leading role and Brando had far less screen time, the Academy nonetheless went along with Paramount's category placement. Brando was nominated in the Best Actor category and Pacino was shortlisted for the Best Supporting Actor statuette along with both Caan and Duvall. According to Lawrence Grobel, the actor's authorized biographer, Pacino was so insulted at his demotion to the secondary category that he boycotted the Oscar ceremony in protest.[16]

Decades later, the inclusion of Pacino in the supporting category continues to feature prominently in discussions of the strategic miscategorization of performances by studios and publicists at awards time. Film blogger Joe Reid recently ranked Pacino's nomination as the most egregious example of category fraud writing, "It's Michael (Pacino) who experiences the main character arc of the movie – guess what? *He's* the godfather the title is referring to – and Michael who is the film's true lead [character]."[17] Online commentator Clayton Davis, meanwhile, declared, "The most heinous example [of category fraud] in the history of the Oscars ... is Al Pacino nominated for Best Supporting Actor for *The Godfather*, when Marlon Brando went on to be nominated and win Lead Actor in the Best Picture winner of 1972. ... I cannot see an argument in which Pacino 'supports' anything."[18]

Although Pacino was considered by many to be the favourite, on Oscar night it was National Board of Review co-winner Grey who received the statuette for his performance in *Cabaret*. At the British Academy Awards shortly after, Pacino was among the nominees for the Most Promising Newcomer to Leading Film Roles Award. Given the controversy surrounding Pacino's category placement at the Oscars, it was somewhat ironic that he lost the British Academy Award to Grey for his supporting role in *Cabaret*.

Alternate Nominee – If Al Pacino had instead been considered for the Best Actor category for *The Godfather*, who might have been in the race for the Best Supporting Actor statuette? Unless Marlon Brando was relegated to the Best Supporting Actor category for *The Godfather* where he arguably belonged, the most likely candidates are Golden Globe Award nominee Clive Revill in *Avanti!* and Ned Beatty in *Deliverance*, a nominee for Best Picture and Best Director at the Oscars.

At the Beverly Hilton Hotel in Los Angeles on 24 January 1976, Walter Matthau won the only Golden Globe Award of his career when he took out the prize in the Best Actor (Comedy or Musical) category for his performance as a former vaudeville star in *The Sunshine Boys*. The film earned two other awards that evening: Best Picture (Comedy or Musical) and Best Supporting Actor for Richard Benjamin, who portrayed the long-suffering nephew and agent of Matthau's character.

When asked by reporters backstage whether he thought the win would help his chances at the upcoming Academy Awards Matthau replied, "I don't think my shtick is strong enough for the Academy. This is going to be Jack Nicholson's year."[19] Bookmakers agreed. For his performance in *One Flew Over the Cuckoo's Nest*, Nicholson had made a clean sweep of the three major critics' prizes and collected the Golden Globe Award for Best Actor (Drama) making him an almost unbackable favourite for the Oscar.

With Nicholson on the ascendency, United Artists executives made the somewhat surprising decision to refocus their awards season campaign for *The Sunshine Boys* on the only member of the cast to have been nominated for a Golden Globe but leave the ceremony empty-handed: eighty-year-old George Burns. For his performance as the other half of the titular comedic duo, Burns had been nominated alongside Matthau in the Best Actor (Comedy or Musical) category.[20] Although presenter Debbie Reynolds didn't call out his name when she opened the envelope, Burns nonetheless cheekily accompanied his co-star to the stage and quipped, "I just came up here to help him up, that's all." The audience was delighted.

On the annual Reminder List that accompanied the nominating ballots sent to Academy members, United Artists listed Matthau among candidates for Best Actor and promoted Burns for the Best Supporting Actor category alongside

Benjamin.   The studio had realized that removed from competition with Nicholson, the veteran comedian could very well charm his way to an Oscar.

Neil Simon's play 'The Sunshine Boys' is a comedy about Willy Clark and Al Lewis, a once legendary comedy duo whose four-decade long partnership ended acrimoniously.   A decade later, Clark's agent (who is also his nephew) tries to convince the pair to overcome their animosity and perform their most famous routine on a television special showcasing the history of American comedy.   It opened on Broadway in December 1972 with Jack Albertson and Sam Levene as the protagonists and co-leads and ran for over five hundred performances.   Albertson won the Tony Award for Best Actor in a Play as well as the Drama Desk Award for Outstanding Performance.

While Bob Hope and Bing Crosby were initially considered for the lead roles when work began on a feature film version, the parts were eventually given to veteran comedians Roy Skelton and Jack Benny, well known for their work on television.   While Albertson and Levene had been close in age when they originated the roles on Broadway (sixty-five and sixty-seven, respectively), there was a more considerable age gap between sixty-one-year-old Skelton and eighty-year-old Benny.   Neither actor ended up making the movie, however. Skelton backed out in favour of a lucrative tour as a stand-up comic and Benny was forced to withdraw when he was diagnosed with the pancreatic cancer that would soon take his life.   Skelton was replaced with fifty-four-year-old Matthau while Benny recommended producers cast his close friend Burns, seventy-nine, in his place.

When Burns was cast in *The Sunshine Boys*, he hadn't made a feature film in thirty-six years.   Like Skelton and Benny, however, he was a well-remembered comic from radio and television, especially a long-running situation comedy opposite his wife, Gracie Allen.

Although Burns had less screen time in *The Sunshine Boys* than Matthau, he played one of the narrative's driving characters and is one half of the comic double act that is at the heart of the film.   Burns was accorded joint star billing, above the title, and was recognised by critics has one of the film's two lead performers.   "With Walter Matthau at the top of his most antisocial form as Willy [and] with George Burns giving a keenly funny, brilliantly straight performance as Al ... the movie is extremely easy to take," wrote Vincent Canby in *The New York Times*.

While Jack Nicholson was a clear frontrunner for the Best Actor Academy Award, the field of candidates was relatively weak.   In his annual article about potential Oscar nominees, *Los Angeles Times* critic Charles Champlin had declared, "It wasn't a bad year for movies, it was a terrible year." Given the acclaim for their performances, United Artists would almost certainly have been able to secure Best Actor nominations for both Burns and Matthau had that been their campaign strategy. As it turned out, the nominees in the main category included Nicholson and Matthau alongside Al Pacino in *Dog Day Afternoon* and "two actors in filmed stage plays that were broadcast on Los Angeles' Z Channel": James Whitmore in *Give 'Em Hell, Harry!* and Maximilian Schell in *The Man in the Glass Booth*. Both Whitmore and Schell had been nominated in the Best Actor (Drama) category at the Golden Globe Awards, but neither appeared to have the same level of support as Burns for *The Sunshine Boys*.

With Nicholson regarded a certainty for the Best Actor statuette, it made little strategic sense for the studio to back both Burns and Matthau for nominations in the same category, especially since United Artists was the distributor of both *One Flew Over the Cuckoo's Nest* and *The Sunshine Boys*. With a Best Actor win seemingly locked in, the studio wanted to maximize its chances of a win in the Best Supporting Actor category as well. Executives had initially pinned their hopes on the performance of Brad Dourif as the nervous young patient with a stutter in *One Flew Over the Cuckoo's Nest*, but the young newcomer had been overlooked for the three major critics' awards which had been won by Charles Durning for *Dog Day Afternoon*, Henry Gibson in *Nashville* and Alan Arkin in *Hearts of the West*. At the Golden Globe Awards, however, their fortunes improved with Dourif receiving the award for Best Acting Debut (Male) and Benjamin triumphing in the Best Supporting Actor category.

Despite having these two strong contenders, United Artists opted to try and dominate the category, and thus all-but-guarantee a win, by placing Burns in contention as well. The rationale for the category fraud was a variation of the usual argument about relative fame. As a film star and Oscar winner, the studio regarded Matthau as the lead. Burns as a 'mere' radio and television personality who hadn't been in a film since before the Second World War, was 'evidently' supporting his more bankable co-star. The notion that Burns was supporting Matthau was aided by the fact that Burns was the 'straight man' in the comic double act, a part often erroneously considered to be secondary. The studio's category placement was in direct contravention of Burns' above the title star billing, and was reminiscent of the controversial supporting category nominations of Robert Stack and Dorothy Malone for *Written on the Wind* nearly two decades earlier.

His substantial co-lead role gave Burns an advantage over actors in genuinely supporting parts in the Oscar contest. When the nominations were announced in mid-February, he was shortlisted for the Best Supporting Actor category alongside Dourif and was quickly labelled as the sentimental favourite. [21]   Golden Globe Award winner Benjamin missed out on a nomination, as did all three winners of the major critics' prizes.

At the Academy Awards ceremony "the winner was no surprise". [22] Collecting the statuette, Burns told the audience, "This is all so exciting. I've decided to keep making one movie every thirty-six years. You get to be new again." [23] At eighty-years-old, he was the oldest winner in Oscar history (a record that would stand for almost fifteen years until Jessica Tandy won the Best Actress Oscar for *Driving Miss Daisy*).

United Artists' strategy had paid off. The distributor's two releases had each been rewarded with Academy Awards. *One Flew Over the Cuckoo's Nest* had swept the top awards for Best Picture, Director, Actor, Actress and Adapted Screenplay, while *The Sunshine Boys* had collected the Best Supporting Actor prize. Had it been necessary to switch Burns into the supporting category though? A year later at the British Academy Awards, Burns was not among the contenders for either Best Actor or Best Supporting Actor for his performance in *The Sunshine Boys*. Matthau was a nominee for Best Actor, but lost once again to Nicholson for *One Flew Over the Cuckoo's Nest*. In the Best Supporting Actor category, that year's Oscar winner Jason Robards for *All the President's Men* was among the candidates who lost in a surprise result. The winner was Brad Dourif for *One Flew Over the Cuckoo's Nest*.

The promotion of George Burns for the Best Supporting Actor Oscar, despite his co-lead role and above the title billing, has long been identified as a significant example of category fraud. Less than a decade after his win, Leonard Klady wrote in *The Washington Post*, "the membership [of the Academy] … awarded supporting actor statuettes to George Burns in *The Sunshine Boys* (1975) and Timothy Hutton for *Ordinary People* (1980) in what were unquestionably leading performances." [24] And in a more recent piece about the growing problem of category fraud at the Oscars, Richard Natale in the *Chicago Tribune* commented, "that all began to change in the '70s [when] performers like George Burns in *The Sunshine Boys*, Al Pacino in *The Godfather* … and Tatum

O'Neal in *Paper Moon*, all of whom were co-leads, showed up in the supporting category".[25]

> *Alternate Winner* – If George Burns had instead been considered for the Best Actor category for *The Sunshine Boys*, who might have won the Oscar as Best Supporting Actor of 1975? The winner could well have been Brad Dourif for *One Flew Over the Cuckoo's Nest* as he won the British Academy Award the following year.

> *Alternate Nominee* – If George Burns had instead been considered for the Best Actor category for *The Sunshine Boys*, who might have been in the race for the Best Supporting Actor statuette? The most likely candidate is Golden Globe Award winner Richard Benjamin in *The Sunshine Boys*.

At various times film critics have both condemned and condoned category fraud campaigns by studios and distributors. And on a handful of occasions, they have themselves instigated cases of inappropriate awards season category placement.

When the New York Film Critics' Circle met a few days before Christmas to determine their winners for 1982, Meryl Streep was chosen as Best Actress for her performance as a concentration camp survivor in *Sophie's Choice*. She received fourteen votes on the first ballot ahead of joint runners-up, with three votes each, Diane Keaton as a woman whose marriage is falling apart in *Shoot the Moon*, and Jessica Lange as an actress on a television soap opera in the comedy *Tootsie*. Unusually, members of the group then proceeded to support Lange's same performance for the Best Supporting Actress prize. She narrowly won the award ahead of Glenn Close as the hero's feminist mother in *The World According to Garp*, by thirty-nine votes to thirty-four.

The scenario played out again a fortnight later when the National Society of Film Critics voted for their awards. Streep was again victorious in the Best Actress category ahead of Lange who was considered for her performances in both the comedy *Tootsie* and the drama *Frances* in which she portrayed early Hollywood actress Frances Farmer. As historian Tom O'Neil has explained, "The crix then considered Lange's *Tootsie* role separately for Best Supporting Actress and she won over Glenn Close." [26] The repeat was perhaps not surprising, according to O'Neil, given "the huge overlap in the membership between the Gotham circle and the National Society".[27]

Whether Lange had a lead or supporting role in *Tootsie* continues to be debated by historians and bloggers. It can be argued that the film is simply a vehicle for Dustin Hoffman. His character is the narrative's driving force while Lange only appears on screen for about one quarter of the film's running time and plays a love interest who can be dismissed as merely a narrative device setting up the climatic live-to-air revelation sequence. The importance of both Lange's character and her performance, however, should not be so easily set aside. "Frankly, Julie Nichols is a very thankless part," observes one Academy Awards blogger, "she is the straight character who could easily get lost compared to Dustin Hoffman's cross-dressing, Bill Murray's one-liners or Teri Garr's neurotic hysterics. Julie Nichols has hardly any jokes, her scenes tend to be more serious and could easily become boring next to the comedic brilliance of others. But personally, I consider Jessica Lange the heart and soul of *Tootsie* … she is the emotional glue that holds the story together."[28]

Like George Burns in *The Sunshine Boys*, Lange plays the 'straight man' in the comedy double act that lies at the core of the film. While Hoffman's character drives the plot, it is Lange's character who is the film's emotional centre and the one whose life is transformed.[29] "Beyond the high-drag/high-concept set-up, the film's conceit rests upon the character of Julie and, indeed, it's nearly impossible to imagine *Tootsie*'s success without Jessica Lange's intelligent, human performance in the role," another blogger has recently argued.[30] In his original review in *The New York Times*, it was for bringing a "sort of intelligent gravity" to a situation comedy that Vincent Canby heaped praised on Lange.

With Universal campaigning for Lange to be nominated in the Best Actress category for *Frances*, Columbia executives made the strategic decision to promote Lange's performance in *Tootsie* for honours in the Best Supporting Actress category, taking their cue from the New York Film Critics' Circle and the National Society of Film Critics. It wasn't possible to argue that Lange was a relative newcomer who shouldn't have to compete with established and famous stars in the top category given she was doing precisely that with her performance in *Frances*, so the rationale for her placement in the supporting category fell to her limited screen time and the centrality of Hoffman's character. Lange was listed second and above the title in the opening credits, but then Garr was listed immediately after her, and also above the title, and there was no suggestion that she was anything other than a supporting player.

Lange received double nominations from both the Hollywood Foreign Press Association and the Academy. At the Golden Globe Awards she was shortlisted for the Best Actress (Drama) Award for *Frances* and for the Best Supporting Actress Award for *Tootsie*. At the Oscars, she was likewise nominated as Best Actress for *Frances* and as Best Supporting Actress for *Tootsie*. She was only the third woman in Academy Awards history to receive nominations in both acting categories in the same year (following the double nominations of Fay Bainter in 1938 and Teresa Wright in 1942).

Unimpressed with the studio's category fraud campaign was Teri Garr, whose own supporting performance in *Tootsie* was marginalised as a result. Garr recalled in her autobiography, that she had almost turned down the role of Sandy Lester in *Tootsie* because it "wasn't the lead".[31] Having just played the lead in Francis Ford Coppola's *One from the Heart*, she felt a supporting role was a backwards step for her career. After meeting with director Sydney Pollack, she said, "I squelched my inner diva, who had said she'd only accept the lead, and took what turned out to be one of the most rewarding roles of my life."[32] Overlooked for the Golden Globe Award, Garr was included on the ballot for the Oscar for the first time in her career only to find herself competing with the actress who did get the lead: Lange. "I'm thrilled by [the nomination], but what really hurts is that I think Jessica Lange was the leading lady in this movie," she explained in an interview with Hearst media columnist Eliot Kaplan one week before the Oscar ceremony. "Sydney Pollack told me, 'We can't make you look too good because everyone will want Dustin to come back to you.' So I played the supporting part, and I was a good sport about it. And then to have to share the nomination – well, I am little bugged by that. I mean, she gets to be leading lady *and* gets to be supporting actress? Oh, well. I think Glenn Close deserves to win anyway."[33]

On Oscar night, just days before her thirty-fourth birthday, Lange triumphed in the Best Supporting Actress category in what historian Anthony Holden described as "an almost inevitable victory (like both Bainter and Wright) in the lesser category".[34] As expected, she subsequently lost the Best Actress race to Streep.

The final coda of the saga was played out in London a year later. At the British Academy Awards, Lange's performance in *Tootsie* was nominated in the Best Actress category rather than in the Best Supporting Actress category (where Garr was among the contenders). The winner was Julie Walters for *Educating Rita*.

Alternate Winner – If Jessica Lange had instead been considered for the Best Actress category for *Tootsie*, who might have won the Oscar as Best Supporting Actress of 1982? The winner is likely to have been Los Angeles and National Board of Review winner Glenn Close for her debut in *The World According to Garp*, although some believe respected theatre veteran Kim Stanley would have triumphed for *Frances*.

Alternate Nominee – If Jessica Lange had instead been considered for the Best Actress category for *Tootsie*, who might have been in the race for the Best Supporting Actress statuette? The Academy is likely to have nominated either Golden Globe Award nominee Lainie Kazan for *My Favourite Year*, for which Peter O'Toole was nominated Best Actor, or Cher for *Come Back to the 5 & Dime, Jimmy Dean, Jimmy Dean* for which she was the runner-up for the Los Angeles Film Critics' prize.

"I wanted to write a true triangle," writer-director James L. Brooks explained to *The New York Times* in early January 1988. "The minute one of the men seemed to be winning, I made an effort to shore up the other relationship – to make Jane's choice as difficult as possible ... I wanted to find out whether a dynamic in romance had changed [in the modern, fast-paced world]."[35]

James L. Brooks wrote *Broadcast News* to be a three-handed comedy and it was widely recognised as such upon its release. "Set in the Washington bureau of a television network facing an economic crunch, the film focuses on the tangled professional and romantic relationships among three characters," wrote Stephen Farber in *The New York Times*.[36] His colleague, Vincent Canby concurred, writing in his review, "The movie is mainly concerned with the fortunes of three ambitious colleagues." Canby also praised the "three smashing star performances by William Hurt, Albert Brooks and Holly Hunter" as a rising television news anchor, an old-fashioned reporter and a workaholic producer. The trio of leads were given joint top-billing above the title and appeared together on the film's publicity material, including its theatrical release poster.

Twentieth Century-Fox ran advertisements promoting all three co-stars for awards season recognition in the lead performance categories. This was despite the fact that Hunter was a relative newcomer and that it put Brooks and Hurt in competition for Best Actor honours. At the time, the prospect of two leads of the same gender contesting the same category was still considered acceptable. Only four years earlier, Shirley MacLaine and Debra Winger had each been nominated in the Best Actress category for their performances in *Terms of Endearment*. And in the year after that, both F. Murray Abraham and Tom Hulce had received nominations for Best Actor for their performances in *Amadeus*. Contrary to what has since become the received wisdom that co-stars nominated alongside one another will split the film's vote and allow a rival candidate to win the statuette, both MacLaine and Abraham won Oscars.

Initially, the prospects of the comedy's two male leads receiving nominations seemed good. With performances in the dramas *Kiss of the Spider Woman* and *Children of a Lesser God*, Hurt had established himself as a respected actor and Academy favourite. Having taken home the Best Actor Oscar for *Kiss of the Spider Woman* and having received a nomination the following year for *Children of a Lesser God*, many commentators believed a third consecutive nomination was a definite possibility for his comedic performance in *Broadcast News* as a handsome young news anchor who knows how to sell the story even if he doesn't always understand what he is reading. Brooks, meanwhile, had built on his successful early career as a stand-up comic to become a critically-acclaimed writer-director with a series of comedies in which he also starred, the most notable of which, *Lost In America*, was released just two years prior to *Broadcast News*. The role of the talented, honest reporter had been written specifically for him by his old friend James L. Brooks (no relation) and it brought him some of the best reviews of his career.

When the major critics' groups met to vote on their annual awards, it was Brooks rather than Hurt who garnered attention. As had been the case with Jessica Lange five years earlier, however, there was support for him in both categories. In the voting by the National Society of Film Critics, for example, Brooks finished as the runner-up in the Best Actor category to Steve Martin in *Roxanne* and then finished in third place in the Best Supporting Actor category behind Morgan Freeman in *Street Smart* and Sean Connery in *The Untouchables*. At the Golden Globe Awards in January, meanwhile, it was Hurt who was included among the six nominees for Best Actor (Comedy or Musical) while Brooks was overlooked.[37]

There was genuine surprise when the Academy Award nominations were announced in mid-February. While Twentieth Century-Fox had promoted both Brooks and Hurt for Best Actor honours, the membership of the Academy's acting branch had shortlisted Hurt on the ballot for the Best Actor prize and nominated Brooks in the Best Supporting Actor category. And it wasn't the only example that year of the Academy's members disregarding studio category placements. They also disagreed with Universal's Best Actor campaign for Denzel Washington's co-lead performance in *Cry Freedom*, for which he had already earned a Best Actor (Drama) nomination at the Golden Globe Awards, and nominated him in the Best Supporting Actor category.

The decision of the Academy's membership is difficult to understand. Although he did not have the fame of his co-star, Brooks was an established leading man with above the title billing in a co-lead performance. While Hunter's character drives the narrative in *Broadcast News*, Brooks' character provides the film with its emotional centre. As historian Emanuel Levy has argued, it is Brooks who "gives the saga its soul".[38] In *Broadcast News*, Brooks is neither a supporting player in terms of his status and billing nor in terms of such metrics as screen time and importance to the narrative.

The category fraud appears to have been a case of stereotyping. As a good-looking, Oscar-winning actor acclaimed for his performances in prestige dramas, Hurt apparently struck Academy members as a traditional Hollywood leading man. In contrast, as a former standup comic known for independent productions as a writer-director-actor, Brooks was evidently regarded by his peers as more of a character actor than a star.

Over the years, many commentators have noted the ironic parallel to the dynamic between the characters they portrayed in the film which juxtaposed the smooth, good-looking but not very bright anchor with the intelligent, witty but not very sexy reporter. In one recent article online Joe Reid remarked, "Well, it's hard not to carry over some of that *Broadcast News* narrative and observe that Brooks got a Supporting nod while William Hurt was nominated in Lead because Hurt has the leading-man good looks while Brooks was short and stubby and sweaty."[39]

Having missed out on a Golden Globe Award nomination, Brooks was pleased to have received an Oscar nomination along with his director and two co-stars, regardless of the category. "If the others had gotten nominated and I didn't," he joked to *People* magazine, "I would have killed myself."

Alternate Nominee – If Albert Brooks had instead been considered for the Best Actor category for *Broadcast News*, who might have been in the race for the Best Supporting Actor statuette? The Academy is likely to have nominated Golden Globe Award nominee R. Lee Ermey for his performance as the sergeant in *Full Metal Jacket* for which he had been lauded in reviews by *The New York Times* and *Time* magazine.

On 9 April 1984, fifty-five-year-old Martin Landau sat at home watching the telecast of the annual Academy Awards ceremony. He recalled "having a beer in my underwear, saying 'I should be there'. It was frustrating. I knew what I was able to do; I was at the height of my powers, but no one was giving me the chance."[40] Among the winners that night was Jack Nicholson, one of Landau's former students at the Actors Studio West, who collected the Best Supporting Actor statuette for his performance in *Terms of Endearment*.

Landau's career had stalled since the cancellation of the television series 'Space: 1999' and his marriage to frequent co-star Barbara Bain had recently ended. Watching the Oscars that evening, redoubled his determination to revive the acting career that had begun in 1955 when he was one of only two candidates for The Actors Studio in New York to be selected from two thousand applicants and had subsequently enjoyed success on Broadway, in film and, most notably, in television.

His career comeback began four years later with *Tucker: The Man and His Dream*, directed by Francis Ford Coppola. For his peformance as a financier with good intentions but questionable practices he won the Golden Globe Award for Best Supporting Actor and received his first nomination from the Academy. The following year he took on a lead role in a new comedy by Woody Allen.

Crimes and Misdemeanors is an exploration of infidelity through a pair of parallel stories which are brought together only in the denouement. One half of the film is a drama about a successful opthamologist, played by Landau, who finds himself contemplating the murder of his mistress after she threatens to reveal their liaison. The other half of the film is a comedy in which a struggling documentary filmmaker, played by Allen, is tempted to have an affair with an associate producer.

As the protagonists of the two storylines, Landau and Allen are the film's co-leads, although they only appear in just over half of the film's running time due to its unusual structure. The two actors were featured on the film's theatrical release poster but were credited alphabetically along with the rest of the ensemble cast in the style of all of Allen's films. In his review of the film in *The New York Times*, Vincent Canby described Landau's character as "the pivotal figure" and that he was "splendid in the key role", but that "it's Mr Allen's presence that fuses the various elements, and that, in the film's fine penultimate scene, sets up the coda that is the bittersweet final image."

When the major critics' groups met at the beginning of the annual awards season, there was the same confusion about category placement as there had been previously for Jessica Lange and Albert Brooks. Landau featured in the voting for Best Actor by the Chicago Film Critics but finished as the runner-up for the Best Supporting Actor from the Los Angeles Film Critics. The *Crimes and Misdemeanors* cast member with the best chance of an Oscar nomination, however, appeared to be Alan Alda who collected the Best Supporting Actor prizes from both the National Board of Review and the New York Film Critics' Circle for his performance as a pompous, sleazy television producer in the comedy half of the film.

In something of a surprise, however, when the Academy Award nominations were announced in mid-February, it was Landau rather than Alda whose name appeared on the ballot for Best Supporting Actor. It was his second consecutive mention in the category. While many critics and commentators, such as Richard Natale of the *Los Angeles Times* and historians Damien Bona and Mason Wiley felt that Landau "had a leading role in *Crimes and Misdemeanors*", the members of the Academy's acting branch elected to place him in the secondary category.[41]

A combination of factors probably drove the category fraud. With the two parallel storylines, Landau appeared in only a little more than half of the film, a proportion consistent with the kinds of substantial secondary roles that often received awards season recognition in the supporting categories. Furthermore, Allen's films were routinely presented as ensemble pieces which only contributed to the view that Landau should be considered a supporting performer along with the rest of the cast: with one, notable exception, of course. "On some level," blogger Joe Reid said recently, "if you're in a Woody Allen movie and are not, in fact, Woody Allen, you're probably not going to be considered a lead."[42] Compounding the view that Landau, as part of an ensemble with limited screen time, should be considered a supporting performer was his standing in the industry as a veteran television performer and character actor. Landau had never been a matinee idol or a star. He had played smaller, interesting character parts in films such as *North by Northwest*, *Cleopatra* and *The Greatest Story Ever Told* and then found fame playing principal characters in television serials with ensemble casts such as 'Mission: Impossible' and 'Space: 1999'. His status as a supporting, character actor in the minds of Academy members was only reinforced by the fact that he had been a nominee in the Best Supporting Actor category just the previous year.

Measured by such indicators as importance to theme, narrative and emotional arc and such metrics as character agency and character development, Landau is a lead in *Crimes and Misdemeanors*. As Reid has commented in a recent online article, "who even thinks about Woody Allen's half of this movie? The whole show here is Landau and his moral dilemma. It's his film entirely."[43]

Like Albert Brooks two years earlier, Landau was happy to receive the nomination and was content with being a character actor rather than a leading man. "I think it would have held me back in a certain way," he explained to *The Times* when asked if he regretted never becoming a movie star. "[Others had] great careers and became major stars, but I played more things [and] had more fun!".[44]

> *Alternate Nominee* – If Martin Landau had instead been considered for the Best Actor category for *Crimes and Misdemeanors*, who might have been in the race for the Best Supporting Actor statuette? The Academy is almost certain to have nominated New York Film Critic's Circle winner Alan Alda for his performance in *Crimes and Misdemeanors*.

In the 1990s, Miramax transformed the annual film awards season with a bold approach to Oscar campaigning. "Through a mix of big schmoozy events, whisper campaigns, and old-school cold-calling," explained entertainment reporter Jesse David Fox, "Harvey Weinstein, the co-founder of Miramax and the current co-chairman of the Weinstein Company, pioneered the modern Oscar campaign."[45] While the old studios regarded the company's tactics as aggressive, they yielded impressive results. As critic and commentator David Poland has said, "Harvey and Bob Weinstein's company revolutionized [the] awards season, turned Oscar campaigning into a contact sport, infuriated rivals, led to new Academy campaign regulations, caused a change in the Best Picture rules ... and, along the way, did a very, very good job of winning Oscar nominations and taking home statuettes."[46] Miramax became such a dominant force in the awards season that the studios and other distribution companies had no choice but to respond. "Miramax has gone at the whole idea of campaigning in a way that just hadn't been seen before," said Bruce Davis, the Academy's former executive director. "They see it as a competitive sport, and look for every edge, every angle. And they're not the only ones responsible, because the others have felt the need to step up and match them."[47]

One angle Miramax sought to exploit, was the Academy's unfortunate tradition of category fraud in the acting categories. On sixteen occasions in Oscar history, co-stars from the same film have received nominations alongside one another in the lead categories. Only on five of those occasions was the eventual winner from among the pairs of nominated co-stars. Even though Shirley MacLaine won over co-star Debra Winger for *Terms of Endearment* in 1983 and F. Murray Abraham won over co-star Tom Hucle for *Amadeus* the following year, the infamous shadow of Anne Baxter ruining Bette Davis' chances of an Academy Award for *All About Eve* has stretched over decades of Oscar history to firmly convince studios executives that nominated co-stars will divide the vote of a film's supporters resulting in a third candidate taking home the golden statuette. In the quarter of a century since Geena Davis and Susan Sarandon each received Best Actress nominations for *Thelma and Louise* only to lose to Jodie Foster for *The Silence of the Lambs*, no pair of co-stars have received nominations in the same lead acting category at the Academy Awards. This is principally because of a seminal campaign mounted by Miramax for the stars of the Quentin Tarantino film *Pulp Fiction* in 1994, three years after the Davis and Sarandon nominations and a decade after the nominations of Abraham and Hucle for *Amadeus* (the last pair of Best Actor nominees from the same film).

Three interconnecting stories about gangsters, hit-men and petty criminals form the basis of *Pulp Fiction*, the black comedy which won the Palme d'Or at the Cannes Film Festival before becoming an unexpected box office smash in North America. The two top-billed stars, John Travolta and Samuel L. Jackson, play hit-men seeking to retrieve a briefcase on behalf of their boss. In the view of historian Emanuel Levy, the "pair forms the central core of the film",[48] while critic Janet Maslin praised Travolta and Jackson for their "terrific comic teamwork" in her review in *The New York Times*.

When the Los Angeles Film Critics met in early December, Tommy Lee Jones led the voting for the Best Actor award after the first ballot for his portrayal of baseball player Ty Cobb in the biopic *Cobb*, but was ultimately outpolled by Travolta in a result that, according to *Variety*, was "so close that four recounts had to be taken."[49] Jones was again the early leader in the voting for Best Actor by the New York Film Critics' Circle at their meeting five days later, but finished third in the end. Edging out Jackson by a singe point, the winner was Paul Newman for his performance in *Nobody's Fool*. According to historian Tom O'Neil, Travolta did not feature among the main contenders.[50] Newman was also the choice of the National Society of Film Critics, finishing ahead of Jackson and Travolta in second and third place, respectively. Jackson was also the runner-up for the Society's Best Supporting Actor accolade behind Martin Landau in *Ed Wood*.

The close result in the voting by the Los Angeles Film Critics had been enough to alarm Miramax and the company's concerns were only heightened by the subsequent critics' results. According to *Los Angeles Times* reporter Richard Natale, Miramax "feared that votes for the two actors would cancel out."[51] As a result, according to then Miramax marketing president, Mark Gill, the company discussed the film's Oscar campaign strategy with "all the actors in *Pulp Fiction*, who agreed that John [Travolta] was the lead actor because he is in every section of the film."[52] For the remainder of the awards season, Miramax promoted Travolta as a Best Actor contender and Jackson for recognition in the Best Supporting Actor category.

Despite rumours of his bitter disappointment, Jackson put on a brave face. "In a perfect world, all of us would have been nominated in the supporting category," he told reporters. "[But] it's totally fine with me."[53]

The splitting of co-stars Travolta and Jackson into different categories is most often justified in terms of Travolta's greater amount of screen time. He appears in all three of the film's interwoven storylines whereas Jackson is featured in only two. There is a greater degree of parity between the two actors, however, when consideration is given to narrative agency, character development and other similar metrics. Jackson's character is a protagonist whose actions materially progress the plot and who experiences significant change during the course of the movie. And in several notable scenes, it is Jackson's character who is dominant and Jackson's performance that is the focus. While present and accumulating screen time, Travolta is providing support to his co-star in these sequences. Like Walter Matthau and George

Burns, they are a double act jointly creating an on-screen dynamic despite different amounts of screen time.

"The lead campaign for John Travolta was a no-brainer in 1994," says blogger Joe Reid, "[as] he was the comeback story of the year. And the rationale for him getting placement over Jackson makes a sort of sense on the surface. After all Vincent Vega (Travolta) gets a whole section of the movie with Mia Wallace (Uma Thurman) that Jules (Jackson) isn't a part of. But the two major sections where Vincent and Jules are together – jacking those kids for Marcellus's briefcase and the diner robbery – prove it would be a fallacy to call them equal scene partners. Jackson *towers* over Travolta in both sequences, nearly blowing him off the screen. He'd earned his shot as a lead."[54]

Many agreed at the time. According to Natale, one Miramax insider suggested that Jackson's performance, "particularly his riveting fire-and-brimstone speech in the film's last scene, stays with audiences as they leave the theater", rather than Travolta's.[55] And at the Independent Spirit Awards ceremony, held two days before the Oscars, it was Jackson who collected the trophy for Best Actor. Travolta was not even among the nominees.

Aside from the Independent Spirit Awards, Miramax's strategy of splitting the two lead actors into separate categories succeeded. At the Golden Globe Awards, the Screen Actors Guild Awards, the Academy Awards and the British Academy Awards, Travolta received Best Actor nominations and Jackson earned Best Supporting Actor nominations. Travolta lost on all four occasions (three times to Tom Hanks for *Forrest Gump* and once to Hugh Grant for *Four Weddings and a Funeral*). Jackson lost three of the prizes, including the Oscar, to Martin Landau for *Ed Wood* but took home the British Academy Award.

Although the company was unable to secure golden statuettes for either Travolta or Jackson, the success of scoring nominations for them both in separate categories where they didn't have to compete with one another, became the template for dozens of campaigns over the following two decades, many instances pushing category fraud to new degrees of outrageousness and audacity. Marketing directors and campaign strategists have become so wary of co-stars cancelling out each other's votes that only two pairs of performers have been promoted for the same lead acting category since Miramax's *Pulp Fiction* campaign. Ironically, this pursuit of category fraud has been in defiant disregard of the three times during the same period that an actress has successfully collected the Best Supporting Actress Academy Award from a field that included another nominee from the same film: three times from the eight occasions in which two performers from the same film have been nominated alongside one another in that category.

> *Alternate Nominee* – If Samuel L. Jackson had instead been considered for the Best Actor category for *Pulp Fiction*, who might have been in the race for the Best Supporting Actor statuette? The most likely contender is John Turturro for his performance in *Quiz Show* for which he was nominated for the Golden Globe Award and the Screen Actors Guild Award.

Directed by Antoine Fuqua from a screenplay by David Ayer, *Training Day* is a two-handed drama about Jake Hoyt, a young Los Angeles police recruit, drawn into a violent web of corruption by Alonzo Harris, a charismatic narcotics officer, on the first day of his assignment to undercover operations. While Hoyt is the audience surrogate and the straightman in the on-screen double act, Harris is the sort of flashy role almost guaranteed to grab the attention of Academy members. When Denzel Washington was cast as Harris, Warner Bros. began positioning the film as an awards vehicle for him.

While the film received some mixed reviews upon its release, the response to Washington's performance was overwhelmingly positive and provided Warner Bros. with the perfect launching pad for its campaign. In *The New York Times*, Elvis Mitchell said Washington "demonstrates every trick of one-upmanship that an actor could employ" in a notable performance that "deserves regard ... his powerhouse virtuosity will almost guarantee him an Oscar nomination." Reviewing the film for the *Los Angeles Times*, Kenneth Turan wrote "Washington's exceptional acting elevates *Training Day* to a place it wouldn't otherwise occupy ... It's a driving, galvanic piece of acting that Washington seems to relish". Writing in *Variety*, Todd McCarthy agreed, describing Washington's work as "a flashy, cool and supremely charismatic performance ... it's the way Washington socks over his role that makes the picture genuinely worth seeing."

Washington was named Best Actor by the Los Angeles Film Critics, finished runner-up for the National Society of Film Critics' award and placed third in the voting by the New York Film Critics. His main rival for the industry plaudits seemed to be Russell Crowe for his portrayal of economist John Forbes Nash Jr in *A Beautiful Mind*, a performance that brought him the Best

Actor prize from the Broadcast Film Critics. The two actors had been among the frontrunners for the Best Actor Academy Award two years earlier: Washington for his portrayal of boxer Rubin Carter in *The Hurricane* and Crowe for his performance in *The Insider*. In the end they had both lost to Kevin Spacey for *American Beauty* and many observers put the result down to the damage to Washington's chances caused by controversy surrounding misrepresentations of Carter's life and the legal case at the centre of the film's plot.

In an ironic reversal of fortune, as the awards season got underway two years later similar accusations were levelled at *A Beautiful Mind* for which Universal was seeking to secure a second consecutive Best Actor Oscar for Crowe following his victory the previous year for *Gladiator*. The biopic was criticised for omitting key facts about Nash's marriage and sexuality while Crowe's image was tarnished by media reports of 'bad boy' movie star behaviour. "The Oscar campaigns have certainly become nastier, more aggressive, more expensive and more sophisticated," film critic Emanuel Levy said. "But I am not sure I would call it 'dirty'. I would call it aggressive – or desperate."[56] Many others, however, were soon deploring the tactics being used. "Everyone is saying that this year is the worst," said *Los Angeles Times* reporter Patrick Goldstein.[57] Historian Peter Biskind later remarked, "The Oscar jockeying that year was unusually ugly … [*A Beautiful Mind*] became the the target of a smear campaign unprecedented in the history of the Academy Awards for its viciousness."[58]

In the context of an increasingly bruising race towards the Oscars, Warner Bros. decided to take no chances with its campaign for Washington. For his performance as Jake Hoyt, the other lead role in *Training Day*, Ethan Hawke had received the best reviews of his career. "Mr Hawke plays shock and disgust so well it is almost as it his Jake is having a real-life chemical reaction to Alonzo's bullying perfidy," wrote Elvis Mitchell in *The New York Times*. Meanwhile in *Variety*, Todd McCarthy said, "For his part, Hawke … show signs of coming to new life as a screen actor … [he] adds feisty and cunning flourishes to his part that allow him to respectably hold his own under formidable circumstances." To ensure that Hawke could not siphon any votes away from Washington, the studio listed him on the annual Reminder List in the supporting category. The studio had no intention of promoting the younger actor, it just wanted him safely out of the picture. As awards season commentator Joe Reid explained, Warner Bros.' campaign "was designed for one thing only: to win Denzel Washington his second Oscar."[59]

It was a huge surprise, therefore, when Hawke received Best Supporting Actor nominations from both the Screen Actors Guild and the Academy. Even the actor was shocked. "I feel really lucky because I was so completely not expecting it," he told the media soon after the Oscar nominations had been revealed. [60]   One key reason that Hawke himself was surprised by the nomination was the fact that he hadn't been pushing for one. "Hawke did no campaigning," explains historian Damien Bona. "In fact, in terms of his attitude to Hollywood glitz and awards, he can be thought of as the anti-Sally Kirkland. Academy members saw the film, loved Hawke's subtle, gutsy and extraordinarily affecting work and voted for him simply because of the quality of his performance – which given all the time and money spent on soliciting Oscar voters is something rare and quite wonderful."[61]

Another reason for the surprise at Hawke's Oscar nomination was the sheer audacity of the category fraud involved. The members of the Screen Actors Guild were not able to vote for his performance in the lead category because of Warner Bros.' strategic categorisation of his role as supporting. Under the Academy's rules, however, the members of the Actors Branch were at liberty to cast votes for Hawke in the Best Actor category, but instead chose to accept the studio's placement. In so doing they ignored the size and importance of his role as well as his star status and billing.

Jake Hoyt is the protagonist in *Training Day*. While Alonzo Harris is the manipulative antagonist, Hoyt is the character who must negotiate the unfolding scenario and is the character who makes choices and grows and changes as a result of his experiences. The film opens with him waking to the first day of his assignment and ends with him returning to his home and family. Hawke is central to both the film's narrative and its emotional arc. He appears in almost every single scene and has more screen time than Washington. According to an analysis conducted by *The Wall Street Journal*, Hawke has one hundred and forty-eight minutes of screen time and appears in a staggering ninety-four percent of the movie. By comparison, Washington has ninety-five minutes of screen time and appears in only eighty-three percent of the film. Astonishingly, Hawke had more screen time in terms of percentage of running time, than four of that year's Best Actor nominees and was on screen for more minutes than all four of that year's Best Actress nominees. When compared to the other candidates in the Best Supporting Actor category, he had more than twice the on-screen time than Jim Broadbent in *Iris*, the nominee with the next most sizeable role (fifty-two minutes of screen time appearing in sixty percent of the film).[62]

In addition to playing a lead character, Hawke was billed as a star in *Training Day*. The thirty-year-old actor had starred in numerous films including *Reality Bites*, *Before Sunrise*, *Gattaca*, *Great Expectations*, *Snow Falling on Cedars* and *Hamlet* and, appropriately, was billed after Washington above the title on the film's theatrical release poster and other publicity material. With his nomination, he joined Robert Stack, Dorothy Malone, Jessica Lange, Albert Brooks, Samuel L. Jackson and others as an established, top-billed above-the-title star shortlisted in the supporting categories by the Academy for a performance in a lead role.

Having never expected Hawke to make the Oscar ballot, Warner Bros. suddenly had to rationalise their category placement to puzzled journalists. "It's a tough call to make," Dawn Taubin, president of marketing at the studio, admittedly awkwardly. "I think Ethan's character is more reactive to Denzel's character. Denzel is sort of the motivator for what happens in the movie."[63] The focus on the metric of character agency in her comments is in sharp contrast to the line usually spun by publicists when justifying category fraud. Marketing executives normally emphasise relative fame and billing over consideration of agency when trying to justify blatant disregard of screen time.

For his part, Hawke appeared content to defer to Washington as the star and box office draw. *"Training Day* was my best experience in Hollywood," he said a few years later, "and a lot of that you have to give up to the fact that, pure and simple, Denzel Washington is a great movie star. Each generation there's two or three – and he's it."[64] The film was also a revelation for Hawke, demonstrating that critical and commercial success don't have to be mutually exclusive. "When you can thread that needle," he said, "a movie that doesn't pander, but is still entertainment, that's a great goal."[65]

While Warner Bros. executives rationalised Hawke's category placement at the time based on who was acting and who was reacting in *Training Day*, other commentators have more recently explained it in terms of protagonist versus antagonist. "There's a history at the Oscars of actors playing sinister villains, but in secondary roles, scoring Best Actor nods instead of the film's true lead, whose roles are less showy," says Kevin Fallon at *The Daily Beast*. In addition to Washington and Hawke, Fallon cites the nominations of Forest Whitaker instead of James McAvoy for *The Last King of Scotland*, Meryl Streep rather than Anne Hathaway for *The Devil Wears Prada* and Steve Carrell at the expense of

Channing Tatum in *Foxcatcher*.[66] Daniel Day-Lewis for *Gangs of New York* rather than Leonardo DiCaprio is another example that could have been added to that list.

What sets Hawke apart from DiCaprio, McAvoy, Hathaway and Tatum, however, is the fact that he received an Oscar nomination in a supporting category for his lead performance. In that regard, he is more analogous to George Burns in *The Sunshine Boys*: both played lead 'straight man' roles in a double act for which they received a nomination in the supporting category, despite their billing and narrative importance, while their partner received recognition in the lead category for the flashier of the two lead roles (the comic in the case of Walter Matthau and the villain in the case of Denzel Washington).

But more important than the tradition from which Hawke's nomination arose, was the future that it ushered in. The willingness of the Academy to accept Warner Bros.' classification of Hawke's performance in *Training Day* as supporting confirmed to studios, distributors and publicists that the nomination of Samuel L. Jackson for *Pulp Fiction* was no outlier. Over the decade and half that followed, marketing strategists desperately looking for every edge and any angle in the campaign to secure nominations for their films and statuettes for their performers seized on the Academy's nomination of Hawke with alacrity.

> *Alternate Nominee* – If Ethan Hawke had instead been considered for the Best Actor category for *Training Day*, who might have been in the race for the Best Supporting Actor statuette? The most likely contender is Steve Buscemi for his performance in *Ghost World* for which he was nominated for the Golden Globe Award and the American Film Institute Award and for which he won the New York Film Critics' Circle prize and the National Society of Film Critics accolade.

Julianne Moore had two leading roles in prestige feature films released in 2002: *Far From Heaven* and *The Hours*. In both instances she played a housewife in post-war America.

Written and directed by Todd Haynes, the drama *Far From Heaven* is set in an affluent Connecticut suburb in 1957 and explores contemporary issues about gender roles, sexuality and race while stylistically playing homage to the films of Douglas Sirk. Moore plays Cathy Whitaker whose seemingly perfect world as wife, mother, homemaker and hostess suddenly falls apart. Cathy is the film's sole central character. She drives the narrative and her experiences and character growth provide the emotional arc. Moore was the film's top-billed star and featured prominently on its poster and other publicity material. USA Films had financed the film, but its awards season campaign was handled by Focus Features, a new production and distribution entity, created by the merger of USA Films with Universal Focus and Good Machine

In *The Hours*, Moore shares the screen, and the theatrical release poster, with co-stars Nicole Kidman and Meryl Streep. "The film concerns three different women, two of whom are hyperarticulate – one of them is Virginia Woolf, and the other is a publisher in modern New York – but the third of whom is not articulate at all," explained playwright David Hare, who adapted the screenplay from the novel by Michael Cunningham.[67] The film intricately interconnected the stories of three women in different times and places whose lives are affected by the novel 'Mrs Dalloway' by Virginia Woolf. In the segment set in England in the 1920s, Kidman portrays the writer as she struggled with depression while trying to complete the novel. Streep plays a woman in New York preparing a party for a long-time friend who seems to be a contemporary version of the novel's title character. And finally, Moore plays a pregnant housewife in post-war California who feels trapped and suffocated by the confines of her suburban life as a wife and mother and struggles with the pressure to be perfect. The three actresses received equal billing above the title and shared the theatrical release poster (Streep and Kidman stand one either side with Moore appearing immediately behind them in the centre). *The Hours* was principally financed by Paramount, which handled the film's North American distribution and therefore also its awards season promotion, however Miramax had a secondary stake in its backing and had the international distribution rights.

In early September, *Far From Heaven* premiered at the Venice Film Festival to an enthusiastic response. Moore's performance was singled out for particular praise and she subsequently collected the festival's prestigious Best Actress trophy. Even before the film had opened in the United States, pundits declared her to be the favourite for the Academy Award. Focus Features executives and Moore's representatives at Creative Artists Agency, however, were concerned about Moore having two performances in contention for the Best Actress category, especially with the similarities between the two roles. They feared that awards voters would be confused or unable to decide which to support. At their urging, Moore herself requested that Paramount list her performance in *The Hours* for consideration in the Best Supporting Actress category.[68] Paramount publicists, still debating how to promote three female co-leads, welcomed the suggestion.

It was also a good result for the powerful and influential agent Kevin Huvane of Creative Artists Agency who handled the careers of all three actresses. The agreement to place Moore in the supporting contest for *The Hours* ensured that her performances wouldn't compete and potentially cancel each other out when Academy members cast their ballots in the nominating stage. It also raised the prospect of her receiving a double nomination, a feat that was also a possibility for Streep. In addition to her co-lead performance in *The Hours*, Streep had a substantial supporting role in *Adaptation*, a comedy directed by Spike Jonze and distributed by Columbia. The category fraud placement of Moore in the supporting category for *The Hours* along with the dual campaigns for Streep and a push for Kidman to be included in one category or the other (Paramount was yet to decide its strategy with regard to her performance) meant that the three Huvane clients could potentially receive five Oscar nominations between them for their work in three different films.

There is no obvious rationale for the placement of Moore in the supporting category for her work in *The Hours*. As a famous movie star who shares above the title billing with her co-leads and is featured with equal prominence in the marketing material, she carried the film at the box office as much as Kidman and Streep. The justifications for category fraud regarding relative marquee value that are so often made by studio representatives are not applicable in Moore's case.

Further, it is not possible to mount an argument that Moore is a supporting player in *The Hours* on the basis of such metrics as screen time, agency or emotional resonance. In an article in *The New York Times*, Rick Lyman wrote, "A stopwatch taken to the film shows that the actresses appear fairly equally: Ms Streep for 42 minutes, Ms Moore for 33 minutes and Ms Kidman for about 30."[69] Each is the lead in their section of the movie, each play the protagonist in their section of the movie and each drives the narrative forward. And they advance the film's themes and emotional arc collectively. As director Stephen Daldry explained to *The New Yorker*, "the hardest thing was that the actresses never met, and the difficulty, I think, on the whole was not being in control of their emotional arc, because the emotional arc is essentially the film's. So they couldn't articulate, they couldn't create, they weren't in charge, in control of how to make a whole sweep, because the whole sweep in the end is a very complicated mathematical combination between three characters."[70]

Given Moore shares top billing and plays one of the three protagonists at the centre of one of the narrative strands as well as the film's collective emotional arc, her classification as a supporting actress can only be regarded as strategic. In a piece in *The New York Times* printed two weeks before the announcement of the Academy Awards nominations, film historian and industry analyst Pete Hammond remarked, "If Julianne Moore gets nominated for supporting for *The Hours*, then I think that's all about the advertising and the Oscar campaign. I do not think that any actor watching the film would think that any of the three actresses is supporting the others. Either they're all supporting, or they're all leads."[71]

In a recent article on category fraud in *Variety*, Tim Gray put the placement of Moore's performance down to "practical considerations" which Hammond summarized as "to avoid cannibalizing her own chances for lead actress in *Far From Heaven*."[72] The strategy was bad news, however, for Toni Collette who appeared alongside Moore in the post-war segment of *The Hours* in the supporting role of an emotionally repressed neighbour. With Moore shifting into the supporting contest, Collette's chances of a nomination were doomed. "Forget past faves Toni Collette in *The Hours* or Emily Watson in *Punch-Drunk Love*," declared Tom King in a mid-January article in *The Wall Street Journal* canvassing the likely Oscar nominees. "With their studios not pushing them, it's unlikely their peers will."[73]

Moore had an ideal start to the awards season. In early December, she won the Best Actress prize from the National Board of Review for her performance in *Far From Heaven* and two weeks later collected the Best Actress accolade from the Los Angeles Film Critics, who cited her for both *Far From Heaven* and *The Hours*. In the Best Actress voting by the New York Film Critics' Circle her performance in *Far From Heaven* finished as runner-up to Diane Lane's turn in *Unfaithful*.

Other campaigns, meanwhile, faltered during this early part of the awards season. Miramax had been backing Martin Scorsese' violent historical drama *Gangs of New York*, but the film did not collect Best Picture prizes from the major critics' groups. With the film failing to generate the awards buzz he had anticipated, Miramax boss Harvey Weinstein hastily switched horses mid-race. "As an Oscar contender, Harvey ignored *Chicago*, just as he did *In the Bedroom* the year before, until the film on which he had placed his bets, *Gangs of New*

York, foundered," explains historian Peter Biskind. "In both instances, his gut, his instinct, misled him, but like a studio executive, he played the percentages, taking his cues from the marketplace, and moved his money when and where the numbers told him to."[74]

When the musical 'Chicago' premiered on Broadway in June 1975, it starred Chita Rivera as Velma Kelly, Gwen Verdon as Roxie Hart and Jerry Orbach as Billy Flynn. With music by John Kander, lyrics by Fred Ebb and a book by Fred Ebb and Bob Fosse, the production was based on a 1926 play of the same name by reporter Maurine Dallas Watkins who had been assigned to cover the trials of accused murderers Beulah Annan and Belva Gaertner for the *Chicago Tribune* two years earlier. While the original play focussed on Roxie and Billy, the part of Velma was expanded in the musical version, turning the story into a triangle between the three lead characters. At the Tony Awards, both Rivera and Verdon were nominated for the Best Performance by a Leading Actress in a Musical prize while Orbach was shortlisted for the Best Performance by a Leading Actor in a Musical category. When the musical was revived twenty years later, Bebe Neuwirth won the Tony Award for Outsanding Actress in a Musical for her performance as Velma.

The film version of the musical starred Renée Zellweger as Roxie, Catherine Zeta-Jones as Velma and Richard Gere as Billy. As has been the case in *The Hours*, the three leads received equal billing above the title and shared the theatrical release poster (Zeta-Jones and Zellweger stand on either side with Gere appearing immediately behind them in the centre).

With a strong performance by Zellweger, who was at the height of her popularity following the box office success of *Bridget Jones's Diary* the previous year (for which she had been a Best Actress Oscar nominee), and a breakthrough turn by Zeta-Jones, who had begun her career in musical theatre in London including a lead role in a revival of '42nd Street' while still a teenager, Miramax had two serious contenders for the Best Actress category. Weinstein, however, wasn't taking any chances – he saw an opportunity for payback. According to Haynes, when he chose to make *Far From Heaven* at USA Films with former Miramax employee Scott Greenstein rather than at Miramax, Weinstein had subjected him to a tirade of abuse over the phone and threatened to spend $10million to prevent Moore from getting an Oscar for *Far From Heaven*.[75] Following the strategy employed for co-leads John Travolta and Samuel L. Jackson in *Pulp Fiction*, Miramax declared that Zellweger, as the bigger box office draw and a previous Best Actress Oscar nominee, would be promoted for Best Actress honours while Zeta-Jones would be listed as a supporting actress. To make up for lost time, the studio unleashed an advertising campaign unprecedented in its size.

The media quickly called out the placement of Zeta-Jones in the supporting contest as category fraud. In *The New York Times*, Lyman commented that, "In *Chicago*, Renée Zellweger is being positioned for a best actress Oscar for playing Roxie Hart, the floozy with dreams of fame, and Richard Gere is going for best actor as the lawyer who defends her, yet Catherine Zeta-Jones, as another incarcerated chanteuse who has every bit as much screen time and importance to the story as Mr Gere, is going for a supporting Oscar."[76] In *The Wall Street Journal*, meanwhile, King wrote, "Miramax, in its tree-killing onslaught of 'For Your Consideration' ads in the trade papers, is trying to get voters to consider Catherine Zeta-Jones as a supporting actress in *Chicago*. She has a leading role, but they're pushing Ms Zellweger as Best Actress. ... if Miramax's category-conjuring is ... successful with Oscar voters, Ms Zeta-Jones will be a shoo-in as supporting actress."[77] With Zeta-Jones contesting the supporting category alongside Moore for her performance in *The Hours*, awards voters found themselves faced with two blatant category fraud campaigns on behalf of above-the-title stars in lead roles. "This year in particular there has been a lot of blurring of the lines," lamented Hammond.[78]

Just as a serious threat for the Best Actress Academy Award emerged with the backing of the awards-juggernaut Miramax stable, Focus Features appeared to drop the ball on its campaign for *Far From Heaven*. Haynes expressed concern that the distributor's attention had switched to Roman Polanski's drama *The Pianist*, perhaps believing that *Far From Heaven* had sufficient momentum to allow them to ease back on the campaign and bring a second contender into the equation. In an interview with Biskind for his revealing book 'Down and Dirty Pictures', Haynes recalled, "People would say, 'Focus isn't pushing it enough, don't you wish you were with Miramax?' I could say no, because the most important thing for me, hands down, is to finish the film the way I want. And someone interfering in the production process, that's worse than a lacklustre marketing campaign." His producer Christine Vachon explained, "*Far From Heaven* just wasn't Focus's movie. It was a leftover, an orphan." On 4 January, *The Pianist* collected the Best Picture, Director and Actor awards from the National Society of Film Critics. Moore's performance in *Far From Heaven* did not even finish in the top three in the Society's voting for Best Actress.[79]

As Miramax flooded the media with a flashy campaign promoting *Chicago*, producer Scott Rudin became increasingly unhappy with Paramount's awards season campaign for *The Hours*. In a piece in *Esquire* magazine Kim Masters revealed, "Almost every morning throughout the anxiety-filled Oscar campaign, [Rudin] has picked up the papers and decided that he's getting shorted again. There are little black-and-white ads for his movie, *The Hours*, while other studios have bought big, splashy spreads for their contenders. Despite his years of turning out hit movies ... this is the powerful producer's first shot ever at a Best Picture award, and he is convinced that Paramount is blowing it." According to Masters, Rudin slammed Paramount chief Sherry Lansing over the size of the studio's advertisements compared to those being taken out by rival Miramax. While acknowledging that the ads were good, "my issue was with the spend," he explained.[80]

In contrast to Miramax's strategy for *Chicago*, Paramount was putting both Streep and Kidman forward for the Best Actress prize, making them the first pair of leads in a major awards contender to be promoted for nominations alongside one another in the same lead category in a decade. Streep, however, was reluctant to participate in the modern campaign circus. "I find it alarming that all the campaigning for Oscars is getting like a political campaign," she told the *Daily Telegraph* in London. "It really is distasteful. It won't be long before they start paying for television commercials for best picture, best actor and all those things."[81] Kidman, however, had no such qualms. "Ms Kidman gets extra kudos ... for campaigning like mad," said King in *The Wall Street Journal*. "Beyond doing the talk shows, she's been making personal appearances at screenings ... [and taking] audience questions."[82]

Several commentators believed that Paramount should have listed Kidman in the supporting category where her chances of winning were considered to be better.[83] There were others who contended that campaigning for her in the Best Actress race was category fraud, primarily because of her screen time. According to one report, Kidman herself had considered the role of Woolf to be a supporting part and that she had accepted the role to support Streep, an actress she idolized.[84] The same arguments canvassed above about Moore's status as one of three lead protagonists who together provide the film with an emotional arc, apply equally to Kidman. Indeed, the film's screenwriter viewed Kidman's character as the lynchpin of the movie. "I sort of made Virginia Woolf the substitute author of the whole thing," Hare explained to *The New Yorker*. "And that's how it tied together."[85]

At the Critics Choice Awards ceremony on 17 January 2003, Moore emerged victorious in the Best Actress category for her performance in *Far From Heaven* defeating three other contenders, including Kidman. The result seemed to indicate that her march to the Oscar was still on track. In the supporting category, Zeta-Jones collected her first significant trophy for the season defeating a field of candidates that included Streep for *Adaptation*.

Just two days later, however, the race tightened at the Golden Globe Awards. The Hollywood Foreign Press Association had rejected the category fraud campaigns mounted for Moore in *The Hours* and Zeta-Jones in *Chicago*. The former was excluded from the Best Supporting Actress category and the latter was nominated alongside Zellweger in the Best Actress (Comedy or Musical) category as a lead performer. In the Best Actress (Drama) category, Moore was up against both Kidman and Streep. With Zeta-Jones not in contention, Streep collected the Best Supporting Actress prize for *Adaptation*. Later in the evening, the two Best Actress awards were presented to Zellweger and Kidman.

Having split the Globes, the new Oscar frontrunners then split the two remaining major precursors. In late February, Kidman collected the British Academy Award in London outpolling Zellweger and co-star Streep among others. A fortnight later, the tables were turned as Zellweger took home the Screen Actors Guild Award from a field of nominees that included Kidman and Moore. At both ceremonies, Zeta-Jones won the accolades in the Best Supporting Actress category. Interestingly, Moore's request to be listed as a supporting actress in *The Hours* to ensure votes for her two lead performances didn't cancel each other out was seemingly vindicated by the Screen Actors Guild Awards. According to Sony Pictures, a studio employee had erroneously put Streep forward as a lead actress for her performance in *Adaptation*, thus putting her into competition with herself in *The Hours*.[86] Many industry observers cited the mistake as the reason she was not among the five nominees for Best Actress at the Screen Actors Guild Awards that year.

Streep did not receive a Best Actress nomination from the Academy either. She was included in the Best Supporting Actress category for her work in *Adaptation* but was overlooked in the top category for her performance in *The Hours*. Unlike the members of the Hollywood Foreign Press Association, the Academy's acting branch blindly accepted the category fraud campaigns pushed by Paramount and Miramax and nominated both Moore for *The Hours* and Zeta-Jones for *Chicago* in the Best Supporting Actress category alongside Streep.

Also nominated were Kathy Bates for *About Schmidt* and Queen Latifah for her performance as the prison matron in *Chicago*. In the Best Actress category, Moore, Kidman and Zellweger received nominations along with Diane Lane for *Unfaithful* and Salma Hayek for *Frida*, another Miramax release.

At the Academy Awards ceremony in late March, category fraud paid off for Catherine Zeta-Jones, who triumphed as Best Supporting Actress, but not for Moore. Despite avoiding a competition with herself in the lead category stakes and receiving a rare double nomination, the early favourite for the Best Actress statuette went home empty-handed. The victor was her co-star in *The Hours*, Nicole Kidman. Perpetuating the myth of the vote-splitting rule and the phobia of having two leads in the same film nominated together, many observers cited the unexpected absence of Streep from the ballot as having made the difference for Kidman in what was thought to have been a tight race against Zellweger. The fact that Zeta-Jones had won an Oscar from a field that included another nominee from the same film was conveniently ignored. The industry took a completely different lesson away from that result: category fraud pays.

> *Alternate Winner* – If Catherine Zeta-Jones had instead been considered for the Best Actress category for *Chicago*, who might have won the Oscar as Best Supporting Actress of 2002? The winner may have been Screen Actors Guild winner Meryl Streep for *Adaptation* although there is likely to have been support for Kathy Bates in *About Schmidt* for which she won the National Board of Review prize and was runner-up for the Los Angeles Film Critics' accolade.

> *Alternate Nominee* – If Julianne Moore and Catherine Zeta-Jones had instead been considered for the Best Actress category for *The Hours* and *Chicago*, who might have been in the race for the Best Supporting Actress statuette? The most likely contender is Patricia Clarkson for her performance in *Far From Heaven* for which she won the New York Film Critics' Circle prize and the National Society of Film Critics accolade. The other place on the ballot is likely to have gone to either Toni Collette for *The Hours* or Screen Actors Guild nominee Michelle Pfeiffer for *White Oleander*.

The season after Julianne Moore asked to be listed as a supporting actress in *The Hours* so as not to compete with herself in *Far From Heaven*, Sean Penn found himself with two acclaimed lead performances in films generating awards season buzz, each distributed by a different company.

In *Mystic River*, a drama directed by Clint Eastwood and distributed by Warner Bros., Penn plays a rehabilitated ex-criminal who is quietly raising a family and running a small grocery store when his daughter's murder brings past secrets to the surface. The film premiered in competition at the Cannes Film Festival in May before screening at the Toronto and New York Film Festivals and opening in cinemas in October. Pundits identified Penn's performance as a frontrunner for the Best Actor Academy Award from an early stage.

In *21 Grams*, a drama directed by Alejandro González Iñárritu and distributed in North America by Focus Features, Penn plays a mathematics professor who receives a heart transplant and becomes involved in the obsession for revenge carried by the grieving widow of his organ donor. The film premiered at the Venice Film Festival in September before screening at the Toronto and New York Film Festivals and opening in cinemas in November. The praise for his performance added to the pre-awards season buzz already generated by his work in *Mystic River*.

The received wisdom in Hollywood was that having two award-worthy performances in the same year posed the serious risk of cancelling each other out in the voting. Many observers believed that Meryl Streep missed out on a Screen Actors Guild nomination as Best Actress in 2002 for *The Hours* because Sony Pictures mistakenly listed her performance in *Adaptation* in the leading rather than supporting category, resulting in her performances competing against one another for inclusion in the same category. Given the Academy's rules prohibit performers from being nominated twice in the same category, one industry insider explained to the Associated Foreign Press "studios and agents have to be very careful how they pitch their actors for nominations. They have to make sure that they push that actor for nominations in both lead and supporting actor and not a double nomination in the same category, which could put them out of the running altogether."[87]

As the awards season approached, the balance was heavily in favour of Penn's work in *Mystic River* getting the attention of the Academy. Firstly, the reviews had been extraordinarily good. In *The New York Times*, for example, A. O. Scott had declared, "Mr Penn, his eyes darting as if in anticipation of another blow, his shoulders tensed to return it, is almost beyond praise … [He gives] not only one of the best performances of the year, but also one of the definitive pieces of screen acting in the last half-century." And then there was the Motion Picture Association of America's ban on studios and distributors sending screeners to awards season voters. A film such as *Mystic River* in general release on numerous screens and promoted with a well-funded publicity campaign by a major studio, was not particularly affected. The ban had a massive adverse impact, however, on features such as *21 Grams*, which were playing on fewer screens and were backed by a smaller marketing budget.

Although the MPAA argued the ban was necessary to combat digital piracy, many in the industry saw it as a cynical move by the major studios' trade association to curtail the success of the studios' art cinema divisions and independent companies at the Oscars. Patrick Goldstein reported in the *Los Angeles Times*, "it's an open secret in Hollywood that the Oscar screener ban was instigated by Warner Bros. Chief Executive Barry Meyer."[88] In the *New York Post*, Lou Lumenick declared "the screener ban isn't about piracy – but is a blatant attempt by the old-line Hollywood studios to take back control of the Oscars which have been increasingly dominated by the indies, almost all of which are based in New York." Lumenick particularly noted that Warner Bros. had initiated the ban just when it had "its first serious Oscar contender in years in *Mystic River*."[89]

According to David Brooks, the Focus Features marketing president at the time, "there was a lot of discussion" internally about the company's campaign strategy for *21 Grams* given the acclaim for Penn's performance in *Mystic River* and the impact of the screener ban on the company's ability to garner attention for their releases. In the end, Penn consented to Focus Features promoting his performance in *21 Grams* for Best Actor honours in direct competition with his performance in *Mystic River*. "Given that his character opens and closes *21 Grams* and is such a key figure, it only made sense to put him in the lead category," explained Brooks. "You let the chips fall where they will."[90]

Focus Features didn't let all the chips fall where they will though. While the company couldn't avoid Penn's two lead performances competing in the Best Actor stakes, it did follow Miramax's *Pulp Fiction* playbook and manouveur the film's other male lead into the Best Supporting Actor contest.

Iñárritu's *21 Grams* is a drama centred on three lead characters whose stories are revealed through a nonlinear juxtaposition of sequences. Geoff King, Professor of Film Studies at Brunel University London, summarized the plot in his paper 'Weighing Up the Qualities of Independence: *21 Grams* in Focus' writing, "told bluntly, the core narrative synopsis is rather conventional: man and children knocked down by careless driver; man's heart given to transplant candidate who starts an affair with the victim's grieving wife, at whose urging he sets out to kill the driver, who is himself wracked by guilt."[91] In *The New York Times*, Elvis Mitchell called the movie a "triptych of psychological affliction" performed by "stars Sean Penn, Benicio Del Toro and Naomi Watts". Penn plays the transplant recipient who becomes an instrument of revenge, Del Toro the guilt-ridden driver and Watts the grieving widow whose life has collapsed around her. Like the three leads in *The Hours*, Penn, Del Toro and Watts play characters at the centre of their own storyline who each interact with one another and with the supporting cast. And like *The Hours*, the emotional arc of *21 Grams* comes from the interweaving of their three stories rather than from the performances on their own. Each of the three leads, who were all billed above the title, have significant screen time.

"In *21 Grams*, Benicio Del Toro will go for best-supporting actor ... leaving the way for Penn as best actor," announced Liam Lacey in the *Globe and Mail* a few days before the first of the major critics groups voted for their annual awards.[92] The rationale for category placement was relative box office clout. As blogger Joe Reid later explained, "Penn was a bigger star, and Del Toro had already established himself as a supporting player with his [Oscar] win in 2000 for *Traffic*."[93] The decision to list Del Toro as a supporting actor in *21 Grams*, however, was really a strategic move.

Given it was so apparent that Penn's performance in *Mystic River* would be the one that grabbed the Academy's attention, it begs the question: why didn't Focus Features push Del Toro as their candidate for Best Actor honours? His previous Oscar win had established him as a high-profile actor capable of carrying a film at the box office as had been demonstrated six months prior to the release of *21 Grams* when he was the centre of the publicity for the action film *The Hunted* in which he had a lead role and received above the title billing. And his capacity to win major accolades against Hollywood's biggest names had been demonstrated three years earlier when his performance in the ensemble drama *Traffic* had been listed for the lead actor category at the Screen Actors Guild Awards. Not only did Del Toro receive a nomination, he won the trophy from a field of nominees that included that year's subsequent Best Actor Oscar winner Russell Crowe in *Gladiator* and previous Best Actor Academy Award winners Tom Hanks and Geoffrey Rush. The answer, of course, was that Focus Features already had a strong candidate in the Best Actor race. The category fraud of placing Del Toro in the supporting race for *21 Grams* wasn't about getting him out of the way of Penn, who was primarily a contender for Warner Bros.' *Mystic River*. It was about getting him out of the way of Focus Features' contender: Bill Murray in *Lost in Translation*.

"There are two real buzz performances this year: Penn in *Mystic River* and Bill Murray in *Lost In Translation*," said Lacey in his preview of the approaching awards season. "Penn's performance is a demonstration of sheer ability, starting with Method naturalism and ending up looking like Greek tragedy. In contrast, Murray is all soft touch, ironically playing off his persona as the wistful clown."[94] Focus Features had used the same path to the awards season for Sofia Coppola's *Lost in Translation* starring Bill Murray and Scarlett Johansson as it had for *21 Grams*. The film premiered at the Venice Film Festival in September before screening at the Toronto and New York Film Festivals. It went into release in North America several weeks earlier, however, opening in early October. By the time awards voters were seeing *21 Grams*, the focus was already firmly on Penn and Murray as the Best Actor frontrunners.

The British Academy rejected Focus Features' category fraud that year. When the British Academy Award nominees were announced in mid-January, Del Toro was shortlisted for the Best Actor Award. Penn was nominated in that category twice, receiving separate nods for *Mystic River* and *21 Grams*. At both the Screen Actors Guild Awards and the Academy Awards, however, Del Toro appeared on the ballot for Best Supporting Actor.

As expected, the Best Actor race came down to a contest between Penn and Murray, who took home the Golden Globe Awards for Best Actor in a Drama and Best Actor in a Comedy or Musical, respectively. Perhaps proving the industry's fears about vote splitting to have some basis, the double-nominated Penn lost the British Academy Award to Murray. At the Oscars, however, where he was in contention for only one performance, Penn collected his first golden statuette. Del Toro, meanwhile, went home empty-handed.

Alternate Nominee – If Benicio Del Toro had instead been considered for the Best Actor category for *21 Grams*, who might have been in the race for the Best Supporting Actor statuette?

The most likely contender is Albert Finney for his performance in
Big Fish for which he was a Golden Globe Award and British
Academy Award nominee.

Released in August 2004 and taking over $100million at the North
American box office, Michael Mann's *Collateral* was an unusual awards season
contender. The film received positive notices for Mann's stylish direction and
the against-type performance by Tom Cruise, but action thriller was not a genre
that Academy members had traditionally embraced. It was only when the
critical reception for Steven Spielberg's *The Terminal* starring Tom Hanks and
Catherine Zeta-Jones proved to be less enthusiastic than the studio had hoped,
leaving *Collateral* as its only viable candidate, that DreamWorks launched an
awards season campaign.

The studio began by scrambling to get the film out on DVD earlier than had
been planned originally. "DVD releases have become a key strategy in Oscar
campaigns," explained Mike Snider in *USA Today*, "[They are] a way of
reminding critics and awards voters about a film – especially one that came out
long before the year-end rush ... *Collateral* arrives on DVD [on] Tuesday, timed
to boost the movie's chances for year-end awards consideration."[95] The studio
then listed the two male lead actors for consideration in different categories.

The central character in *Collateral* is a Los Angeles taxi driver, played by
Jaime Foxx. The film recounts his experiences over the course of one night
after he picks up a passenger who turns out to be a psychotic hitman, played by
Cruise. As the film progresses, wrote Manohla Dargis in *The New York Times*,
"the story shifts from a two-hander to a road movie, a tourist-board nightmare
and a bloodied valentine to the director's adopted hometown. [It is] a portrait
of radically different souls clinging to radically different paths". The film's
dynamic is reminiscent of the partnership between Denzel Washington and
Ethan Hawke in *Training Day*. Like Washington before him, Cruise plays a
flashy villain contrary to his established screen image. And like Hawke in the
earlier film, Foxx plays the 'straight-man' role in the double act with the more
famous star, carrying the narrative and the emotional arc as the central
character with the larger share of screen time. Like Hawke, he plays the
protagonist and audience surrogate but manages to avoid being completely
overshadowed by his co-star's attention-getting role. "Mr Foxx can't have had
an easy time playing foil to the world's biggest movie star, but he holds his own

gracefully" remarked Dargis. Meanwhile *Rolling Stone* praised Cruise and Foxx for "their teamwork".

Given the obvious similarities between the co-lead actor pairings in *Training Day* and *Collateral*, it made sense for DreamWorks to pursue a category fraud strategy, especially since Academy members had themselves endorsed the placement of Hawke in the supporting category by nominating him in the absence of a publicity push by his studio or a campaign drive by the actor himself. Studio executives clearly felt that they could secure a Best Actor nomination for Cruise on the basis of his star power and the kudos he received for playing an antagonist despite the fact that Foxx had more screen time and played the plot's pivotal character. In addition to the example of Washington's nomination for *Training Day* there was also that of Daniel Day-Lewis' nomination the following year for *Gangs of New York*, a film in which he had a showy role as a villain opposite Leonardo DiCaprio as the protagonist with the larger share of screen time. As Kevin Fallon noted on *The Daily Beast*, and already quoted previously, "There's a history at the Oscars of actors playing sinister villains, but in secondary roles, scoring Best Actor nods instead of the film's true lead, whose roles are less showy." Key to earning a nomination for Cruise, the studio believed, was moving Foxx out of the same category: a strategy which could yield the additional dividend of a supporting nomination for Foxx as it had for Hawke.

DreamWorks had a second motivation for promoting Foxx for supporting honours that year. In addition to getting him out of the way of a Best Actor push for Cruise, the studio wanted to capitalise on the attention Foxx was receiving as the Best Actor frontrunner for his portrayal of Ray Charles in the biographical movie *Ray*, distributed by Universal Pictures. The studio hoped the critical acclaim and awards buzz around Foxx would result in a rare double Oscar nomination as it had for Julianne Moore when she had lead roles in *Far From Heaven* and *The Hours* but was promoted for the lead and supporting categories for her performances, respectively. As *Rolling Stone* had declared in its review of *Collateral*, "This is Foxx's year!". In addition to a lengthy career in television comedy, Foxx had appeared in numerous films over the previous decade such as *Any Given Sunday* and *Ali*. With his performances in *Ray* and *Collateral* he had broken into the ranks of Hollywood's leading men and bankable stars and had earned respect as a dramatic actor as well as a popular comedian. Like Hawke before him, Foxx did not enter the awards season as either a newcomer or an unknown.

In a highly competitive year, DreamWorks' campaign for a Best Actor nomination for Cruise was unsuccessful. He did not feature in the voting by any of the major critics groups nor receive nominations from the Academy or any of the major industry groups. Foxx, however, not only collected numerous accolades in the lead category, including the Academy Award as Best Actor for *Ray*, but also received several prominent nominations in the supporting category in the second half of the awards season. The critics groups dismissed the attempted category fraud either by simply ignoring Foxx's performance in *Collateral* when voting for Best Supporting Actor winners or by including both of his lead performances in *Ray* and *Collateral* in the citations for Best Actor honours as was the case when the National Society of Film Critics selected their winner. It was a different story, however, when it came to the Hollywood Foreign Press Association and the major industry organizations on either side of the Atlantic. At the Golden Globe Awards, the Screen Actors Guild Awards, the British Academy Awards and the Academy Awards, Foxx received nominations in the Best Supporting Actor category for his performance in *Collateral* making him a double nominee in each instance.

The nomination of Foxx as a supporting player in *Collateral* at the Oscars remains one of the most commonly cited examples of egregious category fraud. In one recent piece online, Nathaniel Rogers wrote "It's one thing to accept the rare instances when a child leads a film and is demoted to supporting ... But its quite another to nominate bonafide adult stars in supporting when they are the protagonist of their film: Jamie Foxx in *Collateral* anyone?!".[96] Meanwhile, Joe Reid at Film.com ranked Foxx at number three on his recent list of category frauds. "Absent a Cruise nomination, Foxx's miscategorization just ends up looking stupid," Reid said, "And greedy, since Foxx was already steamrolling to a win in Best Actor that year."[97]

> *Alternate Nominee* – If Jaime Foxx had instead been considered for the Best Actor category for *Collateral*, who might have been in the race for the Best Supporting Actor statuette? There is no obvious candidate but possibilities include Golden Globe Award nominee David Carradine for *Kill Bill Vol. 2*, Screen Actors Guild Award nominee James Garner in *The Notebook* and British Academy Award nominee Phil Davis in *Vera Drake*.

DreamWorks' campaign for Jaime Foxx in *Collateral* wasn't the only example of category fraud perpetrated that year. Almost half a century after Robert Stack and Dorothy Malone were nominated in the supporting categories for their co-lead performances in the four-handed melodrama *Written on the Wind* in flagrant disregard of their star billing above the title, history repeated itself with the nominations of Clive Owen and Natalie Portman for their performances in *Closer*.

Adapted from Patrick Marber's four-character drama of the same title, *Closer* stars Julia Roberts, Jude Law, Natalie Portman and Clive Owen as two couples living in London whose lives become complicated by attraction, jealousy and betrayal after a chance meeting. The four co-leads share both the film and its publicity material equally. Their characters drive the narrative forward in what A. O. Scott in *The New York Times* called "a tight, ever-shifting grid of jealousy, longing and deceit" and, like the trio in *The Hours*, deliver the film's emotional arc together. It is impossible to make sense of the film's story, themes or emotional resonance without considering all four characters and the performances of all four of the leads. None has significantly more screen time than the other three. That *Closer* is a genuine four-handed drama is evident simply from the looking at the theatrical release poster: all four actors are featured equally, their names listed above the title.

Given both contemporary Hollywood's aversion to promoting co-lead performers of the same gender for honours in lead categories and the willingness of the Academy's members to go along with blatant category fraud, it was evident to industry observers that Columbia would divide the quartet into the four different acting categories. In late November, a week before the first of the major critics groups met to select their annual winners, critic Emanuel Levy wrote, "Is Natalie Portman, who gives this year's breakthrough performance, a lead or supporting in *Closer*? I think lead, although I'm certain that Columbia will campaign for her in the secondary category so that Julia Roberts can gave the lead field for herself."[98] This is, of course, precisely what happened. Columbia Pictures, by that time a division of Sony, promoted Roberts for Best Actress honours and listed Portman for consideration as a supporting actress. Similarly, Law was placed in the Best Actor category while Owen was put forward as supporting actor. The determining factor and rationale for these divisions was the relative fame of the four performers, just as had been the case nearly five decades earlier in regard to Stack and Malone. As established stars, Roberts and Law were placed in the prestigious lead category while rising stars Portman and Owen were allocated to the supporting category.

Not only did Columbia's marketing team believe that Portman and Owen stood a better chance of securing nominations in the secondary category, they also saw a strategic opportunity to reduce the competition for a frontrunner in a film released by one of their sister companies. Sony Classics, another division of the Sony conglomerate, was promoting Annette Bening for Best Actress honours that season for her performance in *Being Julia*. With the flashier role, Portman had garnered more attention for *Closer* than Roberts and placing her in the supporting category meant that she would not go up against Bening. Sony's chances of bagging a Best Actress statuette for Bening would thus be improved and the company would also have a shot at grabbing the other statuette with Portman.

Columbia's strategy for *Closer* was only half successful. Neither Roberts nor Law garnered significant nominations for their performances in the lead categories. In the supporting categories, however, Portman and Owen appeared on ballots regularly and collected several major accolades. It was an eerie echo of the outcome of the *Written on the Wind* campaign which yielded supporting nominations for Stack and Malone for their flashy roles but garnered nothing in the lead categories for Rock Hudson and Lauren Bacall in less showy parts. Ten days after *Closer* was released in cinemas, Owen was chosen by the New York Film Critics' Circle as Best Supporting Actor. Later in the season he collected both the Golden Globe Award and the British Academy Award and was favoured by many to win the Oscar as a result, but lost to Morgan Freeman for his performance in *Million Dollar Baby*, the Academy's Best Picture choice. Portman, meanwhile, also won the Golden Globe Award as Best Supporting Actress and received nominations from the British Academy and the Academy in Hollywood. In fact, the only significant organization not to shortlist the pair was the Screen Actors Guild who snubbed *Closer* entirely. Even though the cast had won the Best Ensemble prize from the National Board of Review, the Guild did not even shortlist the quartet for the equivalent award at their annual gala.

In 1958, the inclusion of stars Stack and Malone in the supporting categories at the Oscars for substantial co-lead roles for which they have received equal top-billing above the title had provoked outrage among leading members of the Screen Actors Guild, generated media coverage and resulted in a rule change by the Academy. Half a century later, the nominations of Portman and Owen in the supporting categories by the Academy, even though they had been billed above the title for their co-lead roles, were accepted with little controversy. Even the most egregious strain of category fraud had become normal.

> *Alternate Nominee* – If Clive Owen had instead been considered for the Best Actor category for *Closer*, who might have been in the race for the Best Supporting Actor statuette? There is no obvious candidate but possibilities include Golden Globe Award nominee David Carradine for *Kill Bill Vol. 2*, Screen Actors Guild Award nominee James Garner in *The Notebook* and British Academy Award nominee Phil Davis in *Vera Drake*.

> *Alternate Nominee* – If Natalie Portman had instead been considered for the Best Actress category for *Closer*, who might have been in the race for the Best Supporting Actress statuette? There is no obvious candidate but possibilities include Screen Actors Guild Award nominee Cloris Leachman in *Spanglish* and Meryl Streep who was a Golden Globe Award and British Academy Award nominee for *The Manchurian Candidate*.

"By 2005, the accepted wisdom was that campaigning two leads from the same movie was Oscar death, so no one really blinked an eye when Heath Ledger – the recipient of better reviews – was declared the true lead while Jake was demoted," said critic Joe Reid recently in reference to the Oscar nominations of Heath Ledger and Jake Gyllenhaal for their performances in the romance drama *Brokeback Mountain*. The placement of Gyllenhaal in the supporting category was, in Reid's opinion, an audacious case of category fraud. "This one takes some balls," he wrote. "The entire reason this movie exists is to tell a love story between two people, yet you're gonna tell me one was more prominent than the other?"[99]

Adapted from a short story by Annie Proulx and directed by Ang Lee, *Brokeback Mountain* was the year's most acclaimed film and an unexpected box office success. Distributed by Focus Features, it was the first gay romance to find success with mainstream audiences grossing $178million worldwide. The movie centres on the relationship between two ranch hands, Ennis Del Mar and Jack Twist, who spend brief periods of time with one another periodically over the course of twenty years. Their time together is contrasted with the lives they lead apart from one another as married men and fathers. The two main characters are both protagonists and are equally important to the narrative. Each experiences character development, contributing to the film's emotional arc. They were portrayed by two of the industry's rising stars, young actors with experience as leading men who received equal billing above the title and were featured with equal prominence on the film's publicity material.

Unwilling to promote Ledger and Gyllenhaal alongside and against one another for Best Actor honours, however, Focus Features listed Ledger for consideration in the Best Actor category and put Gyllenhaal forward for recognition in the supporting category, ostensibly on the basis of Gyllenhaal's slightly lesser amount of screen time and absence from the film's final sequences.   Absurdly, this decision resulted in Gyllenhaal contesting the supporting categories in parallel with the film's supporting actresses Michelle Williams and Anne Hathaway, both of whom had significantly less screen time than Gyllenhaal. MSNBC correspondent Sarah D. Bunting was among those in the media unimpressed at the time.   In her preview of the Oscars on the website of the 'Today' morning television show she wrote, "Jake Gyllenhaal has a shot, even though he doesn't really belong in this category. Yes, he spent slightly less time on-screen than Heath Ledger did in *Brokeback Mountain*, but that doesn't mean Jack Twist is a supporting role – it's a leading role."[100]

Focus Features weren't alone in pursuing category fraud strategy that season. Warner Bros.' flip-flopping category placement of George Clooney's performance in the thriller *Syriana* was even more brazen and similarly drew the ire of Bunting and other commentators.

Loosely based on the memoirs of a CIA case officer, *Syriana* weaves together several, parallel storylines and features an ensemble cast headed by Clooney, the top-billed star who served as executive producer on the film. The screenplay was written by Stephen Gaghan, best known as the Oscar-winning writer on Steven Soderbergh's *Traffic*. Gaghan also directed the movie.

Five years earlier, the ensemble cast of *Traffic* had all been listed for awards consideration in the supporting categories and industry observers initially assumed that the ensemble of *Syriana* would follow suit. According to a report in the *Los Angeles Times*, however, when a preview audience reacted negatively to the first cut of the thriller, complaining that it was too long, Gaghan re-edited the material. A plotline centred on a character played by Michelle Monaghan was eliminated entirely from the new version and Clooney's share of the screen time was apparently increased. As a result, said the *Los Angeles Times* in early November, "there's an official new category declaration: Clooney's definitely going lead and screening tattletales claim he's got a real shot at winning. Not only does he give a powerhouse perf as a conspiracy-snooping CIA trooper, but Clooney's got that whole body transformation thing going on. Voters love it when pretty stars go ugly, of course, and Clooney accommodates them by growing a scruffy beard, shaving back his hairline and packing on 30 pounds." The reporter then speculated, "one of two things has gone on behind the scenes. Either Clooney has finally piped in about category placement, disagreeing with his studio and campaign advisors. Or else that Vegas-loving star and his advisors have all just had a change of heart together and decided – what the heck – to gamble for higher stakes. Either way his studio reps and campaigners have recently changed their Oscar plans."[101]

The decision to separate Clooney from the ensemble and promote him for Best Actor honours was consistent with the traditional approach to the Academy Awards in which major film stars who were carrying the film at the box office were recognised in the lead category regardless of their screen time. Clooney was the film's most bankable box office draw. He was top-billed and appeared on the various theatrical release posters either alone or featured the most prominently relative to co-stars Matt Damon and Jeffrey Wright. One blogger recently argued that Clooney belonged in the lead actor category "because *Syriana* revolves around his character's choices: he's what brings the film's disparate threads together in time for the gut-wrenching and explosive finale."[102]

Debate within the Clooney team and executives and publicists at Warner Bros. evidently continued, however. Just two weeks later the *Los Angeles Times* was reporting a complete about-face. "This time he means it," the paper announced, "George Clooney will campaign for the best supporting actor Oscar for his role in *Syriana*."[103] A spokesperson for Warner Bros' was then quoted as explaining, "We've been listening carefully to members of the Screen Actors Guild, National Board of Review, the Hollywood Foreign Press Association and to film reviewers. Everyone decided, because this was best for the movie."[104] It was a brazen statement. The studio was admitting that its category placement was based purely on an assessment of Clooney's best chances for a nomination and a win, after consulting a sample of awards voters. Rather than offering a rationale about limited screen time or the collegiate nature of an ensemble, the studio was simply saying that their category placement of Clooney's performance was purely strategic; what was "best for the movie".

The studio's assessment of Clooney's best path to Oscar success was shared by leading industry commentators. The *Los Angeles Times* concluded that it was "unlikely that Clooney, with limited screen time, could have squeezed into the crowded best actor category, which is dominated by more than a half-dozen strong front-runners."[105] Leading film critic Pete Hammond later remarked, "Clooney was originally going for lead ... where he almost certainly would have lost to Philip Seymour Hoffman, but strategically dropped to support".[106]

As well as improving his chances of winning a golden statuette, the placement of Clooney in the supporting race was also in the interests of the actor's other awards contender that season: *Good Night, and Good Luck*, a small-budget black-and-white drama about the clash between television anchor Edward R. Murrow and U.S. Senator Joseph McCarthy. Clooney had directed the film and co-written the screenplay. The film's distributor, Warner Independent Pictures, was mounting a Best Actor campaign for the film's lead actor, David Strathairn. By allowing his name to be put forward for the supporting category for his work in *Syriana*, Clooney was bolstering Strathairn's chances of making the Academy's shortlist.

Some commentators were critical of the placement of Clooney in the supporting race given he was the top-billed star of *Syriana* and the film's principal box office draw. Bunting followed up her criticism of Gyllenhaal's inclusion in the Best Supporting Actor category by lamenting Warner Bros.' decision to promote Clooney for the category when several of the film's genuine supporting actors had given award-worthy performances, albeit in less showy roles. Bunting felt the Academy was eager to reward Clooney for his body of work. "The Academy really wanted to nominate George Clooney for *Syriana*, to the exclusion of everyone else in the cast," she wrote. "The nomination is not *completely* out of left field, as Clooney is an immensely likable actor (and personage, generally) who got a lot of publicity for the Bob Barnes role, but his chief accomplishment seems to have been de-sexy-fying himself with a paunch and a beard. He's just not doing a lot, acting-wise, that we haven't already seen from him. The Academy may have favored Clooney with this nomination as a potential consolation prize, in case he doesn't take the best original screenplay or best director awards for *Good Night, and Good Luck* but the voters ought to have let that film stand on its own — especially since other actors in *Syriana* did stronger work."[107]

Category fraud proved to be a successful strategy for both Focus Features and Warner Bros. that season. The slew of stars in co-lead performances nominated in the supporting categories despite the fame and above the title billing of the actors and actresses concerned had rendered blatant category fraud campaigns practically routine and awards voters had become disappointingly blasé. Gyllenhaal won the National Board of Review's Best Supporting Actor prize and received nominations in the supporting category for the Screen Actors Guild Award, the British Academy Award and the Academy Award. Clooney, meanwhile, was a multiple nominee at the Golden Globe Awards, the British Academy Awards and the Academy Awards. At all three awards ceremonies he was a nominee in the Best Director and Best Original Screenplay categories for *Good Night, and Good Luck* and was in contention for the Best Supporting Actor category for *Syriana*. At the British Academy Awards he was nominated alongside himself in the Best Supporting Actor category, receiving a mention for his small role in *Good Night, and Good Luck* as well as for his performance in *Syriana*. The Screen Actors Guild, meanwhile, nominated him in the secondary category for *Syriana*.

The three main precursor awards in the lead up to the Academy Awards were split between three of the Oscar nominees making it difficult for pundits to pick a clear favourite. Clooney won the Golden Globe Award and Gyllenhaal took home the British Academy Award. The Screen Actors Guild, meanwhile, chose Paul Giamatti for *Cinderella Man*. At the Academy Awards, although he was unsuccessful in the screenplay and directing categories, Clooney nonetheless collected a golden statuette by triumphing in the Best Supporting Actor. It was the ultimate reward for the decision by the Warner Bros. team to put their star in the supporting category despite his above the title billing and movie star status.

Gyllenhaal's *Brokeback Mountain* co-star was nominated in the Best Actor category, as was the leading man in Clooney's *Good Night, and Good Luck*. Neither Ledger nor Strathairn were victorious, however, despite the clear run given each of them by the miscategorization of Gyllenhaal and Clooney as supporting players. The winner was Philip Seymour Hoffman for his performance in *Capote*. Just seven years later, Hoffman would himself follow Gyllenhaal and Clooney into the supporting actor stakes for a performance in a co-lead role for which he received above the title billing. With the success of each category fraud campaign, the studios and distributors simply became bolder and bolder, testing the limits of credulity and yet finding reward time and again.

> *Alternate Winner* – If George Clooney had instead been considered for the Best Actor category for *Syriana*, who might have won the Oscar as Best Supporting Actor of 2005? The winner may have been Screen Actors Guild winner Paul Giamatti for *Cinderella Man* after he had been controversially overlooked for an Oscar nomination the previous year for his lead performance in *Sideways*.

> *Alternate Nominee* – If George Clooney and Jake Gyllenhaal had instead been considered for the Best Actor category for *Syriana* and *Brokeback Mountain*, who might have been in the race for the Best Supporting Actor statuette? The most likely contender is Don Cheadle for his performance in *Crash* for which he won a Screen Actors Guild Award and was a British Academy Award nominee. Other possibilities include Golden Globe Award nominee Bob Hoskins for *Mrs Henderson Presents* and Frank Langella for *Good Night, and Good Luck*.

In May 2005, Fox Searchlight announced, "Oscar winners Judi Dench and Cate Blanchett will headline *Notes on a Scandal*, based on Zoë Heller's award-winning novel of the same name". With a screenplay adapted by Patrick Marber, directed by Richard Eyre and produced by Scott Rudin, production began in London three months later. Dench and Blanchett shared billing above the title, were given equal prominence on the theatrical release poster and other publicity material, and played the two main characters.

Described by the distributor as "a story of loneliness, loyalty, envy and love", the film centres on Barbara Covett, a veteran schoolteacher who befriends Sheba Hart, the school's new art teacher, and becomes the keeper of her secret when Sheba begins an illicit affair with a student. Dench took on the role of Barbara, the antagonist, while Blanchett played Sheba, the protagonist. In Heller's novel, events are described from Barbara's point of view and Marber's adaptation echoes this aspect of the original source material with the character of Barbara providing key passages of narration. On one hand it puts Dench's character at the heart of the film, but on the other it renders her an observer rather than an initiator of action. Blanchett's character, although she has less screen time, is the active protagonist and the object of desire and envy. "Is this Judi's film or Cate's, Barbara's or Sheba's?" asked Manohla Dargis in her review in *The New York Times*.

The answer is both. "There's an argument to be made that Judi Dench shoulders a bit more of the storytelling burden," says critic Joe Reid, "however, this is a classic two-lead movie."[108] In his review for the *Chicago Sun-Times*, Roger Ebert called Dench and Blanchett "perhaps the most impressive acting duo in any film of 2006."

Fox Searchlight wasn't about to have both actresses vie for the same awards, however. Not when the now all-too accepted category fraud strategy gave the distributor an opportunity to go after two statuettes. On the basis of her greater screen time, narrative voice and status as a respected industry veteran, Dench was listed for Best Actress honours. Blanchett's name appeared on the annual Reminder Lists for consideration in the Best Supporting Actress category. "The studio just looked at Supporting Actress as the path of least resistance to a nomination for Blanchett," explains Reid, "especially since Best Actress that year was being stacked with names like Streep, Winslet and Mirren."[109]

Reid ranks the placement of Blanchett in the supporting category for *Notes on a Scandal* as the sixth most egregious example of category fraud in Oscar history. Other commentators and film bloggers share his assessment. "Blanchett's nomination in [the supporting] category is a bit puzzling as Sheba is clearly a leading character as the movie follows her just as much as it follows Judi Dench's Barbara," says one.[110] "In essential ways, Blanchett's Sheba is the center of this film … Blanchett's on camera for nearly two-thirds of the film and, even in most of the scenes where Blanchett does not appear, the character of Sheba remains the focus of attention or discussion," writes another.[111] "It's so clearly a lead role," a third states, "not only is she onscreen most of the time but the story focuses on her when she's not and she has scenes without Dench who some people claim is the sole lead just because she narrates".[112]

Fox Searchlight dropped *Notes on a Scandal* into the awards season at the very last moment, giving the film a limited release in North America on Christmas Day. Having thus qualified for awards consideration, the movie did not open wide until January and only appeared in cinemas internationally in February and the months that followed. It was a risky strategy, but one that had some advantages. While the film wasn't considered by the major critics' groups in the early part of the season and thus did not have the opportunity to build momentum, it came fresh to awards voters just when the major industry organizations were casting their nominating ballots. The strategy had proven successful for Warner Bros. with *Million Dollar Baby* and Focus Features with *The Pianist*. It would become the basis of the 'sneak attack' strategy Fox Searchlight would employ in subsequent years for *Crazy Heart* and *Hitchcock*. "A sneak attack essentially involves telling everyone at the start of an awards season that a film won't open until the following year, and then notifying them later on – after many have grown tired of the existing contenders and narratives – that for one reason or another, that's no longer the case. That the film will, in fact, receive an awards-qualifying run," explains Scott Feinberg of *The Hollywood Reporter*.[113]

The late release and the category placement strategy for the two stars paid off for Fox Searchlight. In the lead up to the Oscars, Dench and Blanchett received Best Actress and Best Supporting Actress nominations, respectively, for both the Golden Globe Awards and the Screen Actors Guild Awards. The actresses missed out on the nomination pairing only at the British Academy Awards where Dench was shortlisted for the main prize but Blanchett was overlooked. The British Academy has the strongest record of dismissing blatant attempts at miscategorization and its members may have baulked at the suggestion that Blanchett was a supporting player in *Notes on a Scandal*, one of the year's most acclaimed independent British productions. Interestingly, Blanchett had also missed out on a nomination from the London Film Critics' Circle, perhaps indicating that category fraud campaigns had less success on the other side of the Atlantic where voters were more removed from the onslaught of awards season advertisements in trade publications and newspapers.

The members of the Academy in Hollywood, however, were evidently only too happy to accept Fox Searchlight's suggestion that Cate Blanchett had been supporting Judi Dench in *Notes on a Scandal*. Both actresses received Oscar nominations that year: Dench in the Best Actress category and Blanchett as Best Supporting Actress.

> *Alternate Nominee* – If Cate Blanchett had instead been considered for the Best Actress category for *Notes on a Scandal*, who might have been in the race for the Best Supporting Actress statuette? The most likely contender is Golden Globe Award nominee Emily Blunt for her performance in *The Devil Wears Prada* for

which Meryl Streep was nominated by the Academy in the Best Actress category.

In the space of just six years, ten established movie stars received Oscar nominations in the supporting categories for lead performances in films for which they were credited above the title: Ethan Hawke, Julianne Moore, Catherine Zeta-Jones, Benicio Del Toro, Jaime Foxx, Clive Owen, Natalie Portman, George Clooney, Jake Gyllenhaal and Cate Blanchett. Their inclusion on the ballot in the secondary category was a major extension of the tradition of category fraud (canvassed in the previous chapter) in which character players, newcomers, relative unknowns, children and juveniles contested the supporting categories for performances in significant leading roles. The industry had allowed these ordinary actors and actresses to get away with category fraud because they lacked fame or experience and because they weren't marquee attractions with above the title billing. Many believed it wasn't fair to make them to compete against famous movie stars in the top categories. In the new era of ruthless awards campaigning, however, the definition of supporting had somehow been extended to include any member of the cast other than the single most famous star. A slew of famous performers in lead roles with equal top billing began to crowd out genuine supporting players in the race for supporting accolades. The members of the Academy accepted the studio's fraudulent campaigns and allowed it to happen. Except on one notable occasion.

When initially offered the role of Hanna Schmitz in *The Reader*, Kate Winslet turned it down. The shooting schedule for Stephen Daldry's adaptation of Bernhard Schlink's best-selling novel conflicted with the filming dates for *Revolutionary Road*, a marital drama directed by Winslet's then husband, Sam Mendes, to which she was already committed.[114] Daldry instead gave the part to Nicole Kidman with whom he he had recently completed *The Hours*.

Principal production on *Revolutionary Road* took place in Connecticut in the northern hemisphere summer in 2007. Adapted from the acclaimed 1961 novel by Richard Yates, the film is a portrait of a deeply unhappy couple whose personal dreams have been stifled by the conventions of a seemingly picture-perfect marriage in the 1950s. Winslet co-starred as April Wheeler, an aspiring actress who finds herself as a suburban wife and mother, opposite Leonardo DiCaprio as Frank Wheeler, an office worker bored with his monotonous routine. It was the first time Winslet and DiCaprio had appeared together onscreen since they had starred in *Titanic* over a decade earlier. Given the stature of everyone involved in the production and the prestigious source material, distributor Paramount Vantage and producer Scott Rudin carefully positioned the film for the awards season by scheduling a North American release date of 26 December 2008.

Daldry began filming *The Reader* in Germany in September 2007. Principal photography was already well underway when Kidman, who was yet to film any scenes, suddenly had to withdraw from the project because she was pregnant. With work on *Revolutionary Road* complete, the director turned to Winslet once again. "[It] became impossible for her because she was having a child," Winslet later recalled. "When it came back to me, the schedule had changed and I was able to do it. Fate had worked in my favour."[115] In January 2008, after an eight-week hiatus in production, Winslet took on the role of Hanna Schmitz, a former SS guard who has an affair with a schoolboy in post-war Germany and, some years later, is put on trial for her actions during the war. Winslet portrayed Schmitz at various times in her life: as an SS guard during the war; as a tram conductor in the 1950s who has an affair with a schoolboy; as a defendant on trial in the 1960s for war crimes; and as a prisoner in the 1980s. The movie's other central character is Michael Berg, who encounters Schmitz as a schoolboy and who later observes her trial as a law student and finally sends her recordings of books read on audio cassette tape. In the sequences set in the 1950s and 60s, Berg is played by David Kross. The role of Berg as an older man is played by Ralph Fiennes. Production on the film took place over an unusually extended period with the scenes shot out of narrative sequence. The sex scenes involving the two main characters in the 1950s sections of the film were shot last, after Kross had turned eighteen.[116] Filming finally concluded in Cologne on 14 July 2008.

Just six weeks later, Daldry's initial edit of *The Reader* was shown in New York City at a screening arranged by the film's North American distributor The Weinstein Company. The next day, citing the positive response from the screening audience, The Weinstein Company announced that the film would be released by the end of the year in order to qualify for the Academy Awards.[117] The distributor reportedly demanded delivery of the final edit by early October.[118]

Contractually guaranteed final cut approval and other rights, Daldry, with the backing of producer Scott Rudin, resisted. In an email to Harvey Weinstein, leaked to the media, Daldry wrote, "I simply cannot – and will not – do the work in the very short time that remains. You are asking me to cram months of work into perhaps 24 hours of editing time. It can't happen. It won't happen. I will not be able to work with the composer. I will not be present at the recording of the score. I will not be able to mix the film. This work is my job … I cannot be party to a process that strips me of my ability to make my work good. … I am desperately committed to finishing this movie well so that it is worth the pain that this process has been for all of us. … I am not able to continue in this process this way. I cannot make this date – and it's not for a lack of desire or a lack of effort. It's for a simple finite, irrefutable lack of hours."[119]

An ugly battle ensued between the distribution company and the film's producer and director, much of it played out in the media as a result of leaked emails and statements by the high-powered legal teams that became involved.[120] Among the numerous media stories were reports that Rudin, Daldry and Winslet threatened not to support an awards campaign for *The Reader*.[121] Rudin and Winslet, of course, had understandable concerns about *Revolutionary Road* and *The Reader* contesting the same season and Winslet's two lead performances competing against one another for Best Actress honours.

While Rudin already had *Revolutionary Road* and *Doubt* in contention for the awards season, which meant two Best Actress candidates in Kate Winslet and Meryl Streep respectively, Weinstein's only Oscar contender was the comedy *Vicky Christina Barcelona*. Bringing *The Reader* into contention gave The Weinstein Company a candidate for Best Picture, Best Director and Best Actress. According to reporter Nikki Finke, the company's bid to have the film released by the end of the year was also driven by "The Weinstein Co's money woes".[122]

Eventually, an agreement was struck. "We are issuing this statement together to emphasize the fact that we are in complete agreement on the date we have chosen to release *The Reader*," said a joint statement by Rudin and Weinstein on 28 September. "Working together, we developed a plan to extend the post-production schedule in order to given Stephen Daldry the additional time he needs to successfully complete the film in time to release it on December 12, 2008."[123] Under the deal, Rudin won an additional five weeks for Daldry, but it came at a price. Weeks later, the producer left the project and removed his name from the film.[124]

There also appeared to be another element to the deal reached on that last weekend in September. While Paramount Vantage was promoting Winslet for Best Actress honours for her performance in *Revolutionary Road*, The Weinstein Company announced that it would be promoting her performance in *The Reader* for recognition in the Best Supporting Actress category. "Some sort of deal was struck," says Scott Feinberg of *The Hollywood Reporter*.[125] Industry observers were sceptical. "Winslet's role in the Holocaust drama is decidedly a lead, and a dominant one at that. She is the center of the story," declared critic Emanuel Levy.[126] Catherine Shoard agreed, writing in *The Guardian*, "Winslet is being put forward by the film's distributors not for the best actress accolade, but best supporting actress. It seems, if you've seen the film, like potty logic. She's unquestionably the star: the joint chief character, the actor with the most screen time, the centre of the whole enterprise."[127] In the *Philadelphia Inquirer*, Steven Rea concluded, "the supporting actress [listing] does a disservice to her work in *The Reader* … This is a lead role, and a rich, morally tricky one."[128] Blogger Matt Brennan, meanwhile, dismissed the category placement as "laughable" and "more obviously fraudulent (and craven) than the Clooney case" for *Syriana* three years earlier.[129]

Industry commentators also expressed surprise at The Weinstein Company's placement of Winslet in the supporting category for *The Reader* since the move put her performance in direct competition with the company's only other serious Oscar contender that season: supporting player Penélope Cruz in Woody Allen's *Vicky Christina Barcelona*.

When *Revolutionary Road* and *The Reader* were finally released in December, both films received generally positive reviews from leading film critics, with a few notable exceptions. Overall, however, the response was more respectful than enthusiastic, especially since both releases were decidedly downbeat. Many wondered whether *The Reader*, in particular, could obtain traction with Academy members. "The general impression appears to be that it's intelligent, well-crafted and delicately performed," observed Guy Lodge, "[but] there are concerns that it may prove too distant and cerebral for many audiences … including Oscar voters."[130] At the heart of the issue was the unsympathetic central character, which several commentators suggested was likely to also hamper any major awards push for Winslet's performance. The actress herself, however, had no regrets about how she had approached the role. "I didn't try to make her sympathetic. I knew that would be a mistake – I knew it would be wrong to demand the sympathy of an audience. I'm playing a woman who is an SS guard. We're not supposed to sympathize with SS guards," she told Monica Hesse of *The Washington Post*. "But I knew that I had to understand her. I had to really understand her to come to her in very profound and complicated ways and develop my own relationship with her."[131]

There appeared to be wisdom in the strategy to push Winslet's performances in separate categories when the Hollywood Foreign Press Association announced its annual Golden Globe Award nominations. Winslet received double nominations as Best Actress in a Drama for *Revolutionary Road* and Best Supporting Actress for *The Reader*. Both films were included among the candidates in the Best Picture (Drama) category and Daldry and Mendes were each shortlisted for the Best Director prize. *The Reader*'s unexpectedly strong showing vindicated Weinstein. He told one prominent blogger, "That wasn't a surprise to me. It's very moving, it's a very emotional film. I was never in doubt, because I knew the movie was strong."[132]

While Weinstein may not have been surprised by how many Golden Globe nominations *The Reader* received, everyone was surprised when Winslet won both trophies for her performances at the ceremony in mid-January. The unprecedented double victory thrust her into firm Oscar favouritism just when buzz about her two starring vehicles had begun to wane. In critic Eric Henderson's opinion, "The HFPA's actions have essentially hit the reset button on Winslet's campaign, which up until about last week appeared to be barely surviving, mostly on the maxim 'strength in numbers' given both of Winslet's performances this year are housed in what we expect to be revealed next Thursday as failed Oscar bait that no one particularly likes".[133]

A fortnight after the Golden Globe Awards ceremony, Winslet triumphed again in the Best Supporting Actress category for *The Reader* at the Screen Actors Guild Awards where she was again a double nominee. She lost in the Best Actress category, however, to Meryl Streep for her performance in *Doubt*. By then, however, there were early indications that there may yet by a surprise ending to the awards season.

While the Hollywood Foreign Press Association had accepted the distributors' category classifications of Winslet's two lead performances and the Screen Actors Guild had followed suit (the Guild's members not having the freedom to nominate performers in a category contrary to a studio detemination), the British Academy had dismissed The Weinstein Company's strategy. In London, Winslet received two nominations in the Best Actress category for her pair of lead performances. And in what would prove to be a telling sign, *The Reader* received nominations for Best Film and Best Director while *Revolutionary Road* was overlooked in both of those categories. The dual Best Actress nominations for Winslet defied the prevailing wisdom in the industry "that two strong roles in the same category will cancel each other out, or split the Academy voters".[134] The maxim was discredited altogether by her subsequent victory in the category, which was for *The Reader* rather than for *Revolutionary Road*.

The fact that Winslet was nominated in the lead category for *The Reader* at the British Academy Awards and ultimately took home the accolade for that performance rather than her work in *Revolutionary Road*, indicates that there were many in the major industry organisations who were unconvinced by The Weinstein Company's classification of Hanna Schmitz as a supporting role. According to many around Hollywood, Weinstein's staff were seizing on this sentiment in the lead up to Oscar nominations and were unofficially encouraging voters at screenings and press parties and through bloggers to ignore the official classification when completing their nomination ballots and to support Winslet's performance in *The Reader* in the Best Actress category ahead of her performance in *Revolutionary Road*. If such rumours are true, it was a high-risk strategy, but one based not only on a belief that support for the Mendes marital drama was cooling but also on a keen understanding of the Academy's rules. "The leading role and supporting role categories will be tabulated simultaneously," states the Academy's rules governing the acting categories. "If any performance should receive votes in both categories, the achievement shall be placed only on the ballot in that category in which, during the tabulation process, it first receives the required number of votes to be nominated." The by-laws go on to declare that, "In the event that two achievements by an actor or actress receive sufficient votes to be nominated in the same category, only one shall be nominated using the preferential tabulation process and such other allied procedures as may be necessary to achieve that result."

When the Academy announced the annual Oscar nominations on 22 January 2009, Winslet's name appeared on the ballot only once. She received a Best Actress nomination for her portrayal of Hanna Schmitz in *The Reader*. The film received four other nominations, including Best Picture and Best Director for Daldry. Paramount Vantage's *Revolutionary Road*, meanwhile, was notably absent from the top categories.

When the Academy Awards were presented a month later, The Weinstein Company enjoyed victories in both the female acting categories. In the Best Supporting Actress category, in the absence of the Golden Globe Award and Screen Actors Guild Award winner, the golden statuette was collected by Penélope Cruz for *Vicky Christina Barcelona*. And in the Best Actress category, Kate Winslet took home the Oscar for *The Reader*.

Coming just five years after the Academy had dismissed Newmarket Films' promotion of Keisha Castle-Hughes as a supporting actress in *Whale Rider* by instead nominating her in the Best Actress category, many commentators were delighted that the Academy had similarly resisted the attempted category fraud for Kate Winslet in *The Reader*. "The Academy went their own way," said Erin Whitney in an article about category fraud on the website ScreenCrush. "Winslet's role in *Revolutionary Road* got shut out of the Oscars, but she got nominated and won Best Actress for *The Reader*." In *The Hollywood Reporter*, meanwhile, Scott Feinberg wrote, "[the] Academy acting branch members revolted and nominated her in lead for *Reader* and not at all for *Road*. They do have a mind of their own sometimes!"[135]

While the outcome could have been a turning point for the modern form of category fraud in which marketing executives pushed established stars with above the title billing into the supporting categories for performances in lead roles, it didn't. Winslet's case was an example of the relatively rare occurrence in which a performer has two acclaimed performances in leading roles in the same year. Most cases of category fraud, however, were occurring when a distributor was handling an awards season contender featuring two stars of the same gender. And just two years later, Hollywood's beliefs about the shortcomings of promoting a pair of co-leads for accolades in the same category were reconfirmed. The practice of category fraud was given renewed impetus as a result.

Industry commentators and bloggers have been amongst the most strident critics of category fraud in recent years. There are those in the professional and associated media, however, who have not only helped the studios to get away with such campaigns but have actively encouraged them to do so.

In 2010, Focus Features was the distributor of *The Kids Are All Right*, an independent comedy-drama about a married lesbian couple raising two children in Los Angeles. Directed by Lisa Cholodenko from a screenplay she co-wrote with Stuart Blumberg, the film starred Annette Bening and Julianne Moore. It was a hit with audiences at the Sundance Film Festival, received glowing reviews from critics and was released on DVD at the start of the annual awards season.

At the time, Bening and Moore were generally regarded as the two most respected American actresses of their generation to have never won an Oscar. Between them they had received seven nominations without collecting a statuette. In *The Kids Are All Right*, they both play protagonists and have similar amounts of screen time given their characters rarely appeared apart. Unable to separate the co-leads, Focus Features listed both for consideration in the Best Actress category for their performances. After more than a decade of supporting campaigns for stars in co-lead roles, the reactions of pundits in trade publication and on the internet was mixed. Some supported the dual listing, but others pushed the company to pursue the sort of category fraud that had become such a regular feature of recent Oscar history.

"Julianne Moore: Drop down to supporting – That's an order!" barked the headline of an article by influential film critic and industry commentator Tom O'Neil on his Gold Derby website just a few weeks before the first of the major critics' groups were due to vote on their annual awards. "Let's dispense with the niceties and make this point as firmly as possible," he wrote in his public letter to Moore, "if you want to do the right thing this Oscar season for *The Kids Are All Right*, your costar Annette Bening and yourself, you will immediately quit the Best Actress race and campaign in supporting. You and Bening have the best shots at winning Oscars as a result. Stay in the lead race and you may ruin both of your hopes. Frankly, you have no realistic chance of winning the lead actress contest. … However, if you drop down to supporting, you have a decent chance to win. That race is wide open and you'll be campaigning with a lead-role advantage … It hardly seems fair, I know. You've lost more Oscars than Annette Bening (four to her three), so, if anybody should be stepping out of the way, theoretically it should be Bening so that you can finally prevail. But sorry – that's not how the dynamics of this particular situation stack up."[136]

O'Neil presented no arguments for placing Moore in the supporting category based on screen time or narrative agency. His rationale was pure strategic expediency. At the time, Bening was considered the favourite to win the Best Actress Academy Award. Having Moore on the ballot alongside her appeared to be a potential spoiler. The dual nominations of Bette Davis and

Anne Baxter for *All About Eve* sixty years earlier cast a long shadow over the film's campaign and were even mentioned by O'Neil in his article. "You can't win for the same reason Anne Baxter had no prayer of beating Bette Davis in a similar situation," he wrote. "Davis was the sympathetic centre of *All About Eve*. Baxter was the bad-girl spoiler both on screen and off. ... In *The Kids Are All Right*, you portray the spoiler of a happy lesbian family because you hop in the sack with Mark Ruffalo. Oscar voters are not going to side with you over your betrayed lover (Bening). Ain't gonna happen."[137] As far as O'Neil was concerned, Focus Features should have been promoting Bening for Best Actress and Moore for Best Supporting Actress in order to prevent competition between the two co-stars from derailing Bening's chances of victory and to give Moore a strong chance of taking home a statuette herself, albeit in the secondary category. There was nothing at play in this scenario other than strategy.

Several of O'Neil's colleagues condemned the suggestion that Focus Features promote Moore's performance in the supporting category in the same way Paramount had listed her performance in *The Hours* in that category. "That's not gonna fly with *The Kids Are All Right*, since Bening and Moore are rarely on screen without each other ... making it virtually impossible to argue that one is a leading part supported by the other," said critic Scott Feinberg.[138] Over at *Variety*, leading critic and editor Guy Lodge agreed writing, "Those suggesting Moore move to support risk reductively branding the flightier character the flimsier one. Recently, a counter-argument that Bening should be the one demoted hews closer to screenwriting-manual logic: Bening's character's decisions don't imperil as many characters as Moore's do, ergo, she is the less integral character. They're both wrong. The women's performances amount to a *pas de deux* marking out the shifting distribution of power in any marriage; to suggest that one is subsidiary is to miss the message of the entire film."[139]

Despite claims that the promotion of both women for Best Actress honours would result in votes cancelled out and support split, Bening remained a strong contender in the lead up to the Academy Awards. Early in the season she was named Best Actress by the New York Film Critics' Circle and was runner-up for the National Society of Film Critics' prize. At both the Golden Globe Awards and the British Academy Awards, Bening and Moore received nominations alongside each other in the lead category. Bening won the Golden Globe Award for Best Actress in a Comedy or Musical, but lost the British

Academy Award to Natalie Portman for her performance in *Black Swan*. Portman had also triumphed at the Screen Actors Guild Awards, where Bening was shortlisted for the Best Actress trophy but Moore was not. It was that scenario that later played out again at the Oscars. Academy members nominated Bening, but not Moore. On the big night, it was Portman who took home the golden statuette.

With Moore overlooked for a nomination, Bening's loss to Portman couldn't be blamed on a split vote nor on the distributor's campaign strategy. Moving Moore into the supporting category wouldn't have changed the outcome in the lead actress category. Nonetheless, marketing executives and the publicists responsible for awards season campaigns took careful note. By pursuing a dual contender strategy for Bening and Moore in the same category, Focus Features had secured just a single nomination for one of the co-stars. The fraudulent practice of dividing co-leads of the same gender into separate categories, in contrast, had repeatedly yielded nominations for both performers. The lesson was clear: why settle for just one nomination when you could get two?

When the first trailer for Paul Thomas Anderson's drama *The Master* landed in July 2012, industry experts and awards bloggers quickly declared the film to be a likely critic's favourite and major awards contender. The campaign strategy that distributor The Weinstein Company would adopt was also quite evident. "I'm already dreading the Oscar Campaign Category Fraud that's on its way because *The Master* is obviously a mano a mano movie, a two male lead battle," wrote Nathaniel Rogers at The Film Experience blog site. "Who goes supporting fraudulently? What worthy supporting player character actor will have to sacrifice a once-in-a-lifetime nomination so that Phoenix and Hoffman can have their third and fourth, respectively?"[140]

The Weinstein Company was juggling several awards contenders that season. Also on the slate were Quentin Tarantino's *Django Unchained* and David O. Russell's *Silver Linings Playbook*. Between the three releases, the company had five actors in lead roles and two in supporting roles vying for awards attention. Having decided to promote both Jaime Foxx and Christoph Waltz for Best Actor honours for their performances in *Django Unchained*, it was unsurprising when the company confirmed rumours that Phoenix would be listed as the lead in *The Master* while Hoffman's name would be put in contention for the Best Supporting Actor prizes.

As Rogers identified, *The Master* is a mano a mano psychological drama about the encounter between Freddie Quell, a war veteran struggling to adjust in post-war society and Lancaster Dodd, the charismatic leader of a new religious movement. Hoffman had appeared in four of the director's five previous films and Anderson wrote the title role with the actor in mind. Phoenix was brought onto the project to play the drifting veteran after a lengthy production delay caused by financing problems had forced Jeremy Renner to give up the role. The dynamic between the two main characters portrayed by Hoffman and Phoenix provides the conflict at the crux of the film. "Some of the film's drama resides in the struggle between the two characters – and perhaps the two actors – for supremacy," said critic A. O. Scott in *The New York Times* when the movie was released in September. Two weeks earlier, Hoffman and Phoenix had shared the Volpi Cup for Best Actor at the Venice Film Festival.

While their characters are equally important to the narrative, Phoenix's alcoholic war veteran has a greater share of the screen time. Hoffman's cult leader doesn't appear until the film's opening twenty minutes have elapsed. While Hoffman, playing the antagonist, dominates the scenes they share and the viewer often observes events from his perspective, it is Phoenix's protagonist who develops during the course of the film, brings the audience into the events portrayed and carries the emotional arc. The film opens and closes with Phoenix, not Hoffman, a rationale given by the marketing president of Focus Features for placing Sean Penn in lead for *21 Grams* while putting Benicio Del Toro in support. A. O. Scott formed the view that *"The Master* is really more Freddie's story than Dodd's" and several bloggers agreed, including Pat Mullen who wrote, "Hoffman arguably has a role secondary to Joaquin Phoenix."[141]

The rationale for The Weinstein Company's categorization of Hoffman as a supporting player, however, was purely strategic. For years, studio publicists had insisted that screen time was not a factor in determining a performer's category placement. The relative fame and marquee value of the stars, as evidenced by their billing, was allegedly the key consideration. It is hard to argue, however, that Phoenix was a bigger star than Hoffman, a Best Actor Oscar winner and regarded as one of the great actors of his generation. As critic Pete Hammond observed, Hoffman was "every bit the match for Phoenix … but in order to avoid [them] competing in the same category, the Weinstein Company is campaigning Hoffman for supporting."[142] The company's strategy was all about getting nominations for both actors in the two categories rather than just for one in the lead category. As Mullen remarked at the time, "a loose interpretation of the world 'supporting' might let *The Master* double dip."[143] As a result, said critic Joe Reid, "one of half of one of the year's most intense give-and-take pairs [has been] placed in a subordinate category to his co-star."[144]

As it turned out, the company's strategy ended up at crossed-purposes. Once the season was underway, the company was forced to adjust its campaign for *Django Unchained* and move Waltz into the supporting campaign where he went into competition with Hoffman and also Robert De Niro for *Silver Linings Playbook*. All three were strong contenders for the Academy Award. The company's candidates in the Best Actor category, in contrast, were proving no match for Daniel Day-Lewis in *Lincoln*. Phoenix's performance had been lauded by critics as exceptional and had garnered the Best Actor prize from the Los Angeles Film Critics. His chances of taking home the Academy Award, however, were severely curtailed by remarks he made to the magazine *Interview* at the start of the awards season. "I'm just saying that I think it's bullshit. I think it's total, utter bullshit, and I don't want to be a part of it. I don't believe in it," he said. "It's totally subjective. Pitting people against each other – it's the stupidest thing in the whole world. It was one of the most uncomfortable periods of my life when *Walk the Line* was going through all the awards stuff and all that. I never want to have that experience again."[145] A month later, he offered an apology saying, "I didn't mean that … I know that first of all, I wouldn't have the career that I have if it weren't for the Oscars. I haven't been in a lot of movies that have made a lot of money … And getting nominated for a movie has probably helped my career tremendously. But in some ways it's the antithesis of what you want to be as an actor."[146] His performance in *The Master* was shortlisted for the Best Actor Academy Award, but in the view of industry insiders, the damage was done.

In the light of Phoenix's remarks, it is likely a campaign for both Hoffman and Phoenix for Best Actor recognition would have resulted in a nomination for Hoffman, but not for Phoenix. While this would have meant one less nomination for *The Master*, it would have left The Weinstein Company with a better chance of defeating Day-Lewis, who was seeking an unprecedented third Best Actor statuette. In *The New York Times*, Scott had praised Hoffman for bringing his character to life "with the flair and precision of a great concert pianist" and called his portrayal "integrated, highly nuanced". His work may not have been enough to win the Oscar ahead of Day-Lewis, but he would probably have come closer than Phoenix, whose anti-Oscar words were still ringing in the ears of Academy members.

As it turned out, De Niro, Hoffman and Waltz all lined up in the supporting actor contest at the Academy Awards. Following wins at both the Golden Globe Awards and the British Academy Awards, it was rumoured that The Weinstein Company was favouring Waltz, especially after *The Master* failed to secure Oscar nominations outside of the acting categories. On the night, Waltz collected his second golden statuette and Day-Lewis took home his third. The Weinstein Company's category fraud had secured nominations for both Hoffman and Phoenix for their co-lead performances, but they left the ceremony empty-handed. Had the company promoted them both for the Best Actor category, the outcome might have been different.

> *Alternate Nominee* – If Philip Seymour Hoffman had instead been considered for the Best Actor category for *The Master*, who might have been in the race for the Best Supporting Actor statuette? The most likely candidates appear to be Leonardo DiCaprio, a nominee at the Golden Globe Awards and the winner of the National Board of Review prize for *Django Unchained*, and Javier Bardem, a Screen Actors Guild and British Academy Award nominee for playing the villain in the James Bond film *Skyfall*.

At the 2008 Tony Awards, the black comedy 'August: Osage County' won five awards including Best Play. Two months earlier, the play's writer, Tracy Letts, was honoured with the Pultizer Prize for Drama. Given the acclaim for the source material, when a film version was announced, industry observers immediately earmarked it as a potential Oscar contender.

The play is a portrait of dysfunctional family who have gathered at a farmhouse for a funeral. The narrative is a ferocious battle of wills between Violet Weston, the family's razor-tongued matriarch, and Barbara Fordham, her eldest daughter. In both the original production by the Steppenwolf Theatre Company in Chicago and the subsequent Broadway run, the central roles of Violet and Barbara were played by Deanna Dunagan and Amy Morton, respectively. The actresses earned strong praised from critic Charles Isherwood in *The New York Times*. "Ms Dunagan is simply magnificent in this fabuously meaty role," he wrote. "The cast does not have a weak link, and the other major female roles, in particular, are rewarding and perfectly played … Perhaps finest of all is Ms Morton's Barbara". Both women received nominations in the Best Leading Actress in a Play category at the Tony Awards and also in the Outstanding Actress in a Play category at the Drama Desk Awards. In both instances, Dunagan emerged victorious for her galvanizing performance of the monstrous Violet. At the Tony Awards, supporting player Rondi Reed also collected a prize for her performance as Violet's sister, Mattie Fae Aiken. Reed won the Tony for Best Featured Actress in a Play.

Letts adapted his own material for the film version, directed by John Wells. Three-time Oscar winner Meryl Streep took on the role of Violet and Oscar winner Julia Roberts played Barbara. With two of the most famous actresses in the world in a cinematic *pas a deux* for which they were billed at the head of an ensemble of acclaimed performers, many industry experts were outraged when The Weinstein Company once again turned to its by then all too familiar category fraud playbook.

In mid-August, critic Tom O'Neil announced on his blog, "Streep has agreed to drop down to the supporting race for her role as Violet, the pill-popping, booze-swilling momma in *August: Osage County*, a Weinstein Company source tells [me]." The category placement, he said, "is a shockeroo".[147] Over at The Film Experience website, blogger Nathaniel Rogers responded to the news writing, "I wasn't at all surprised to hear that *August: Osage County*, which has in every incarnation had two leads (Barbara & Violet), suddenly only had one for its future Oscar campaigns according to Gold Derby. I am, however, a bit surprised that it's Violet/Streep who all the action centres on who has mysteriously become a 'supporting' character."[148] Industry commentator Kris Tapley, meanwhile, was critical of the distributor's reported categorization. "It's a clear leading role in a play with two of them," he wrote, "Both, in fact, were nominated for Tonys, but the 'bigger' role of Violet naturally brought in the attention and, ergo, the awards. So I don't quite know how you shuffle that performance, particularly coming from Streep, over to a supporting actress campaign."[149]

The Weinstein Company appeared to back away from its intended strategy after the outcry from online media commentators. Company representatives told Tapley that the campaign was "not finalized"[150] and O'Neil published a follow-up piece stating that the strategy might be changed based on reactions to screenings for industry insiders and the premiere at the Toronto Film Festival in early September.[151]

The response to the film in Toronto proved to be mixed, but Streep's performance was singled out for attention. "Streep is every bit as mercurial, ferocious and funny as one would expect," declared David Rooney in *The Hollywood Reporter*. Roberts' work was overshadowed. The film is "a thespian cage match," said A. O. Scott in *The New York Times*, "Within a circumscribed space, a bunch of unquestionably talented performers is assembled with no instructions other than to top one another ... It goes without saying that nobody can beat Ms Streep at this game ... [She] smokes, rants, bites her fingers, slurs her speech and spews obscenities with the gusto of a tornado laying waste to a small town. Julia Roberts, playing Barbara, tries to hold her own by refusing to smile. She also slaps a face and breaks a plate. It's hardly a fair contest."

In *The Hollywood Reporter*, critic Scott Feinberg gave his assessment of the film after the Toronto premiere. "I imagine that the film could do decent business," he wrote, "but, as far as awards, I'm not sure it will live up to the massive expectations many have had for it. ... The dialogue-heavy dramedy, in the hands of Wells, unfolds largely like a play that has been filmed, as opposed to opened up." Feinberg cited the work of the strong cast as the main reason for seeing the film, particularly the performances of Streep in the lead role of Violet and supporting actress Margo Martindale as Violet's sister, Mattie Fae Aiken. "My guess is that, if any members of this massive ensemble are to receive individual nominations – which become harder to come by when so many actors and actresses are splitting each other's votes – it would be Streep for best actress and Martindale for best supporting actress. (In a highly competitive year, I'm not sure I see picture or director noms in the cards, and even the aforementioned [acting] noms won't come without work.)".[152] Over at Deadline.com, Steven Hammond chimed in to say, "Some were saying Roberts could be shoehorned into supporting as so as not to compete against Streep but I see this as the same kind of situation as 1983's *Terms of Endearment* where Shirley MacLaine and Debra Winger, also playing a mother/daughter combo like this one, squared off, with MacLaine triumphing in the end. Consideration in the supporting categories should also go to a wonderful Margo Martindale."[153]

The clear expectation among industry experts and commentators was that The Weinstein Company would move Streep back into the Best Actress category and campaign for her as lead and Martindale as support. Based on the response to the film, the company quickly announced that Streep would be listed for consideration in the Best Actress category, but the strategy reversal came with another quite unexpected twist. "The Weinstein Company has switched the Oscar strategy of the top stars in *August: Osage County*," announced O'Neil on his Gold Derby website. "Meryl Streep will return to the lead race, according to one of the studio's Oscar campaigners. But here's the shockeroo: Julia Roberts will drop to supporting ... Last week, the studio hinted that Streep might go back up to lead based upon reactions to early screenings of a new, final cut of the film. But there was no hint that Roberts might be shuffled too."[154]

While the role of Violet, the narrative's antagonist, is the more flashy and attention-grabbing, there is no question that Barbara is also a lead role in *August: Osage County*. A. O. Scott noted in his review of the play's Broadway production, the real tragedy of the piece is watching as Barbara "gradually – and frightfully – begins to metamorphose before our eyes into a boozing, brutalizing mirror image of her mother." Barbara is the protagonist in *August: Osage County*. In the family's distorted dynamics, it is Barbara who tries to be an agent of change and she, more than any other, is the character who grows and is transformed.

The centrality of Barbara was further emphasised by the controversial ending of the film adaptation. The stage version ends with Violet sitting alone on the stairs of the house she once dominated having been abandoned by the three daughters whose lives she has made into a misery. The film, however, ends with a coda in which Barbara is seen driving away. The ending "essentially concedes the fact Roberts is the lead as it nicely wraps up her character's arc, establishing Barbara as the story's central figure," explains blogger and critic Brad Brevet. [155] Promoting Roberts for supporting actress honours was completely at odds with the importance of her character in terms of the narrative and emotional arc of the film, the amount of screen time she had, her status as one of the world's most famous movie stars and her billing, along with Streep, at the head of the film's ensemble.

The first cut of the movie ended, just as the play had, with a shot of Violet alone on the stairs but audiences at preview screenings had responded negatively. "We tested it over and over again and people rebelled in the theater," Wells said in an inteview. "They were terrified about what happened to Barbara."[156] At the urging of The Weinstein Company and the film's producers, the additional sequence was added to the end for the premiere at Toronto. A tense dispute was soon unfolding over the ending between the producers and distributor on one hand and the writer and the director on the other. "I'm not sure I'm OK with doing it that way," Wells said in reference to the edit shown at the premiere with the denouement of Barbara driving away. "I don't want to say there's anything wrong with the current ending, because there isn't. But it's something we're still talking about. We don't open for three months, and it's possible you'll see something different." [157] Ultimately, the film opened in December in the same form that had screened in Toronto. Critics were positive, particularly about the performances, but the reviews were not glowing and the film was not the major awards contender the company had hoped for. "I have only myself to blame for pushing John Wells to try and be ready for a festival," Harvey Weinstein later reflected, "It was my call, and it was not the right call." [158]

The decision to "shoehorn" Roberts in the supporting category for her co-lead performance was shamelessly strategic. "Roberts, clearly a co-lead in *August: Osage County*, was demoted to supporting to avoid competing against co-star Streep as a lead," said Susan Wloszczyna at Indie Wire. [159] The executives at The Weinstein Company did not even attempt to provide any sort of rationale for the decision based on any of the familiar metrics and were brazen about their motivation. "We have to look at Best Actress this way," a spokesperson told O'Neil, "Who's strong enough to beat [frontrunner] Cate Blanchett? It's Meryl." [160] The objective merits of the category placements were not considered. The approach that gave the distributor the best chance of collecting statuettes was all the mattered.

The listing of Roberts in the supporting category dashed any prospects of Margo Martindale and Julianne Nicholson receiving recognition for their genuine supporting performances as Violet's sister and youngest daughter, respectively. Both were respected character actresses who had never previously been shortlisted by the Academy. Their acclaimed performances were overlooked throughout the awards season. Three quarters of a century after the Academy had introduced the supporting categories so that the work of lesser known featured players could be rewarded without them having to complete against famous movie stars, it was ironic and also rather sad to see the award-worthy performances of Martindale and Nicholson overshadowed and completely shut out of contention by the presence in the secondary category of the star they had been supporting: one of the biggest names in film history giving a performance in a co-lead role for which she had received top billing.

Frustratingly, the major awards organisations acquiesced in the category fraud purported by The Weinstein Company that season. The Hollywood Foreign Press Association shortlisted Streep for the Best Actress in a Motion Picture Musical or Comedy category and included Roberts among the candidates for the Best Supporting Actress Golden Globe. Their peers for the Screen Actors Guild Awards likewise nominated the two women in the lead and support categories, and Roberts earned a Best Supporting Actress nomination from the British Academy in London.

The members of the Academy's acting branch, who can choose to nominate performers in either category regardes of the campaigns mounted by studios and distributors, nonetheless included Streep on the ballot for Best Actress and Roberts for Best Supporting Actress. They were the film's only nominations. Martindale and Nicholson missed out. At the Awards ceremony in early March 2014, Blanchett won the Best Actress statuette for *Blue Jasmine* ahead of Streep. In the secondary category, Roberts went home empty-handed, losing to Lupita Nyong'o for *12 Years A Slave*. Among industry leaders, the egregious category fraud went unremarked upon. In less than two decades, the phenomenon had reached its zenith and become unremarkable and normalized.

> *Alternate Nominee* – If Julia Roberts had instead been considered for the Best Actress category for *August: Osage County*, who might have been in the race for the Best Supporting Actor statuette? The most likely candidates appear to be Oprah Winfrey in *The Butler*, for which she was a Screen Actors Guild Award and British Academy Award nominee, and Margo Martindale in *August: Osage County*.

When Rooney Mara was first offered the role of Therese Belivet, the young department store sales assistant whose life is transformed by an encounter with a glamorous older woman, she turned it down. "I passed on *Carol*," she told Kathryn Shattuck of *The New York Times*, "which when I think about it now is insane to me, because Cate is one of my favourite actresses in the world. Working with her is like a dream come true, so the fact that I passed up on that opportunity – I can only imagine the state of mind I must have been in."[161]

Mara was offered the part shortly after completing *The Girl with the Dragon Tattoo*, the thriller that made her a star and for which she received an Academy

Award nomination as Best Actress. The seventh-month production had been gruelling and Mara had found portraying the central character to be a confronting experience. The publicity schedule that followed was also punishing and she had difficulty adjusting to her sudden fame and the attendant media scrutiny. She took a break and then appeared in films for directors Steven Soderbergh, Spike Jonze, David Lowery and Terrence Malick. When she was once again approached for *Carol*, she did not let the chance pass a second time, especially since director Todd Haynes was by then attached to the project. "The script and Cate would have been enough, but Todd is brilliant, and I wanted to work with him terribly," she said.[162]

In 1952, Patricia Highsmith published 'The Price of Salt', the novel that was the basis for the film, under a pseudonym because it explicitly deals with a lesbian relationship. The novel is written entirely from the perspective of Therese. While Carol emerges as a fully developed character through dialogue and action, the reader is privy only to the thoughts and self-reflection of Therese. In adapting the work for the screen, however, Phyllis Nagy gave voice to both. "By the time we come back to the scene at the very end, we understand the story through both characters' perspectives and we now find ourselves in Carol's realm," explains Haynes.[163] As a result, the film emerges as a genuinely two-handed romantic drama. Carol is the title character and the active protagonist who drives the narrative forward, while Therese is the audience surrogate and the character who undergoes transformation and carries the emotional arc. Of the two co-leads, Mara has the greater amount of screen time but Blanchett received top billing.

The film, which took its title from the 1990 reprinting of the novel as 'Carol', premiered at the Cannes Film Festival. There had been much speculation that Blanchett would receive the festival's Best Actress prize, adding to the Academy Award she had won two years previously for her performance in *Blue Jasmine*. In a surprise result, however, it was Mara who was favoured by the jury, sharing the accolade with Emmanuelle Bercot for *Mon Roi*. While some industry commentators began speculating about dual Best Actress nominations for the film's two stars, such an outcome was always highly unlikely. For The Weinstein Company, the film's North American distributor, category fraud had become a modus operandi when handling an awards contender with two leads of the same gender.

In the lead up to the film's screening at the Telluride Film Festival in early September, rumours began swirling on the internet that The Weinstein

Company would campaign for Blanchett in the supporting category and promote Mara for Best Actress honours. "If it were to go that way the reasoning is clear," said blogger Nathaniel Rogers, "to have Cate avoid competing with herself in *Truth* ... and defer to Rooney Mara since [she] took Best Actress at Cannes."[164] Distributed by Sony Picture Classics, the political drama *Truth*, in which Blanchett portrayed television news producer Mary Mapes, was scheduled to premiere a fortnight later at the Toronto Film Festival. The rumours, however, did not circulate for very long before Blanchett's agent denied them.

Two days after the screening of *Truth* in Toronto, it was confirmed by The Weinstein Company that they would be pushing Blanchett for Best Actress recognition and Mara for Best Supporting Actress honours for their performances in *Carol*. According to Kris Tapley at *Variety*, the company had decided to favour "Blanchett's fiery and showier turn in lead" and place "Mara's more reserved and passive portrayal" in the supporting category.[165] The rationale echoed the category placements for the stars of *Training Day* in which Denzel Washington's flashier but smaller role as the antagonist was pushed for the main category while Ethan Hawke's more subdued performance as the narrative's central character and protagonist was classified as supporting. Blanchett's greater fame and top billing was also a factor as David Sims explained in *The Atlantic*. "The two are undoubtedly co-leads," said Sims, "but Blanchett is the bigger name, so she'll get the bigger stage so as not to split the vote."[166]

Not splitting the vote was the principal factor behind the distributor's cynical ploy. "The movie may be titled after Blanchett's character, and Blanchett does give an unflinching performance, but Mara's Therese Belivet is entirely on her co-star's level," said blogger Erin Whitney at ScreenCrush, "Mara undoubtedly deserves a spot next to her co-star on awards ballots ... [but] putting Mara up against Blanchett is a risky move with an outcome no one could predict."[167] The opportunity to garner two nominations rather than one and increase the chances of collecting a statuette was another consideration. "The Weinsteins, of course, know this game inside out: why put both your leading eggs in one basket when you could try eking out a statuette for both?" explained Guy Lodge in *Variety*.[168]

The decision to place Mara in the supporting category was criticised by leading industry commentators as well as bloggers. "Blanchett may play the title role, but by no measure can she be considered a sole protagonist," wrote

Lodge. "It's Mara's character's perspective that guides the film from beginning to end. Were the film a heterosexual romance, there can be little doubt that roles of equivalent size and construction would be campaigned for best actress and best actor."[169] Film critic Steve Katz agreed, "the concept of Rooney Mara having a supporting role in that film is odious. She is certainly more of a lead than her co-star Cate Blanchett, providing the point of reference and the journey of growth that comes to define Todd Haynes' film."[170] In the *Los Angeles Times*, meanwhile, influential critic Kenneth Turan labelled the listing of Mara for supporting actress honours as "controversial".[171]

The maelstrom on the internet and in the trade publications became so widespread that Harvey Weinstein felt the need to address the matter in an opinion piece published in *The Hollywood Reporter* at the start of the awards voting period. "I know there's been controversy about Rooney Mara competing in the best supporting actress category for *Carol*," he wrote. "We, as a company, went back and forth and concluded, at the end of the day, that it was the right decision ... we decided, for the good of the movie, that we had to play as a team with this one."[172]

The decision had nothing to do with objective metrics or relative fame. Issues such as screen time, billing, active agency and passive perspective were simply excuses used to justify a calculated strategic move. "The film opens and closes on Mara's shrinking violet of a character," observed Sims.[173] Opening and closing the film had been cited by the marketing president of Focus Features as a key reason for placing Sean Penn in lead for *21 Grams* while putting Benicio Del Toro in support, and had been a factor in The Weinstein Company's decision to promote Joaquin Phoenix for Best Actor for *The Master* while classifying Philip Seymour Hoffman's performance as support. But opening and closing the film didn't secure Mara a place in the lead contest any more than it had made a difference for Hawke in *Training Day*. Equally inconsistent was the application of the notion that Blanchett was the lead in *Carol* because she played the title character. That reasoning hadn't resulted a lead actor categorization for Hoffman in *The Master* two years earlier. Such inconsistencies from one year to another, even when the same distributor was involved, arise from the fact that they are rationales for strategic decisions applied after the fact rather than genuine considerations influencing the decision-making process. Strategy was the only determining factor at play in The Weinstein Company's decision to place co-stars Blanchett and Mara in different categories for their co-lead performances in *Carol*. In Weinstein's parlance, playing as a team was code for placing performers in categories that maximised the film's chances of Oscar success overall, regardless of the objective merits of the placements in terms of each individual performer's role.

And at least one member of Weinstein's team was not at all happy. When asked by Shattuck about reports that the distributor would promote her as a supporting actress and Blanchett as a lead, Mara is said to have "prickled slightly" and then curtly replied, "I don't think it's decided." When asked if it would even be possible for the company to campaign for both co-stars as lead performers, she replied coolly, "It would be possible if we were man and woman."[174]

Mara wasn't the only one unimpressed with the distributor's tactics. In mid-November, one major awards group dismissed a pair of category fraud proposals, including that Mara be considered a supporting player in *Carol*. "After The Weinstein Co. and Focus Features, rather controversially to some, decided on supporting actress campaigns for Rooney Mara and Alicia Vikander in *Carol* and *The Danish Girl*, respectively, the Hollywood Foreign Press Association has called foul," reported Kris Tapley in *Variety*. "I'm told the international press group, which puts on the annual Golden Globe Awards, has vetoed the studios' submissions. Both performances will compete in the lead actress – drama category." [175] A month later, both actresses received nominations, alongside Blanchett, in the Best Actress in a Motion Picture (Drama) category. At the Independent Spirit Awards, meanwhile, Blanchett and Mara were likewise included in the Best Female Lead category alongside one another for their performances in *Carol*.

The decision by the Hollywood Foreign Press Association in particular was hailed as a victory for attempts to combat the rise of increasingly egregious category fraud. But the major industry organisations did not follow suit. Bound to adhere to studio category placements, the Screen Actors Guild shortlisted Mara in the secondary category. The members of both the British Academy and the Academy, although able make their own determinations regarding category placements, accepted The Weinstein Company's strategic classification and nominated Mara for their Best Supporting Actress awards. She lost all three contests: two to Vikander and one to Kate Winslet for *Steve Jobs*.

"Instead of refusing to take the bait, the Academy mindlessly went along with the studio's efforts at category fraud, a ridiculous development considering Mara has more screen time than co-star (and Best Actress nominee) Cate

Blanchett," railed film critic Matt Brunson in *Connect Savannah*. "The Academy's blunder will continue to allow the studios to get away with such nonsense."[176]

> *Alternate Nominee* – If Rooney Mara had instead been considered for the Best Actress category for *Carol*, who might have been in the race for the Best Supporting Actress statuette? Likely nominees appear to be Kristen Stewart in *Clouds of Sils Maria* for which she was the first American actress to win a Cesar, or Jane Fonda in *Youth* for which she was a Golden Globe Award nominee.

In her interview with Kathryn Shattuck in *The New York Times*, Rooney Mara indicated she believed that her performance in *Carol* would have been promoted for Best Actress honours if her co-star had been a man. Leading film critic Guy Lodge made the same point in an article that season in *Variety*. The suggestion is debatable. Had her co-star been Ryan Gosling or James McAvoy, she may well have found herself in the Best Actress contest the way Felicity Jones had a year earlier for her performance in *The Theory of Everything* opposite Eddie Redmayne. Had her co-star been George Clooney or Brad Pitt, however, there is every possibility that she may have nonetheless been pushed for the supporting category as Alicia Vikander was that season for *The Danish Girl* and as Jennifer Connelly had been fifteen years earlier for her work in *A Beautiful Mind* opposite Russell Crowe. Marketing agents and publicists pursue category fraud campaigns whenever and wherever they see an advantage for their film or performer. In recent years, however, it has become most obvious when a distributor has been handling a film with two leads of the same gender, or when a performer has two award-worthy performances in contention for honours in the same season.

There have been questionable category placements from the very first year the Academy introduced the supporting categories. The merit of most instances is open to debate because the classification of roles and performances as leading or supporting is contested. For studios and agents, the issue of whether a performer is carrying the release at the box office with their name on the marquee is paramount. Film critics and industry observers tend to give greater weight to objective metrics such as screen time, narrative agency and importance to the emotional arc.

In recent years, however, there has been a surge in campaigns for actors and actresses who conform to neither of the traditional views of what is a supporting performance. Distributors have mounted supporting category campaigns for established stars billed above the title for performances in the roles that afford them substantial screen time playing protagonists who are crucial to plot, theme and emotional arc. In just fifteen years, thirteen established movie stars have received Oscar nominations in the supporting categories for lead performances in films for which they were credited above the title: Ethan Hawke, Julianne Moore, Catherine Zeta-Jones, Benicio Del Toro, Jaime Foxx, Clive Owen, Natalie Portman, George Clooney, Jake Gyllenhaal, Cate Blanchett, Philip Seymour Hoffman, Julia Roberts and Rooney Mara. In the new era of ruthless awards campaigning, with distributors desperate to avoid co-stars splitting votes and keen to maximise the total number of nominations for their films, the definition of supporting has been stretched to include any member of the cast other than the single most famous star.

While the Hollywood Foreign Press Association and the British Academy have resisted these fraudulent campaigns on several notable occasions, the membership of the Academy's acting branch has proven all too willing to accept the studios' category placements. The phenomenon has the most significant impact on the genuine supporting players who are crowded out of the race for prestigious supporting accolades by their famous peers. Performers whose careers could have been substantially transformed by awards season recognition are missing out as a result of category fraud campaigns and the willingness of awards organizations and industry leaders to acquiesce in these campaigns. Also impacted is the reputation of the Academy in general and its annual awards in particular. The Academy's Board of Governors is acutely aware of the impact of excessive and questionable campaigning on the image of the Oscars. Its efforts to address issues in this area, however, have so far fallen short of the kinds of reform that are necessary. That the issue of category fraud is increasingly discussed in traditional, mainstream media and not just online among bloggers and industry commentators, demonstrates the reputational risk the practice poses to the Academy and its Oscars.

When rising stars Robert Stack and Dorothy Malone received Academy Award nominations in the supporting categories for their co-lead performances in roles for which they had received billing above the title, there was an outcry among industry heavyweights. Within a year, the Academy had changed its rules. Outrageous nominations in the supporting categories in recent years, such Jaime Foxx in *Collateral*, Cate Blanchett in *Notes on a Scandal* and Julia Roberts in *August: Osage County*, have not yet raised the ire of Hollywood's leading performers and directors the way that such nominations did six decades ago. The need for action on category fraud by the Academy's Board of Governors, however, is clear. It's long passed the time for reform.

Epilogue

The #OscarSoWhite Whiplash

"Every year we review the awards season process in every way, to modify, clarify, improve, and to do whatever is needed for more clarity," Cheryl Boone Isaacs, President of the Academy, told *Variety* in early 2014. "It all comes down to the integrity of the awards process."[1]

The integrity of the Oscars has been a contested issue for over twenty years, with the modern style of campaigning clearly the most vexed issue. "I really do think that the integrity of the Oscars has suffered in the past two years, and I think they have to do something about it. They can't keep a blind eye to it any more," film critic Nikki Finke said back in 2000. "If you look at the rules, they're so broad and they're so unenforceable that it's ridiculous. They really should specify what is and isn't allowed, but again that's part of the lackadaisical clubby Academy atmosphere."[2] Over the ensuing years, the Academy has reformed its rules and regulations in attempts to counter and curb the excesses of awards season campaigning, but often changes have been introduced too slowly and the measures have been inadequate.

In February 2011, businesswoman Ariana Huffington hosted a party at her Brentwood home promoting *The King's Speech*, an Oscar frontrunner distributed by The Weinstein Company. The film's stars and director were in attendance, along with Hollywood personalities such as Oliver Stone, John Cusack and Maria Bello, rubbing shoulders with celebrities including Charles Spencer, the 9th Earl Spencer, brother of the late Princess of Wales. "The party generated tons of press and publicity, and was clearly designed to create buzz for the film," reported the *Los Angeles Times*.[3]

The event became emblematic of the excess of awards season campaigning and not only roused concern among industry commentators but caught the attention of the Academy's leadership. "It's really a perception problem for us," Ric Robertson, the Academy's Chief Operating Officer, acknowledged. "The Oscars are about what our members see on screen and think is quality work. To the extent that the public dialogue about the Oscars is who threw a good party or ran a successful campaign versus the quality of the work, that's off-point for us. We want people to be talking about the work."[4]

Following its annual mid-year review of the recent awards season, the Academy announced a raft of new restrictions on how studios and distributors could promote films for recognition at the Oscars, particularly targetting campaign events such as meet-and-greet cocktail parties, post-screening interview sessions and DVD launches. At the heart of the changes was a prohibition on post-screening receptions in the period between the announcement of the nominations and the Oscar ceremony. The Academy also decreed that members could be invited to a maximum of two panels involving performers and filmmakers during the same period. A year later this limitation was revised to four with a fifth permitted if held in the United Kingdom. The service of complimentary food and beverage at such events was banned. "These new rules help us maintain a level playing field for all of the nominees and protect the integrity of the Awards process," said then Academy President Tom Sherak.[5]

The new rules were swiftly dismissed as inadequate. Citing the infamous Huffington party, Patrick Goldstein and James Rainey wrote in the *Los Angeles Times*, "According to the new rules, a similar party this year could offer just as much pomp and circumstance, just as long as it happened two weeks earlier, before the nominations were announced. ... Instead of truly cracking down on the lavish parties and endless stream of celebrity-studded Q-and-A screenings, the academy has embraced a half-hearted compromise. It has essentially decreed that in terms of parties and celebrity screenings, anything goes until the nominations are announced ... [then] all the fun has to stop."[6] After quickly surveying publicists and awards season consultants, meanwhile, Gregg Kilday at *The Hollywood Reporter* concluded the changes "are likely to have two effects ... the months leading up to the nominations could become more frenetic than ever.　And the restricted weeks [after the nomination are announced] could become a social minefield."[7]

It wasn't until five years later than the Academy finally introduced the complete prohibition on awards season parties that industry commentators had been recommending. "Academy members may not be invited to or attend any non-screening event, party or dinner that is reasonably perceived to unduly influence members or undermine the integrity of the vote," stated the revised campaign regulations announced by the Academy in June 2016. Violations of the ban would result in a one-year suspension for the first offense and expulsion for a second explained the Academy.[8]

While the Academy was slow to address the perceived influence of cocktail receptions and post-screening parties on the Oscars, its Board of Governors responded swiftly to counter mounting public criticism of the lack of diversity in the Academy's membership and in the field of Oscar nominees. In early 2016, key African-American filmmakers condemned the Academy and called for a boycott of the ceremony when it was revealed that the twenty nominees in the acting categories were all white performers for the second year in a row. The hashtag #OscarSoWhite quickly trended on social media and accusations of racism were levied at the Academy in a media controversy that rapidly began to spin out of control. Just four days after the announcement of the nominations, Boone Isaacs issued a statement on the growing controversy. "I am both heartbroken and frustrated about the lack of inclusion," she said, "This is a difficult but important conversation, and it's time for big changes. The Academy is taking dramatic steps to alter the makeup of our membership."[9] Within a week, an unusual special meeting of the Board unanimously endorsed measures to increase the number of female and minority members, broaden representation in the governing structures of the Academy, and reform the eligibility criteria for voting for the Oscars.

The speed of the Academy's reaction to the controversy was surprising, particularly as many believed the organization was copping criticism that was more appropriately levelled at the major Hollywood studios. "The protests were angry at Hollywood's longtime failure to recognize racial and gender diversity in the country," explained Tim Gray in *Variety*. "Studio decision-makers are overwhelmingly white and male, which is reflected in their films and especially their awards hopefuls. Out of 305 eligible films, only a handful were made by directors of racial minority; only a few were directed by women."[10] This lack of diversity in the films produced by the industry limited the

Academy's options for inclusivity when it came to the Oscar nominations, explained Scott Feinberg in *The Hollywood Reporter*. "The root of the problem is less with the Academy than with the film industry as a whole," he wrote. "Even in 2016, very few people of color direct or star in major American movies. That is the result of decisions made not by the Academy, but by the studios that finance and produce movies – for reasons of commerce and/or bigotry and/or cowardice. This leaves the Academy with a pool of options lacking diversity, in terms of eligible films and individuals."[11]

Several leading filmmakers and performers made the same point. "The academy is the endgame," producer Stephanie Allen told *The New York Times*, "But the beginning of the game is the industry … [female and minority filmmakers] just need jobs. That's how we're really going to solve the problem – not by more programs or committees".[12] Academy Award winner Whoopi Goldberg, meanwhile, questioned the wisdom of a boycott of the Oscar ceremony, especially as it was to be hosted by comedian Chris Rock. "You want to boycott something?" she asked on the television program 'The View', "Don't go see movies that don't have your representation. That's the boycott you want."[13]

In *The New York Times*, meanwhile, Michael Cieply noted that in the decade leading up to the 2014 awards season in which *12 Years A Slave* won the Oscar as Best Picture, "24 of the 200 acting nomines were black, approximately matching the proporation of blacks in the North American movie audience and population."[14] And while the #OscarSoWhite controversy focused on the omission of Will Smith and Idris Elba from the acting categories and was driven by public comments by Jada Pinkett-Smith and Spike Lee, it was actually performers and filmmakers of Asian, Hispanic and Native American heritage who were grossly under-represented on the Oscar ballot each year.

The Academy moved rapidly to counter criticism of the lack of diversity among the nominees and over the course of several years has taken steps to counter perceptions of undue influence on the voting process of receptions and parties associated with studio campaigns. In explaining reforms and rule changes, successive Academy Presidents have consistently referred to the integrity of the awards process. This has been understandable given the negative impact media reports of lavish parties and expensive campaigns can have on the view of the Academy Awards held by both the general public and industry insiders. "It's a bit like politics," actor Joaquin Phoenix once commented about awards season campaigning. "It's the money behind you, the machine behind you, that's really effective. There are a lot of brilliant performances that don't register on their [Academy members'] radar. When you see who won, you kind of want to say: 'You're right; out of the 10 movies that ran good campaigns, that was the best'."[15]

And yet, there has been no response at all to more than two decades of criticism about the way studios and distributors have undermined the integrity of the four acting Oscars with their pursuit of blatant category fraud in their campaigns. Frustratingly, the Academy's concerns about campaigns have been limited to the perceived influence of parties on the voting process. The actual influence of campaigns on the nomination process in terms of inappropriate category placements has been studiously ignored even though category fraud has become an issue discussed in mainstream media and is causing the Academy reputational damage. Why has the Academy done so much to regulate campaign activity yet steadfastly refused to reform the nominations process that these campaigns are designed to influence and, in some instances, pervert? How can the Board of Governors be more concerned about the perception that parties undermine the voting process than it is about the reality of how inappropriate category placement tarnishes the integrity of the awards themselves? And why is the Academy unwilling to intervene in the acting categories to protect the integrity of the awards when it is prepared to take decisive action in other categories?

In 2014, the Academy rescinded the nomination in the Best Original Song category of "Alone Yet Not Alone" from the film of the same name. The song had been composed by Bruce Broughton with lyrics by Dennis Spiegel. Broughton, a member of the executive committee of the Academy's music branch, had emailed seventy members of the branch asking them to consider "Alone Yet Not Alone" and attached his name to the bottom of the email. As Tim Gray explained in *Variety*, this was deemed a breach of the Academy's rules. "During the nomination process, the Academy sends a DVD to the 240 members of the music branch that includes scenes from each film showing the use of the song in context ... The Academy specifically does not list composers or lyricists, just the movie and song titles ... the idea being to prevent favoritism and promote unbiased voting. ... The Academy wants members to vote for nominees based solely on the achievement of a particular song in a movie, without regard to who may have written it."[16] Broughton's email was determined to have broken Rule 5.3 and the song was struck from the ballot.

"It all comes down to the integrity of the awards process," explained Boone Isaacs at the time.

The Academy does more than simply enforce the rules, however. Twice in recent years, the Academy has intervened in the screenplay categories to reverse category placements designated by studios and distributors. In 2015, Sony Pictures Classics listed Damien Chazelle's screenplay for *Whiplash* for consideration in the Best Original Screenplay category. Chazelle had written the script without reference to any previously produced or published source material. In order to secure funding for the feature, however, he had directed a short film of the same name. The short was a scene taken from the already-completed screenplay and the subsequent feature was neither based on nor adapted from the short film. In a highly controversial decision, however, the Academy ruled Chazelle's work to be an adapted screenplay because of the existence of the earlier short film. Adding to the controversy was the fact that this ruling was inconsistent with the treatment of writer-director Courtney Hunt's original screenplay for *Frozen River* seven years earlier which had similarly spawned a short film in order to secure feature film funding, but which was nontheless allowed to contest the Best Original Screenplay category at the Oscars. A few years prior to that, Stephen Gaghan based his screenplay for *Syriana* on the book 'See No Evil' by Robert Baer. His screenplay won the Best Adapted Screenplay Award from the National Society of Film Critics, earned a Best Adapted Screenplay nomination for the Writers Guild Awards and was shortlisted for the University of Southern California Scripter Award, a prize given to adapted screenplays and their source material. The Academy, however, decided that the script departed significantly from Baer's book and placed it in the Best Original Screenplay category. Given that Chazelle's screenplay was not based on existing material and that Gaghan's was, the Academy's intervention in these instances attracted considerable criticism. It also raised the critical question of why the Academy was unwilling to intervene in the acting categories over the classification of any given performance as lead or supporting when it was prepared to intervene in the writing categories over the classification of a particular screenplay as adapted or original.

The refusal to arbitrate on the categorization of performers has been all the more puzzling given the fact the Academy has done so in the past. When she announced the Academy would take dramatic steps to alter the makeup of the organization's membership, Boone Isaacs noted, "This isn't unprecedented for the Academy. In the '60s and '70s it was about recruiting younger members to stay vital and relevant. In 2016, the mandate is inclusion in all of its facets: gender, race, ethnicity and sexual orientation."[17] And when the reforms were announced a few days later, the limitation of voting rights to members active in the industry during the previous decade was a revival of a rule originally introduced in the 1970s but that had subsequently been revoked. Precedent is understandably important to the Academy, especially when it comes to the Oscars which draw so much of their prestige from a strong sense of tradition and history. A mechanism through which to address the most egregious cases of category fraud, would not be breaking new ground. Following the outcry over the nominations of co-leads Robert Stack and Dorothy Malone in the supporting categories for their performances in *Written on the Wind*, it was announced that while studios would continue to list performances as lead or supporting, a special committee of the Academy would ultimately determine the appropriateness of these classifications in the event that they were questioned. Regrettably, this reform was abolished just seven years later. It does, however, give the Board of Governors a precedent which could be considered.

The Board could also look at adopting a variation of the contemporary best practice model in place in the theatre world. The Tony Awards Administration Committee is comprised of twenty-four members, of whom ten are designated by the American Theatre Wing, ten by the Broadway League, and one each by the Dramatists Guild, Actors' Equity Association, United Scenic Artists, and the Society of Stage Directors and Choreographers. This elite committee of theatre professionals determines the eligibility for nominations in all awards categories as well as reviews the rules governing the awards. It is the Administration Committee that decides whether performances are placed in the lead or featured player categories at the Tony Awards, not the shows' producers or publicists.

A variation on this approach, proposed by Feinberg in *The Hollywood Reporter*, would be "to determine a certain percentage of the run time (perhaps 50 percent) below which a performance automatically would be considered a supporting role and above which it automatically would be considered a leading role. Contenders who dispute the appropriateness of their categorization would be welcome to appeal to the branch's three representatives on the Board of Governors, who would make the final determination."[18] On the Film Experience website, blogger Nathaniel Rogers chimed in, "my suggestion is an executive committee that makes rulings on the lead vs supporting cases. Our other suggestion – that leading actors pretending to be supporting actors for the sake of prizes have to give back their lead salary perhaps to SAG to support out of work character actors – and accept whatever salary they might have been offered for a non-headlining role in its place."[19]

Regardless of the approach adopted and the rules and regulations surrounding that approach, there is widespread recognition that there is a problem that the Academy needs to address. "It's time for the Academy to put an end to so-called 'category fraud', the acting of campaigning for a performer to receive a nomination in one category – lead or supporting – even though he or she clearly should be considered in the other, all in an attempt to improve the likelihood of garnering a nom and/or a win," Feinberg declared.[20] There is also widespread recognition that the problem is getting worse and garnering more and more attention. "Each year, politics and star power determine which actors get campaigned for in different categories, with frequently illogical results," said David Sims in *The Atlantic* as the awards season began in late 2015.[21]

There are, of course, dissenting voices who dismiss the debate about category fraud as either unimportant or a problem that is unsolvable. Jason Bailey has said, "until there's some kind of objective standard, with official awards-season refs running stopwatches in screenings to meet bylaws about screen-time percentages, we're all gonna have to tend to our own gardens on this one. … the amount of hyperbole and film-geek rage swirling around the nonsense issue of 'category fraud' is altogether disproportionate to the amount of actual relevance even the big bad Oscars have, at least insofar as the quality of the films at hand and what will actually endure about any of them. It's much ado about nothing."[22] And in one controversial article in the influential trade paper *Variety*, Tim Gray cited the handful of instances in which supporting performances have been nominated in the lead categories to spuriously declare that "the Oscar ecosystem balances things out".[23]

Gray titled his article, "Oscar Has a Long and Honorable History of 'Category Fraud'". A longtime advocate for reform to address category fraud, Rogers responded, "believing that something is okay because it has been done for a long time does not mean that it is OK. It merely means that you are complacent … [and] this is not always the way it's been. We are dealing with a distortion of history brought on by exactly this kind of anything-goes complacency … things have definitely gotten worse and the gaming more egregious over the years."[24]

As Rogers has written on his blog, the phenomenon of category fraud is not a victimless crime but rather a "cancer that has eaten away at the Oscars and steals dozens upon dozens of opportunities away from the less famous all the time." [25] Leading industry commentator Guy Lodge concurs, "for every borderline-lead star who takes the path of least resistance to a spot on the supporting ballot, there's an outstanding character actor being edged out of the race because their genuinely supporting part seems less showy by comparison."[26] To date the following actors and actress (many of whom are now deceased) have never received a nomination from the Academy in the acting categories: Richard Attenborough, Richard Benjamin, Emily Blunt, Steven Buscemi, David Carradine, Don Cheadle, Phil Davis, Lou Diamond Phillips, R. Lee Ermey, Lillian Gish, Cedric Hardwicke, Betty Hutton, Lainie Kazan, Brian Keith, Margo Martindale, Kate Reid, Noah Taylor, Jack Thompson and John Turturro. As the previous pages have noted, had it not been for inappropriate category placements of more famous performers and juvenile leads, many would have been honoured by the Academy with a nomination. Such recognition would have had a tremendous impact on many of their careers. And then there are many other performers who would likely have received recognition for the first time at a much earlier point in their careers. How ironic it is that the Academy has recently moved decisively to support inclusion in the acting categories on the basis of ethnicity, and yet stands unconcerned about whether genuine supporting players are getting a fair chance at inclusion in the Best Supporting Actor and Best Supporting Actress categories.

In the mid-1930s, Academy President Frank Capra introduced the supporting categories to win support for the Academy among actors. The new categories were designed to enable the Academy to recognize the contribution of character actors and featured players without them having to compete with famous movie stars in lead roles. This fundamental rationale for the supporting categories needs to be protected by the Academy against the corrupting influence of category fraud.

The Academy's leadership has long acknowledged the problem of category fraud, the impact it has on supporting performers and on the reputation of the Oscars. In early 2002, Tom King wrote an article about category fraud in *The Wall Street Journal* in which he described the nominations of Jennifer Connelly and Ethan Hawke in the supporting categories for their performances in *A Beautiful Mind* and *Training Day* as a "potentially embarrassing development".[27]

As part of the research for the article he spoke to Cheryl Boone Isaacs, a studio publicity executive and long-standing member of the Board of Governors of the Academy at the time. She made clear her own displeasure at obviously fraudulent nominations when she remarked, "Apparently, 'supporting' has taken on a whole new meaning these days."[28] In the fifteen years since then, category fraud has become more blatant and outrageous and Cheryl Boone Isaacs has become the President of the Academy of Motion Picture Arts and Sciences. It's time she and her Board took action to restore the supporting categories to outstanding performers in truly supporting roles.

NOTES

Prologue

[1] John Harkness, *The Academy Awards Handbook*, Pinnacle Books, New York, 1994, p41; Anthony Holden, *Behind the Oscar: The Secret History of the Academy Awards*, Simon & Schuster, New York, 1993, p127; Damien Bona and Mason Wiley, *Inside Oscar: The Unofficial History of the Academy Awards*, Ballatine Books, New York, 1986 (ed 1993), p62

[2] *Behind the Oscar* p127; Joseph McBride, *Frank Capra: The Catastrophe of Success*, Faber & Faber, London, 1992, p337; *Inside Oscar* p62

[3] *Behind the Oscar* p128; Peter H. Brown and Jim Pinkston, *Oscar Dearest: Six Decades of Scandal, Politics and Greed Behind Hollywood's Academy Awards 1927-1986*, Perrenial Library, New York, 1987, p28

[4] *Behind the Oscar* p85-7; *Frank Capra* 225; *Inside Oscar* p2

[5] *Behind the Oscar* p88

[6] Steve Pond, *The Big Show: High Times and Dirty Dealings Backstage at the Academy Awards*, Faber & Faber, New York, 2005, p17

[7] Scott Eyman, *Lion of Hollywood: The Life and Legend of Louis B. Mayer*, Robson Books, London, 2005, p 117

[8] *Behind the Oscar* p92; *Inside Oscar* p3

[9] *Behind the Oscar* p102

[10] *Behind the Oscar* p89

[11] *Academy Awards Handbook* p8; *Behind the Oscar* p88; *Frank Capra* p225; Tom O'Neil, *Movie Awards: The Ultimate, Unofficial Guide to the Oscars, Golden Globes, Critics, Guild & Indie Honors*, Perigee, New York, 2001, p8; *Oscar Dearest* p18

[12] *Academy Awards Handbook* p32; *Behind the Oscar* p111-2; *Frank Capra* p285; *Inside Oscar* p46; *Lion of Hollywood* p178-9; *Oscar Dearest* p22

[13] *Behind the Oscar* p128

[14] *Frank Capra* p324; *Inside Oscar* p55

[15] *Behind the Oscar* p128

[16] *Behind the Oscar* p129-30; *Big Show* p20; *Frank Capra* p337; *Inside Oscar* p63

[17] *Behind the Oscar* p132; *Frank Capra* p338-9

[18] *Behind the Oscar* p132; *Frank Capra* p338; *Inside Oscar* p69-70

[19] *Behind the Oscar* p132; *Inside Oscar* p69

[20] *Behind the Oscar* p106, 133; *Inside Oscar* p70

[21] Emanuel Levy, *And the Winner Is … The History and Politics of the Oscar Awards*, Continuum, New York, 1987 (ed 1991), p59; *Behind the Oscar* p133; *Inside Oscar* p70

[22] *Inside Oscar* p73

[23] *Academy Awards Handbook* p46; *Inside Oscar* p73; *Movie Awards* p47

[24] *Behind the Oscar* p133; *Inside Oscar* p70

[25] *Inside Oscar* p78

[26] *Academy Awards Handbook* p52

[27] *Inside Oscar* p78

[28] *And the Winner Is* p59

[29] *And the Winner Is* p60

[30] *Inside Oscar*, p147

[31] *Behind the Oscar* p136

[32] *Inside Oscar* p144

[33] *And the Winner Is* p60-1

[34] *And the Winner Is* p61

[35] *And the Winner Is* p62

Act One

[1] *Inside Oscar* p74; James Curits, *Spencer Tracy*, Knopf, New York, 2011, p315

[2] *Spencer Tracy* p295
[3] *Spencer Tracy* p282
[4] *Spencer Tracy* p276
[5] *Spencer Tracy* p295
[6] *Spencer Tracy* p277-8
[7] *Spencer Tracy* p294
[8] *Spencer Tracy* p297
[9] *Spencer Tracy* p310
[10] *Inside Oscar* p68
[11] *And the Winner Is* p59
[12] *Inside Oscar* p70; *Movie Awards* p46
[13] *Inside Oscar* p71
[14] *Inside Oscar* p71
[15] *Behind the Oscar* p134; Michael Gebert, *The Encyclopedia of Movie Awards*, St Martin's Paperbacks, New York, 1996, p78; *Movie Awards* p46
[16] *Academy Awards Handbook* p46; *Behind the Oscar* p136; *Movie Awards* p46
[17] *Behind the Oscar* p134-5
[18] Michael Troyan, *A Rose for Mrs Miniver: The Life of Greer Garson*, University of Kentucky Press, Lexington, 1999, p81, 85
[19] *A Rose* p34, 85
[20] *A Rose* p59
[21] *A Rose* p61-2
[22] *A Rose* p73, 76
[23] *A Rose* p78-9
[24] *A Rose* p80-1
[25] Emily W. Leider, *Myrna Loy: The Only Good Girl in Hollywood*, University of California Press, Los Angeles, 2011, p205, 230; *A Rose* p85
[26] *A Rose* p86
[27] *A Rose* p83-4
[28] *A Rose* p94
[29] *Inside Oscar* p94
[30] *A Rose* p97
[31] *A Rose* p97
[32] Sam Staggs, *All About "All About Eve": The Complete Behind-the-Scenes Story of the Bitchiest Film Ever Made*, St Martin's Griffin, New York, 2001, p71
[33] *All About* p14
[34] *All About* p72; Gary Carey with Joseph L. Mankiewicz, *More About All About Eve*, Random House, New York 1972 (reference edition: Bantam edition 1974), p68
[35] *All About* p72; *More About*, p68
[36] *More About*, p68
[37] *All About* p60
[38] *All About* p61
[39] *All About* p207
[40] *All About* p152
[41] *All About* p208
[42] *Oscar Dearest* p160
[43] *All About* p207
[44] Tom O'Neil, "Julianne Moore: Drop down to supporting – That's an order!", www.goldderby.com, 12 August 2013
[45] *And the Winner Is* p61
[46] *All About* p208
[47] *All About* p208
[48] *All About* p215
[49] Chris Chase and Rosalind Russell, *Life Is A Banquet*, Ace Books, New York, 1979, p151

[50] *Life Is A Banquet* p156

[51] *Life Is A Banquet* p184

[52] *Life Is A Banquet* p184

[53] *Life Is A Banquet* p217

[54] Sam Kashner and Jennifer MacNair, *The Bad & The Beautiful: Hollywood in the Fifties*, Little Brown, London 2002, p319

[55] Bernard F. Dick, *Forever Mame: The Life of Rosalind Russell*, University Press of Mississippi, Jackson, 2006, p175

[56] *Life Is A Banquet* p185

[57] *Behind the Oscar* p223, *Inside Oscar* p260

[58] *Forever Mame* p178-9

[59] *And the Winner Is* p63; *Behind the Oscar* p309; *Inside Oscar* p530

[60] Trader Faulkner, *Peter Finch: A Biography*, Angus & Robertson, London, 1979 (reference edition: Pan Books, London, 1980), p321

[61] Danny Peary, *Alternate Oscars: One Critic's Defiant Choices for Best Picture, Actor, and Actress – From 1927 to the Present*, Simon & Schuster, New York, 1993, p232

[62] *And the Winner Is* p63; *Behind the Oscar* p309; *Inside Oscar* p530

[63] *Peter Finch* p321

[64] *Behind the Oscar* p309

[65] Lawrence J. Quirk, *Fasten Your Seatbelts: The Passionate Life of Bette Davis*, Signet, London, 1990, p461

[66] *Behind the Oscar* p309

[67] Pauline Kael, *When the Lights Go Down*, Holt, Reinhart and Winston, New York, 1975, p221

[68] *Inside Oscar* p814

[69] *Inside Oscar* p802

[70] *Behind the Oscar* p452

[71] *Behind the Oscar* p453

[72] *Behind the Oscar* p453

[73] *Behind the Oscar* p453

[74] *Movie Awards* p582

[75] *Alternate Oscars* p306; *Movie Awards* p582

[76] *Alternate Oscars* p307

[77] Erin Whitney, "What Is Category Fraud? A Closer Look at This Year's Big Oscar Controversy", www.screencrush.com, 10 December 2015

[78] David Sims, "Why Oscar Nominations Make No Sense", www.theatlantic.com, 15 October 2015

[79] Steve Katz, "On Category Fraud", www.alphaprimitive.com, 9 December 2015

[80] Richard Natale, "Supporting or lead role? It's anyone's call", *Chicago Tribune*, March 2000

[81] Laurence Olivier, *Confessions of an Actor*, Wheelshare, London, 1982 (reference edition: Coronet, London, 1983), p293

[82] Matt Green, *The Amazing Life of Sir Anthony Hopkins*, Google Play, 2014

[83] Peter Cowie, *Coppola*, Faber and Faber, London, 1990, p69

[84] Joe Reid, "Supporting Noms That Were Actually Leads", www.film.com, 17 January 2013

[85] *Coppola* p62

[86] Pauline Kael, *Deeper Into Movies: The essential Kael collection: from '69 to '72*, Marion Books, London, 1975, p423

[87] Clayton Davis, "The History of the Co-Lead Dilemma or (How It Really Isn't a Problem and the Academy Should Be Honest)", www.awardscircuit.com, 11 August 2015

[88] *Deeper Into Movies* p423

[89] *Movie Awards* p253

[90] Judy Klemesrud, "Do Any of These Actresses Rate an Academy Award?", *The New York Times*, 8 February 1976

[91] *When the Lights* p86

[92] Aljean Hametz, "Louise Fletcher: The Nurse Who Rules the 'Cuckoo's Nest'", *The New York Times*, 30 November 1975

[93] *Academy Awards Handbook* p224

[94] *And the Winner Is* p200

[95] "Nurse Who Rules" (New York Times)
[96] Guy Flatley, "At the Movies", *The New York Times*, 27 August 1976
[97] *Inside Oscar* p521
[98] Tim Gray, "Oscar Has a Long and Honorable History of 'Category Fraud'", www.variety.com, 2 December 2015
[99] Nathaniel Rogers, "Pt 1. Oscar Editorials to Make the Blood Boil: on Category Fraud", www.thefilmexperience.net, 4 December 2015

Act Two

[1] John Oller, *Jean Arthur: The Actress Nobody Knew*, Limelight, New York, 1997 (reference: paperback edition 1999), p64-5
[2] *Jean Arthur* p113
[3] *Jean Arthur* p102
[4] *Jean Arthur* p122
[5] *Jean Arthur* p123
[6] John Dileo, *100 Great Film Performances You Should Remember – But Probably Don't*, Limelight Editions, New York, 2002, p144-45
[7] Jeffrey Meyers, *Gary Cooper: American Hero*, Morrow, New York, 1998 (reference edition: Cooper Square Press, New York, 2001), p139
[8] *Gary Cooper* p139
[9] *Inside Oscar* p110
[10] *Inside Oscar* p90
[11] *Behind the Oscar* p149
[12] *Movie Awards* p70
[13] *Inside Oscar* p54
[14] Bob Tourtellotte, "'Baby' Oscar winners advise 'Sunshine' child star", www.reuters.com, 21 February 2007
[15] "Why Oscar Nominations" (The Atlantic)
[16] *Alternate Oscars* p167
[17] *Inside Oscar* p482
[18] *Academy Awards Handbook* p216; *Behind the Oscar* p297; *Inside Oscar* p482
[19] Charles Higham, "Will the Real Devil Speak Up? Yes!", *The New York Times*, 27 January 1974 p13
[20] *Inside Oscar* p487
[21] *Inside Oscar* p487
[22] Vincent Canby, "Linda or Tatum – Oscar Winners?", *The New York Times*, 3 March 1974 p1
[23] Guy Lodge, "Alicia Vikander and Rooney Mara Campaigns Fuel 'Category Fraud' Debate", *Variety*, 6 October, 2015
[24] *Academy Awards Handbook* p216
[25] Brian J. Robb, *River Phoenix: A Short Life*, Plexus, London, 1994, p77
[26] Gavin Edwards, *Last Night at the Viper Room: River Phoenix and the Hollywood He Left Behind*, Dey St. (for HarperCollins), New York 2013, p95
[27] *River Phoenix* p86
[28] *River Phoenix* p86
[29] "Supporting Noms" (Film.com)
[30] Lisa Gubernick, "The Envelope, Please. 'And the Winner Is …'", *The Wall Street Journal*, 24 March 2000
[31] "The Envelope, Please" (Wall Street Journal)
[32] Patrick Goldstein, "Screeners: Behind the ban", *Los Angeles Times*, 7 October 2003
[33] Lou Lumenick, "Sack Jack! – Valenti's Screener Ban Slaps Indie Pix", *New York Post*, 6 October 2003
[34] Paul Fischer, "Oscar Nominee Keisha Castle-Hughes Is Having A Whale Of A Time", www.femail.com.au, 2004
[35] Megan Neil, "Keisha off to the Oscars", *The Age*, 27 February 2004
[36] Dave McNary and Claude Brodesser, "Actors blast screener compromise", *Variety*, 23 October 2003

[37] uncredited, "True Grit Exclusive", www.au.ign.com, 27 October 2009
[38] "Vikander and Rooney" (Variety)
[39] Nicole Sperling, "Why is *True Grit*'s Hailee Steinfeld in SAG's supporting actress category?", *Los Angeles Times*, 17 December 2010
[40] "On Category Fraud" (Alpha Primitive)
[41] "Why Oscar Nominations" (The Atlantic)
[42] "Why Oscar Nominations" (The Atlantic)
[43] Scott Feinberg, "Awards 'Category Fraud': The Insane Inflation of Supporting Roles", *The Hollywood Reporter*, 24 November 2015
[44] Jason Bailey, "Golden Globes: Shots Fired in the Very Serious Fight Against 'Category Fraud'", www.flavorwire.com, 10 December 2015
[45] "What Is Category Fraud?" (ScreenCrush)
[46] "Awards 'Category Fraud'" (Hollywood Reporter)
[47] "Awards 'Category Fraud'" (Hollywood Reporter)
[48] Joyce Eng, "Oscar Nominations Surprise and Snubs: "Spotlight" Stars Rebound, But Where in the World Is Ridley Scott?", www.tvguide.com, 14 January 2016
[49] Scott Feinberg, "Why 'Nebraska's' Bruce Dern Should Go for Supporting Nom", *The Hollywood Reporter*, 23 August 2013
[50] "Bruce Dern Should" (Hollywood Reporter)
[51] Tim Appelo, "'Nebrasla's' Bruce Dern on Going for the Best Actor Oscar", *The Hollywood Reporter*, 30 August 2013
[52] Axel Nissen, *Actresses of a Certain Character: Forty Familiar Hollywood Faces From the Thirties to the Fifties*, McFarland & Company, New York, 2007, p118
[53] Brian Eugenio Herrera, "Agnes Moorehead in THE MAGNIFICENT AMBERSONS (1942) - Supporting Actress Sundays", www.stinkylulu.blogspot, 28 May 2006
[54] *Movie Awards* p81
[55] *And the Winner Is* p59-60; Emanuel Levy, "Oscar 2004: Supporting Actress – Anything Goes", www.emanuellevy.com, 29 February 2004
[56] Patrick McGilligan, *George Cukor: A Double Life: A Biography of a Gentleman Director*, St Martin's Press, London, 1991, p231; Melvyn Bragg, *Rich: The Life of Richard Burton*, Hodder and Soughton, London, 1988 (reference edition: Coronet Books, London, 1989), p45
[57] *George Cukor* p231; *Rich* p545; Leonard Mosley, *Zanuck: The Rise and Fall of Hollywood's Last Tycoon*, Granada, London 1984 (reference edition: Panther, London, 1985), p368
[58] *Zanuck* p367-8
[59] Antoni Gronowicz, *Garbo: Her Story*, Viking, London, 1990, p413; *George Cukor* p232
[60] *George Cukor* p232
[61] *George Cukor* p232
[62] *Rich* p545
[63] *Inside Oscar* p224
[64] *Inside Oscar* p224
[65] *Movie Awards* p157
[66] *Movie Awards* p157
[67] Joseph McBride, *Searching for John Ford: A Life*, Faber and Faber, New York, 2003p545
[68] *Inside Oscar* p261; *Movie Awards* p182
[69] *John Ford* p547
[70] *John Ford* p548
[71] *John Ford* p551
[72] *Inside Oscar* p261
[73] *Inside Oscar* p262
[74] *Behind the Oscar* p218
[75] Betsy Blair, *The Memory of All That: Love and Politics in New York, Hollywood and Paris*, Alfred A. Knopf, New York, 2003p218
[76] *Memory of All That* p264
[77] *Movie Awards* p180

[78] *Memory of All That* p292
[79] *Behind the Oscar* p218
[80] Leo Verswijver, "Interview with Don Murray", www.filmtalk.com, 11 December 2014
[81] *Bad & the Beautiful* p322
[82] *The Hollywood Reporter*, 16 January 1956 p3
[83] "Don Murray" (Film Talk)
[84] *Movie Awards* p191
[85] "Don Murray" (Film Talk)
[86] *Inside Oscar* p277
[87] Richard Schickel, *Elia Kazan: A Biography*, Harper Collins, New York, 2005 (reference edition: Harper Perennial, New York, 2006), p373
[88] *Elia Kazan* p373
[89] *Elia Kazan* p373
[90] *Inside Oscar* p334
[91] *Inside Oscar* p334
[92] "Awards 'Category Fraud'" (Hollywood Reporter)
[93] *Inside Oscar* p334
[94] *Movie Awards* p236
[95] Ed Sikov, *On Sunset Boulevard: The Life and Times of Billy Wilder*, Hyperion, New York, 1998, p501
[96] *On Sunset* p501
[97] *Inside Oscar* p394; *On Sunset* p500
[98] *And the Winner Is* p62; "Supporting Actress – Anything Goes" (Levy.com)
[99] *And the Winner Is* p62
[100] *Inside Oscar* p393
[101] *Movie Awards* p281
[102] *And the Winner Is* p62
[103] David McIntee, *Beautiful Monsters: The Unofficial and Unauthorised Guide to the Alien and Predator Films*, Telos Publishing, London, 2005, p22
[104] Rachel Abramowitz, *Is That a Gun in Your Pocket? The Truth About Female Power in Hollywood*, Random House, New York, 2000, p430
[105] Ximena Gallardo-C. and C. Jason Smith, *Alien Woman: The Making of Lt. Ellen Ripley*, Bloomsbury Academic, London, 2006, p13-61
[106] "A Long and Honorable History" (Variety)
[107] Sara Vilkomerson, "The Untold Story of Ordinary People", *Entertainment Weekly*, 5 February 2016
[108] *Movie Awards* p430
[109] uncredited, "Award Category Fraud", www.tvtropes.org, undated
[110] "Supporting Noms" (Film.com)
[111] Peter Kramer and Alan Lovell, ed., *Screen Acting*, Routledge, London, 1999, p89
[112] Betty Jo Tucker, *Susan Sarandon: A True Maverick*, Hats Off Books, Tucson, 2004, p25
[113] *And the Winner Is* p63; *Inside Oscar* p606; "A Long and Honorable History" (Variety); Steve Pond, "Sean Penn, Lesley Manville Play Category Roulette", www.thewrap.com, 27 October 2010; Steve Pond, "What's Lead, What's Supporting – and Who Really Decides?", www.thewrap.com, 13 October 2009
[114] *And the Winner Is* p63; *Inside Oscar* p606; Aljean Harmetz, "'Reds' and 'Golden Pond' Top Oscar Nominations", *The New York Times*, 12 February 1982
[115] "Top Oscar Nominations" (New York Times)
[116] "A Long and Honorable History" (Variety)
[117] "Supporting Noms" (Film.com)
[118] "Supporting Noms" (Film.com)
[119] "Award Category Fraud" (TV Tropes)
[120] "Supporting or lead" (Chicago Tribune)
[121] *Inside Oscar 2* p64
[122] "Supporting Noms" (Film.com)
[123] "Supporting Noms" (Film.com)
[124] "A Long and Honorable History" (Variety)

[125] Ed Gonzalez, "Oscar 2002 Nominations Predictions", www.slantmagazine.com, 11 February 2002
[126] Tom King, "What Happens When Leading Roles Are Nominated For Supporting Oscars?", *The Walls Street Journal*, 8 March 2002
[127] "What Happens When" (Wall St Journal)
[128] "What Happens When" (Wall St Journal)
[129] Paul Fischer, "Jennifer Connelly: More Than Just a Beautiful Mind", www.girl.com.au, undated (2002)
[130] Tom Roston, "*Slumdog Millionaire* shoot was rags to riches", *The Hollywood Reporter*, 4 November 2008
[131] Todd Leopold, "A rich night for best picture 'Slumdog Millionaire'", www.edition.cnn.com, 23 February 2009
[132] "Why Oscar Nominations" (The Atlantic)
[133] "Supporting Noms" (Film.com)
[134] "Vikander and Rooney" (Variety)
[135] Adam Markovitz, "Will Smith on turning down 'Django Unchained'", *Entertainment Weekly*, 25 March 2013
[136] Tom O'Neil, "Badass Christoph Waltz leaps up to lead Oscar race in 'Django Unchained'", www.goldderby.com, 8 November 2012
[137] Mike Fleming Jr., "Mike Fleming Q&As Harvey Weinstein", www.deadline.com, 28 January 2013
[138] Tom O'Neil, "Weinstein Company confirms Christoph Waltz back in supporting for 'Django Unchained'", www.goldderby.com, 7 December 2012
[139] Daniel Boneschansker, "Why Christoph Waltz could win Supporting Actor at Oscars despite SAG snub", www.goldderby.com, 21 February 2013
[140] "What Is Category Fraud?" (ScreenCrush)
[141] Nathaniel Rogers, "Acting Pairs and Young Bucks", www.thefilmexperience.net, 18 July 2014
[142] Dina Gachman, "Chris Hemsworth Shines But 'Rush' Belongs to Daniel Brühl", www.ssninsider.com, 25 September 2013
[143] Pete Hammond, "Ron Howard's 'Rush' Takes Victory Lap at Emotional Fest Debut Screening", www.deadline.com, 9 September 2013
[144] Kris Tapley, "Ron Howard and Daniel Brühl Reflect on the SAG and Globe Success of 'Rush'", www.hitfix.com, 12 December 2012
[145] Guy Lodge, "Alicia Vikander May Be The Real Winner From *The Danish Girl*", *Variety*, 5 September 2015
[146] Joey Magidson, "The Biggest Oscar morning snubs this year", www.hollywoodnews.com, 20 January 2016; Ben Zauzmer, "Oscar Nominations Odds: What The Math Says", www.huffingtonpost.com, 13 January 2016; Kevin Fallon and Marlow Stern, "2016 Oscar Nomination Predictions", www.thedailybeast.com, 13 January 2016; Eric Henderson, "Oscar 2016 Nominations Predictions", www.slantmagazine.com, 11 January 2016; Nathaniel Rogers, "Oscar Movements", www.thefilmexperience.net, 14 November 2015; "Shots Fired" (Flavorwire)
[147] "What Is Category Fraud?" (ScreenCrush)
[148] "Awards 'Category Fraud'" (Hollywood Reporter); "Vikander and Rooney" (Variety); "Why Oscar Nominations" (The Atlantic)
[149] "What Is Category Fraud?" (ScreenCrush)
[150] "On Category Fraud" (Alpha Primitive); "Vikander and Rooney" (Variety); "What Is Category Fraud?" (ScreenCrush); "Why Oscar Nominations" (The Atlantic)
[151] "Vikander and Rooney" (Variety)
[152] Scott Feinberg, "Oscar Nominations: Now It's A Whole New Race", *The Hollywood Reporter*, 14 January 2016
[153] Matt Brunson, "Shining a Spotlight on Oscar contenders", *Connect Savannah*, 12 January 2016

Act Three

[1] "Awards 'Category Fraud'" (Hollywood Reporter)
[2] *Inside Oscar* p274
[3] *Behind the Oscar* p218
[4] *Behind the Oscar* p218

[5] Gerald Peary, "Interview with Dorothy Malone", *Toronto Globe and Mail*, 15 April 1985

[6] *Movie Awards* p191

[7] *Movie Awards* p192

[8] *Inside Oscar* p277

[9] Robert Stack with Mark Evans, *Straight Shooting*, MacMillan, New York, 1980 (reference edition: Berkley, New York, 1981)p227, 281

[10] *Movie Awards* p192; *Inside Oscar* p277

[11] *Movie Awards* p192

[12] Thomas M. Pryor, "Oscar Loophole Causes Criticsm", *The New York Times*, 29 March 1957

[13] *Coppola* p62; *Inside Oscar* p469

[14] *Coppola* p62; *Inside Oscar* p469

[15] *Coppola* p69

[16] Lawrence Grobel, *Al Pacino: The Authorized Biography*, Simon & Schuster, London, 2006, pxxi

[17] "Supporting Noms" (Film.com)

[18] "History of the Co-Lead Dilemma" (Awards Circuit)

[19] *Movie Awards* p277

[20] NOTE: At the time of printing, numerous online resources, including the official Golden Globe Awards website, list Burns and Matthau as co-winners of the Best Actor (Comedy or Musical) Award, possibly because Burns accompanied Matthau onto the stage. Contemporary newspapers reports, however, clearly state that Matthau was the sole winner of the award.

[21] *Movie Awards* p378

[22] *Movie Awards* p378

[23] *Inside Oscar* p519; *Movie Awards* p378

[24] Leonard Klady, "Oscar Chase: The Long Campaign", *Washington Post*, 5 February 1984

[25] "Supporting or lead" (Chicago Tribune)

[26] *Movie Awards* p456

[27] *Movie Awards* p456

[28] uncredited, "Number 39: Jessica Lange as Julie Nichols in 'Tootsie'", www.fritzlovesoscars.blogspot, 13 July 2011

[29] Matt Mazur, "Best Supporting Actress Rewind 1982", www.popmatters.com, 5 February 2013

[30] Brian Eugenio Herrera, "Jessica Lange in Tootsie (1982)", www.stinkylulu.blogspot, 8 October 2006

[31] Teri Garr with Henriette Mantel, *Speedbumps: Flooring It Through Hollywood*, Hudson Street Press, New York, 2005 (reference edition Plume, London, 2006), p114

[32] *Speedbumps* p115-6

[33] Eliot Kaplan, "Getting Personal with Teri Garr", *Family Weekly*, 3 April 1983

[34] *Behind the Oscar* p348

[35] Stephen Farber, "The Making of a 'Literary' Film, *The New York Times*, 7 January 1988

[36] "Making of a 'Literary' Film" (New York Times)

[37] *Movie Awards* p519

[38] Emanuel Levy, "Broadcast News (1987)", www.emanuellevy.com, 11 February 2008

[39] "Supporting Noms" (Film.com)

[40] Tim Teeman, "Martin Landau: my affair with Marilyn Monroe", *The Times*, 6 October 2012

[41] Richard Natale, "At Least Miramax Supports Acting Nods", *Los Angeles Times*, 19 March1995; *Inside Oscar* p756

[42] "Supporting Noms" (Film.com)

[43] "Supporting Noms" (Film.com)

[44] "My Affair with Marilyn" (Times)

[45] Jesse David Fox, "A Brief History of Harvey Weinstein's Oscar Campaign Tactics", www.vulture.com, 29 January 2014

[46] Steve Pond, "Farewell, Miramax: Oscar Will Never Be the Same", www.thewrap.com, 28 January 2010

[47] *Big Show* p210

[48] Emanuel Levy, *The Cinema of Outsiders: The Rise of American Independent Film*, New York University Press, New York, 1999, p127

[49] *Movie Awards* p626

[50] *Movie Awards* p627
[51] "At least Miramax" (Los Angeles Times)
[52] "At least Miramax" (Los Angeles Times)
[53] "Supporting Actress – Anything Goes" (Levy.com); "At least Miramax" (Los Angeles Times)
[54] "Supporting Noms" (Film.com)
[55] "At least Miramax" (Los Angeles Times)
[56] Duncan Campbell, "Hollywood knives are out as Oscars get nasty", *The Guardian*, 16 March 2002
[57] "Hollywood knives" (Guardian)
[58] Peter Biskind, *Down and Dirty Pictures: Miramax, Sundance & The Rise of Independent Film*, Bloomsbury, London, 2004, p439
[59] "Supporting Noms" (Film.com)
[60] Tom Brook, "Ethan Hawke's Oscar surprise", www.news.bbc.co.uk, 21 March 2002
[61] Ed Gonzalez, "Oscar 2002 Winner Predictions", www.slantmagazine.com, 20 March 2002
[62] "What Happens When" (Wall St Journal)
[63] "What Happens When" (Wall St Journal)
[64] Dan Halpern, "Another sunrise", *The Guardian*, 8 October 2005
[65] "Another sunrise" (Guardian)
[66] Kevin Fallon, "Oscar Conspiracy Theories Debunked: Explaining the 5 Biggest Oscar Snubs", www.thedailybeast.com, 17 January 2015
[67] David Denby, "How 'The Hours' Happened", *The New Yorker*, 24 March 2003
[68] Rick Lyman, "No 2 Spot Or the Star? For Oscars, It's Strategy", *The New York Times*, 30 January 2003
[69] "No 2 Spot" (New York Times)
[70] "How *The Hours*" (New Yorker)
[71] "No 2 Spot" (New York Times)
[72] Peter Hammond, "Best Supporting Actor & Actress – Nothing Secondary About These Races", www.deadline.com, 11 January 2011
[73] Tom King, "Studios Begin Campaigns For Oscar's Top Prizes", *The Walls Street Journal*, 17 January 2003
[74] *Down and Dirty* p466
[75] *Down and Dirty* p429-30
[76] "No 2 Spot" (New York Times)
[77] "Studios Begin" (Wall St Journal)
[78] "No 2 Spot" (New York Times)
[79] *Down and Dirty* p467
[80] Kim Masters, "Can This Marriage Be Saved?", *Esquire*, 29 January 2007
[81] uncredited, "Streep dismisses Oscars as 'political campaign'", *Sydney Morning Herald*, 5 February 2003
[82] "Studios Begin" (Wall St Journal)
[83] Brett Thomas, "Nicole's dramatic transformation", *Sun Herald*, 22 December 2002
[84] Lucy Ellis and Bryony Sutherland, *Nicole Kidman: The Biography*, Aurum Press, London, 2002, p239, 270
[85] "How *The Hours*" (New Yorker)
[86] "No 2 Spot" (New York Times)
[87] uncredited, "Oscars double-ups predicted", www.abc.net.au, 12 December 2003
[88] "Screeners" (Los Angeles Times)
[89] "Sack Jack!" (New York Post)
[90] "Oscars double-ups" (abc.net.au)
[91] Geoff King, "Weighing Up the Qualities of Independence: '21 Grams' in Focus", www.academia.edu, undated
[92] Liam Lacey, "Onward to the Oscars", *Globe and Mail*, 29 November 2003
[93] "Supporting Noms" (Film.com)
[94] "Onward to the Oscars" (Globe and Mail)
[95] Mike Snider, "*Collateral* DVD: Oscar asset?", *USA Today*, 13 December 2004
[96] "Oscar Editorials" (Film Experience)
[97] "Supporting Noms" (Film.com)
[98] "Supporting Actress – Anything Goes" (Levy.com)
[99] "Supporting Noms" (Film.com)

[100] Sarah D. Bunting, "Best Supporting Actor is an odd fellows club", www.today.com, 5 March 2005

[101] uncredited, "Chunky Clooney bounces back to lead", *Los Angeles Times*, 8 November 2005

[102] Matt Brennan, "The 6 Worst Cases of Golden Globes Category Fraud in the Past Decade: Where Does 'The Martian' Stack Up?", www.indiewire.com/v/thompsononhollywood, 13 November 2015

[103] uncredited, "Clooney drops back to supporting race for *Syriana*", *Los Angeles Times*, 23 November 2005

[104] "Clooney drops back" (Los Angeles Times)

[105] "Clooney drops back" (Los Angeles Times)

[106] "Nothing Secondary" (Deadline.com)

[107] "Clooney drops back" (Today.com)

[108] "Supporting Noms" (Film.com)

[109] "Supporting Noms" (Film.com)

[110] Giuseppe Fadda, "Cate Blanchett in Notes on a Scandal (2006)", www.reviewingperformances.blogspot, 26 June 2016

[111] Herrera, Brian Eugenio, "Cate Blanchett in Notes on a Scandal (2006)", www.stinkylulu.blogspot, 18 February 2007

[112] "Cate Blanchett in Notes" (Stinky Lulu): comment

[113] Scott Feinberg, "Will Fox Searchlight Try the Sneak Attack Again", *The Hollywood Reporter*, 30 June 2013

[114] Steven Rea, "Kate Winslet double-dips: Actress is remarkable in two more dark screen roles", *Philadelphia Inquirer*, 19 December 2008

[115] "Winslet double-dips" (Philadelphia Inquirer)

[116] Nikki Finke, "Harvey Weinstein vs Film World: Scott Rudin Wins War of Wills With TWC: 'The Reader' Director Is Given More Time", www.deadline.com, 28 September 2008

[117] Ryan Adams, "Kate vs, Kate, the return of 'The Reader'", www.awardsdaily.com, 28 August 2008

[118] Willa Paskin, "The Oscar Recession", www.dailybeast.com, 11 November 2008; "Weinstein vs Film World" (Deadline.com)

[119] "Weinstein vs Film World" (Deadline.com)

[120] Anne Thompson, "Scott Rudin leaves *The Reader*", *Variety*, 9 October 2008

[121] "Weinstein vs Film World" (Deadline.com)

[122] "Weinstein vs Film World" (Deadline.com)

[123] "Weinstein vs Film World" (Deadline.com)

[124] "Rudin leaves" (Variety)

[125] "Awards 'Category Fraud'" (Hollywood Reporter); Scott Feinberg and Stephen Galloway, "'The Awards Pundits' on Telluride's Rocky Mountain Highs (and Lows) ", *The Hollywood Reporter*, 7 September 2015

[126] Emanuel Levy, "Kate Winslet's Role in The Reader Lead or Supporting?", www.emanuellevy.com, 15 January 2009

[127] Catherine Shoard, "Could this finally be Kate Winslet's year for an Oscar?", *Guardian*, 12 December 2008

[128] "Winslet double-dips" (Philadelphia Inquirer)

[129] "The 6 Worst Cases" (Thompson)

[130] Guy Lodge, "'Reader' draws praise, but is it too remote for Oscar?", *Variety*, 30 November 2008

[131] Monica Hesse, "Ahead of Her Class: No Oscar Yet, but Kate Winslet's Career Is the One to Watch", *The Washington Post*, 24 December 2008

[132] Lane Brown, "Harvey Weinstein on Yesterday's Golden Globe Nominations", www.vulture.com, 12 December 2008

[133] Eric Henderson, "Oscar 2009 Nomination Predictions: Supporting Actress", www.slantmagazine.com, 15 January 2009

[134] "Kate Winslet's Role" (Levy.com)

[135] "What Is Category Fraud?" (ScreenCrush)

[136] "Drop down" (Gold Derby)

[137] "Drop down" (Gold Derby)

[138] Scott Feinberg, "Can the Academy handle 2 women?", www.scottfeinberg.com, 25 July 2010

[139] Guy Lodge, "The Long Shot: Categorical Denial", *Variety*, 20 October 2010

[140] Nathaniel Rogers, "Yes, No, Maybe So: The Master", www.thefilmexperience.net, 21 July 2012

[141] Pat Mullen, "To Lead or Not to Lead", www.cinemablographer.com, 22 October 2012

[142] Pete Hammond, "Oscars: The Supporting Actor Race", www.deadline.com, 8 December 2012

[143] "To Lead or Not to Lead" (Cinemablographer)

[144] "Supporting Noms" (Film.com)

[145] Amanda Dobbins, "Joaquin Phoenix Really Does Not Want an Oscar", www.vulture.com, 18 October 2012

[146] Amanda Dobbins, "And Here Is Joaquin Phoenix's Oscars Non-Apology", www.vulture.com, 13 November 2012

[147] Tom O'Neil, "Meryl Streep drops to supporting, takes on Oprah", www.goldderby.com, 12 August 2013

[148] Nathaniel Rogers, "Meryl Goes 'Supporting' – The Scare Quotes Are Mandatory", www.thefilmexperience.net, 12 August 2013

[149] Kris Tapley, "Will Meryl Streep be campaigned for Best Supporting Actress in 'August: Osage County'?", www.hitfix.com, 12 August 2013

[150] "Will Meryl Streep" (Hit Fix)

[151] Tom O'Neil, "Weinstein Co. may push Meryl Streep back up to lead Oscar race", www.goldderby.com, 30 August 2013

[152] Scott Feinberg, "Toronto: 'August:Osage County' Earns Applause But Divides Pundits", *The Hollywood Reporter*, 10 September 2013

[153] Pete Hammond, "Weinstein's Premiere Marathon Delivers Huge Reaction for Oscar-Bait 'August: Osage County' – But Will It Divide Audiences", www.deadline.com, 10 September 2013

[154] Tom O'Neil, "Oscars flip-flop: Meryl Streep returns to lead, Julia Roberts drop to supporting", www.goldderby.com, 9 September 2013

[155] Brad Brevet, "'August: Osage County' Ending in Flux and Streep Moves Back to Best Actress Category", www.comingsoon.net, 12 September 2013

[156] Steve Zeitchik, "*August: Osage County* ending could be changed for release, *Los Angeles Times*, 11 September 2013

[157] "ending could be changed" (Los Angeles Times)

[158] Mike Fleming Jr., "Harvey Weinstein On His Dark Horse Best Picture Candidate 'Philomena' And, Well, Everything Else", www.deadline.com, 19 February 2014

[159] Susan Wloszczyna, "The Big O: Lead or Supporitng Actress? Depends on Which Category is Likelist to Hit Gold", www.indiewire.com, 24 September 2014

[160] "Oscars flip-flop" (Gold Derby)

[161] Kathryn Shattuck, "Rooney Mara Wears Her Provocative Part Well in *Carol*", *The New York Times*, 30 October 2015

[162] "Rooney Mara Wears" (New York Times)

[163] "Rooney Mara Wears" (New York Times)

[164] Nathaniel Rogers, "Best Actress Updates, Or: Get Right With God. Stop Category Fraud!", www.thefilmexperience.net, 7 September 2015

[165] Kris Tapley, "Cate Blanchett Set for Lead *Carol* Oscar Push, Rooney Mara Supporting", *Variety*, 15 September 2015

[166] "Why Oscar Nominations" (The Atlantic)

[167] "What Is Category Fraud?" (ScreenCrush)

[168] "Vikander and Rooney" (Variety)

[169] "Vikander and Rooney" (Variety)

[170] "On Category Fraud" (Alpha Primitive)

[171] Kenneth Turan, "Oscars 2016: Nominations favored chest-beating action pictures, but there's more to it," *Los Angeles Times*, 14 January 2016

[172] Harvey Weinstein, "Everybody Cannibalized Each Other", *The Hollywood Reporter*, 3 December 2015

[173] "Why Oscar Nominations" (The Atlantic)

[174] "Rooney Mara Wears" (New York Times)

[175] Kris Tapley, "Golden Globes: HFPA Vetoes Rooney Mara, Alicia Vikander Supporting Submissions", *Variety*, 13 November 2015

[176] "Shining a Spotlight" (Connect Savannah)

Epilogue

[1] Tim Gray, "Academy Says Song Decision Was About Oscar 'Integrity'", *Variety*, 1 February 2014

[2] Michael Vincent, "The disorganised state of the Academy Awards", www.abc.net.au, 24 March 2000

[3] Patrick Goldstein and James Rainey, "New Oscar rules – Can the Academy curtail awards season excess?", *Los Angeles Times*, 22 September 2011

[4] Gregg Kilday, "What the New Oscar Campaign Rules Mean for Awards Season", *The Hollywood Reporter*, 21 September 2011

[5] Michael Izzo, "New Oscar Rules Place Restrictions On Screening Invites, Email", *Business Insider*, 26 July 2012

[6] "Can the Academy" (Los Angeles Times)

[7] "What the New Oscar" (Hollywood Reporter)

[8] Steve Pond, "Academy Tweaks Oscar Rules, Campaign Regulations", www.thewrap.com, 30 June 2016

[9] Isaacs, Cheryl Boone, "Statement From Academy President Cheryl Boone Isaacs", www.oscars.org, 18 January 2016

[10] Tim Gray, "Academy Overhauls Membership, Voting Rules to Promote Oscar Diveristy", *Variety*, 22 January 2016

[11] Scott Feinberg, "Omission of Black Actors Upsetting, But Not Inexplicable or Proof of Racism", *The Hollywood Reporter*, 19 January 2016

[12] Michael Cieply, "Academy Board Endorses Changes to Increase Diversity In Oscar Nominees and Itself", *The New York Times*, 22 January 2016

[13] Michelle Maltais, "Will you boycott the Oscars?", *Los Angeles Times*, 19 January 2016

[14] "Academy Board Endorses" (New York Times)

[15] Ravi Somaiya, "For your consideration … and then some", *Guardian*, 13 November 2008

[16] "Academy Says Song" (Variety)

[17] "Statement From" (Oscars.org)

[18] Scott Feinberg, "Five Ways the Academy Can Improve the Show", *The Hollywood Reporter*, 5 January 2016

[19] "Oscar Editorials" (Film Experience)

[20] "Five Ways" (Hollywood Reporter)

[21] "Why Oscar Nominations" (The Atlantic). See also: "Awards 'Category Fraud'" (Hollywood Reporter); "On Category Fraud" (Alpha Primitive); "Vikander and Rooney" (Variety); "What Is Category Fraud?" (ScreenCrush)

[22] "Shots Fired" (Flavorwire)

[23] "A Long and Honorable History" (Variety)

[24] "Oscar Editorials" (Film Experience)

[25] "Meryl Goes" (Film Experience)

[26] "Categorical Denial" (Variety)

[27] "What Happens When" (Wall St Journal)

[28] "What Happens When" (Wall St Journal)

SELECTED BIBLIOGAPHY

Books

Abramowitz, Rachel, *Is That a Gun in Your Pocket? The Truth About Female Power in Hollywood*, Random House, New York, 2000

Biskind, Peter, *Down and Dirty Pictures: Miramax, Sundance & The Rise of Independent Film*, Bloomsbury, London, 2004

Blair, Betsy, *The Memory of All That: Love and Politics in New York, Hollywood and Paris*, Alfred A. Knopf, New York, 2003

Bona, Damien, and Wiley, Mason, *Inside Oscar: The Unofficial History of the Academy Awards*, Ballatine Books, New York, 1986 (ed 1993)

Bona, Damien, *Inside Oscar 2*, Ballatine Books, New York, 2002

Bragg, Melvyn, *Rich: The Life of Richard Burton*, Hodder and Soughton, London, 1988 (reference edition: Coronet Books, London, 1989)

Brown, Peter H., and Pinkston, Jim, *Oscar Dearest: Six Decades of Scandal, Politics and Greed Behind Hollywood's Academy Awards 1927-1986*, Perrenial Library, New York, 1987

Carey, Gary (with Joseph L. Mankiewicz), *More About All About Eve*, Random House, New York 1972 (reference edition: Bantam edition 1974)

Chase, Chris, and Russell, Rosalind, *Life Is A Banquet*, Ace Books, New York, 1979

Cowie, Peter, *Coppola*, Faber and Faber, London, 1990

Curits, James, *Spencer Tracy*, Knopf, New York, 2011

Dick, Bernard F., *Forever Mame: The Life of Rosalind Russell*, University Press of Mississippi, Jackson, 2006

Dileo, John, *100 Great Film Performances You Should Remember – But Probably Don't*, Limelight Editions, New York, 2002

Edwards, Gavin, *Last Night at the Viper Room: River Phoenix and the Hollywood He Left Behind*, Dey St. (for HarperCollins), New York 2013

Ellis, Lucy, and Sutherland, Bryony, *Nicole Kidman: The Biography*, Aurum Press, London, 2002

Eyman, Scott, *Lion of Hollywood: The Life and Legend of Louis B. Mayer*, Robson Books, London, 2005

Faulkner, Trader, *Peter Finch: A Biography*, Angus & Robertson, London, 1979 (reference edition: Pan Books, London, 1980)

Gallardo-C., Ximena and Smith, C. Jason, *Alien Woman: The Making of Lt. Ellen Ripley*, Bloomsbury Academic, London, 2006

Garr, Teri with Mantel, Henriette, *Speedbumps: Flooring It Through Hollywood*, Hudson Street Press, New York, 2005 (reference edition Plume, London, 2006)

Gebert, Michael, *The Encyclopedia of Movie Awards*, St Martin's Paperbacks, New York, 1996

Green, Matt, *The Amazing Life of Sir Anthony Hopkins*, Google Play, 2014

Grobel, Lawrence, *Al Pacino: The Authorized Biography*, Simon & Schuster, London, 2006

Gronowicz, Antoni, *Garbo: Her Story*, Viking, London, 1990

Harkness, John, *The Academy Awards Handbook*, Pinnacle Books, New York, 1994

Holden, Anthony, *Behind the Oscar: The Secret History of the Academy Awards*, Simon & Schuster, New York, 1993

Kael, Pauline, *Deeper Into Movies: The essential Kael collection: from '69 to '72*, Marion Books, London, 1975

Kael, Pauline, *When the Lights Go Down*, Holt, Reinhart and Winston, New York, 1975

Kashner, Sam and MacNair, Jennifer, *The Bad & The Beautiful: Hollywood in the Fifties*, Little Brown, London 2002

Kramer, Peter and Lovell, Alan, ed., *Screen Acting*, Routledge, London, 1999

Leider, Emily W., *Myrna Loy: The Only Good Girl in Hollywood*, University of California Press, Los Angeles, 2011

Levy, Emanuel, *And the Winner Is ... The History and Politics of the Oscar Awards*, Continuum, New York, 1987 (ed 1991)

Levy, Emanuel, *The Cinema of Outsiders: The Rise of American Independent Film*, New York University Press, New York, 1999

McBride, Joseph, *Frank Capra: The Catastrophe of Success*, Faber & Faber, London, 1992

McBride, Joseph, *Searching for John Ford: A Life*, Faber and Faber, New York, 2003

McGilligan, Patrick, *George Cuckor: A Double Life: A Biography of a Gentleman Director*, St Martin's Press, London, 1991

McIntee, David, *Beautiful Monsters: The Unofficial and Unauthorised Guide to the Alien and Predator Films*, Telos Publishing, London, 2005

Meyers, Jeffrey, *Gary Cooper: American Hero*, Morrow, New York, 1998 (reference edition: Cooper Square Press, New York, 2001)

Mosley, Leonard, *Zanuck: The Rise and Fall of Hollywood's Last Tycoon*, Granada, London 1984 (reference edition: Panther, London, 1985)

Nissen, Axel, *Actresses of a Certain Character: Forty Familiar Hollywood Faces From the Thirties to the Fifties*, McFarland & Company, New York, 2007

O'Neil, Tom, *Movie Awards: The Ultimate, Unofficial Guide to the Oscars, Golden Globes, Critics, Guild & Indie Honors*, Perigee, New York, 2001

Olivier, Laurence, *Confessions of an Actor*, Wheelshare, London, 1982 (reference edition: Coronet, London, 1983)

Oller, John, *Jean Arthur: The Actress Nobody Knew*, Limelight, New York, 1997 (reference: paperback edition 1999)

Peary, Danny, *Alternate Oscars: One Critic's Defiant Choices for Best Picture, Actor, and Actress – From 1927 to the Present*, Simon & Schuster, New York, 1993

Pond, Steve, *The Big Show: High Times and Dirty Dealings Backstage at the Academy Awards*, Faber & Faber, New York, 2005

Quirk, Lawrence J., *Fasten Your Seatbelts: The Passionate Life of Bette Davis*, Signet, London, 1990

Robb, Brian J., River Phoenix: A Short Life, Plexus, London, 1994

Schickel, Richard, *Elia Kazan: A Biography*, Harper Collins, New York, 2005 (reference edition: Harper Perennial, New York, 2006)

Sikov, Ed, *On Sunset Boulevard: The Life and Times of Billy Wilder*, Hyperion, New York, 1998

Stack, Robert, with Evans, Mark, *Straight Shooting*, MacMillan, New York, 1980 (reference edition: Berkley, New York, 1981)

Staggs, Sam, *All About "All About Eve": The Complete Behind-the-Scenes Story of the Bitchiest Film Ever Made*, St Martin's Griffin, New York, 2001

Troyan, Michael, *A Rose for Mrs Miniver: The Life of Greer Garson*, University of Kentucky Press, Lexington, 1999

Tucker, Betty Jo, *Susan Sarandon: A True Maverick*, Hats Off Books, Tucson, 2004

Articles

Appelo, Tim, "'Nebraska's' Bruce Dern on Going for the Best Actor Oscar", *The Hollywood Reporter*, 30 August 2013

Brunson, Matt, "Shining a Spotlight on Oscar contenders", *Connect Savannah*, 12 January 2016

Campbell, Duncan, "Hollywood knives are out as Oscars get nasty", *The Guardian*, 16 March 2002

Canby, Vincent, "Linda or Tatum – Oscar Winners?", *The New York Times*, 3 March 1974 p1

Cieply, Michael, "Academy Board Endorses Changes to Increase Diversity In Oscar Nominees and Itself", *The New York Times*, 22 January 2016

Denby, David, "How 'The Hours' Happened", *The New Yorker*, 24 March 2003

Farber, Stephen, "The Making of a 'Literary' Film, *The New York Times*, 7 January 1988

Flatley, Guy, "At the Movies", *The New York Times*, 27 August 1976

Feinberg, Scott, "'August: Osage County' Earns Big Applause But Divides Pundits", *The Hollywood Reporter*, 9 September 2013

Feinberg, Scott, "Awards 'Category Fraud': The Insane Inflation of Supporting Roles", *The Hollywood Reporter*, 24 November 2015

Feinberg, Scott, "Five Ways the Academy Can Improve the Show", *The Hollywood Reporter*, 5 January 2016

Feinberg, Scott, "Omission of Black Actors Upsetting, But Not Inexplicable or Proof of Racism", *The Hollywood Reporter*, 19 January 2016

Feinberg, Scott, "Oscar Nominations: Now It's A Whole New Race", *The Hollywood Reporter*, 14 January 2016

Feinberg, Scott, "Will Fox Searchlight Try the Sneak Attack Again", *The Hollywood Reporter*, 30 June 2013

Feinberg, Scott, "Why 'Nebraska's' Bruce Dern Should Go for Supporting Nom", *The Hollywood Reporter*, 23 August 2013

Feinberg, Scott, and Galloway, Stephen, "'The Awards Pundits' on Telluride's Rocky Mountain Highs (and Lows) ", *The Hollywood Reporter*, 7 September 2015

Goldstein, Patrick, "Screeners: Behind the ban", *Los Angeles Times*, 7 October 2003

Goldstein, Patrick, and Rainey, James, "New Oscar rules – Can the Academy curtail awards season excess?", *Los Angeles Times*, 22 September 2011

Gray, Tim, "Academy Overhauls Membership, Voting Rules to Promote Oscar Diveristy", *Variety*, 22 January 2016

Gray, Tim, "Academy Says Song Decision Was About Oscar 'Integrity'", *Variety*, 1 February 2014

Gubernick, Lisa, "The Envelope, Please. 'And the Winner Is …'", *The Wall Street Journal*, 24 March 2000

Halpern, Dan, "Another sunrise", *The Guardian*, 8 October 2005

Hametz, Aljean, "Louise Fletcher: The Nurse Who Rules the 'Cuckoo's Nest'", *The New York Times*, 30 November 1975

Hametz, Aljean, "'Reds' and 'Golden Pond' Top Oscar Nominations", *The New York Times*, 12 February 1982

Hesse, Monica, "Ahead of Her Class: No Oscar Yet, but Kate Winslet's Career Is the One to Watch", *The Washington Post*, 24 December 2008

Higham, Charles, "Will the Real Devil Speak Up? Yes!", *The New York Times*, 27 January 1974 p13

Izzo, Michael, "New Oscar Rules Place Restrictions On Screening Invites, Email", *Business Insider*, 26 July 2012

Kaplan, Eliot, "Getting Personal with Teri Garr", *Family Weekly*, 3 April 1983

Kilday, Gregg, "What the New Oscar Campaign Rules Mean for Awards Season", *The Hollywood Reporter*, 21 September 2011

King, Tom, "Studios Begin Campaigns For Oscar's Top Prizes", *The Walls Street Journal*, 17 January 2003

King, Tom, "What Happens When Leading Roles Are Nominated For Supporting Oscars?", *The Walls Street Journal*, 8 March 2002

Klady, Leonard, "Oscar Chase: The Long Campaign", *Washington Post*, 5 February 1984

Klemesrud, Judy, "Do Any of These Actresses Rate an Academy Award?", *The New York Times*, 8 February 1976

Lacey, Liam, "Onward to the Oscars", *Globe and Mail*, 29 November 2003

Lodge, Guy, "Alicia Vikander and Rooney Mara Campaigns Fuel 'Category Fraud' Debate", *Variety*, 6 October, 2015

Lodge, Guy, "Alicia Vikander May Be The Real Winner From *The Danish Girl*", *Variety*, 5 September 2015

Lodge, Guy, "The Long Shot: Categorical Denial", *Variety*, 20 October 2010

Lodge, Guy, "'Reader' draws praise, but is it too remote for Oscar?", *Variety*, 30 November 2008

Lumenick, Lou, "Sack Jack! – Valenti's Screener Ban Slaps Indie Pix", *New York Post*, 6 October 2003

Lyman, Rick, "No 2 Spot Or the Star? For Oscars, It's Strategy", *The New York Times*, 30 January 2003

Maltais, Michelle, "Will you boycott the Oscars?", *Los Angeles Times*, 19 January 2016

Markovitz, Adam, "Will Smith on turning down 'Django Unchained'", *Entertainment Weekly*, 25 March 2013

Masters, Kim, "Can This Marriage Be Saved?", *Esquire*, 29 January 2007

McNary, Dave, and Brodesser, Claude, "Actors blast screener compromise", *Variety*, 23 October 2003

Natale, Richard, "At Least Miramax Supports Acting Nods", *Los Angeles Times*, 19 March1995

Natale, Richard, "Supporting or lead role? It's anyone's call", *Chicago Tribune*, March 2000

Neil, Megan, "Keisha off to the Oscars", *The Age*, 27 February 2004

Peary, Gerald, "Interview with Dorothy Malone", *Toronto Globe and Mail*, 15 April 1985

Pryor, Thomas M., "Oscar Loophole Causes Criticsm", *The New York Times*, 29 March 1957

Rea, Steven, "Kate Winslet double-dips: Actress is remarkable in two more dark screen roles", *Philadelphia Inquirer*, 19 December 2008

Roston, Tom, "*Slumdog Millionaire* shoot was rags to riches", *The Hollywood Reporter*, 4 November 2008

Shattuck, Kathryn, "Rooney Mara Wears Her Provocative Part Well in *Carol*", *The New York Times*, 30 October 2015

Shoard, Catherine, "Could this finally be Kate Winslet's year for an Oscar?", *Guardian*, 12 December 2008

Snider, Mike, "*Collateral* DVD: Oscar asset?", *USA Today*, 13 December 2004

Somaiya, Ravi, "For your consideration … and then some", *Guardian*, 13 November 2008

Sperling, Nicole, "Why is *True Grit*'s Hailee Steinfeld in SAG's supporting actress category?", *Los Angeles Times*, 17 December 2010

Tapley, Kris, "Cate Blanchett Set for Lead *Carol* Oscar Push, Rooney Mara Supporting", *Variety*, 15 September 2015

Tapley, Kris, "Golden Globes: HFPA Vetoes Rooney Mara, Alicia Vikander Supporting Submissions", *Variety*, 13 November 2015

Teeman, Tim, "Martin Landau: my affair with Marilyn Monroe", *The Times*, 6 October 2012

Teutsch, Danielle, "How to win an Oscar", *Sun Herald*, 23 January 2005

Thomas, Brett, "Nicole's dramatic transformation", *Sun Herald*, 22 December 2002

Thompson, Anne, "Scott Rudin leaves *The Reader*", *Variety*, 9 October 2008

Turan, Kenneth, "Oscars 2016: Nominations favored chest-beating action pictures, but there's more to it," *Los Angeles Times*, 14 January 2016

Vilkomerson, Sara, "The Untold Story of Ordinary People", *Entertainment Weekly*, 5 February 2016

Weinstein, Harvey, "Everybody Cannibalized Each Other", *The Hollywood Reporter*, 3 December 2015

Zeitchik, Steve, "*August: Osage County* ending could be changed for release, *Los Angeles Times*, 11 September 2013

uncredited, "Chunky Clooney bounces back to lead", *Los Angeles Times*, 8 November 2005

uncredited, "Clooney drops back to supporting race for *Syriana*", *Los Angeles Times*, 23 November 2005

uncredited, "Connelly found playing Crowe's wife exhilarating", *Sun Herald*, 19 February 2002

uncredited, "Streep dismisses Oscars as 'political campaign'", *Sydney Morning Herald*, 5 February 2003

Online Articles

Adams, Ryan, "Kate vs, Kate, the return of 'The Reader'", www.awardsdaily.com, 28 August 2008

Bailey, Jason, "Golden Globes: Shots Fired in the Very Serious Fight Against 'Category Fraud'", www.flavorwire.com, 10 December 2015

Boneschansker, Daniel, "Why Christoph Waltz could win Supporting Actor at Oscars despite SAG snub", www.goldderby.com, 21 February 2013

Brennan, Matt, "The 6 Worst Cases of Golden Globes Category Fraud in the Past Decade: Where Does 'The Martian' Stack Up?", www.indiewire.com/v/thompsononhollywood, 13 November 2015

Brevet, Brad, "'August: Osage County' Ending in Flux and Streep Moves Back to Best Actress Category", www.comingsoon.net, 12 September 2013

Brook, Tom, "Ethan Hawke's Oscar surprise", www.news.bbc.co.uk, 21 March 2002

Brown, Lane, "Harvey Weinstein on Yesterday's Golden Globe Nominations", www.vulture.com, 12 December 2008

Bunting, Sarah D., "Best Supporting Actor is an odd fellows club", www.today.com, 5 March 2005

Davis, Clayton, "The History of the Co-Lead Dilemma or (How It Really Isn't a Problem and the Academy Should Be Honest)", www.awardscircuit.com, 11 August 2015

Dobbins, Amanda, "And Here Is Joaquin Phoenix's Oscars Non-Apology", www.vulture.com, 13 November 2012

Dobbins, Amanda, "Joaquin Phoenix Really Does Not Want an Oscar", www.vulture.com, 18 October 2012

Eng, Joyce, "Oscar Nominations Surprise and Snubs: "Spotlight" Stars Rebound, But Where in the World Is Ridley Scott?", www.tvguide.com, 14 January 2016

Fadda, Giuseppe, "Cate Blanchett in Notes on a Scandal (2006)", www.reviewingperformances.blogspot, 26 June 2016

Fallon, Kevin, and Stern, Marlow, "2016 Oscar Nomination Predictions", www.thedailybeast.com, 13 January 2016

Fallon, Kevin, "Oscar Conspiracy Theories Debunked: Explaining the 5 Biggest Oscar Snubs", www.thedailybeast.com, 17 January 2015

Feinberg, Scott, "Can the Academy handle 2 women?", www.scottfeinberg.com, 25 July 2010

Finke, Nikki, "Harvey Weinstein vs Film World: Scott Rudin Wins War of Wills With TWC: 'The Reader' Director Is Given More Time", www.deadline.com, 28 September 2008

Fischer, Paul, "Jennifer Connelly: More Than Just a Beautiful Mind", www.girl.com.au, undated (2002)

Fischer, Paul, "Oscar Nominee Keisha Castle-Hughes Is Having A Whale Of A Time", www.femail.com.au, undated (2004)

Fleming Jr., Mike, "Harvey Weinstein On His Dark Horse Best Picture Candidate 'Philomena' And, Well, Everything Else", www.deadline.com, 19 February 2014

Fleming Jr., Mike, "Mike Fleming Q&As Harvey Weinstein", www.deadline.com, 28 January 2013

Fox, Jesse David, "A Brief History of Harvey Weinstein's Oscar Campaign Tactics", www.vulture.com, 29 January 2014

Gachman, Dina, "Chris Hemsworth Shines But 'Rush' Belongs to Daniel Brühl", www.ssninsider.com, 25 September 2013

Gonzalez, Ed, "Oscar 2002 Nominations Predictions", www.slantmagazine.com, 11 February 2002

Gonzalez, Ed, "Oscar 2002 Winner Predictions", www.slantmagazine.com, 20 March 2002

Gray, Tim, "Oscar Has a Long and Honorable History of 'Category Fraud'", www.variety.com, 2 December 2015

Hammond, Pete, "Best Supporting Actor & Actress – Nothing Secondary About These Races", www.deadline.com, 11 January 2011

Hammond, Pete, "Ron Howard's 'Rush' Takes Victory Lap at Emotional Fest Debut Screening", www.deadline.com, 9 September 2013

Hammond, Pete, "Oscars: The Supporting Actor Race", www.deadline.com, 8 December 2012

Hammond, Pete, "Weinstein's Premiere Marathon Delivers Huge Reaction for Oscar-Bait 'August: Osage County' – But Will It Divide Audiences", www.deadline.com, 10 September 2013

Henderson, Eric, "Oscar 2009 Nomination Predictions: Supporting Actress", www.slantmagazine.com, 15 January 2009

Henderson, Eric, "Oscar 2016 Nominations Predictions", www.slantmagazine.com, 11 January 2016

Herrera, Brian Eugenio, "Agnes Moorehead in THE MAGNIFICENT AMBERSONS (1942) - Supporting Actress Sundays", www.stinkylulu.blogspot, 28 May 2006

Herrera, Brian Eugenio, "Cate Blanchett in Notes on a Scandal (2006)", www.stinkylulu.blogspot, 18 February 2007

Herrera, Brian Eugenio, "Jessica Lange in Tootsie (1982)", www.stinkylulu.blogspot, 8 October 2006

Isaacs, Cheryl Boone, "Statement From Academy President Cheryl Boone Isaacs", www.oscars.org, 18 January 2016

Katz, Steve, "On Category Fraud", www.alphaprimitive.com, 9 December 2015

King, Geoff, "Weighing Up the Qualities of Independence: '21 Grams' in Focus", www.academia.edu, undated

Leopold, Todd, "A rich night for best picture 'Slumdog Millionaire'", www.edition.cnn.com, 23 February 2009

Levy, Emanuel, "Broadcast News (1987)", www.emanuellevy.com, 11 February 2008

Levy, Emanuel, "Kate Winslet's Role in The Reader Lead or Supporting?", www.emanuellevy.com, 15 January 2009

Levy, Emanuel, "Oscar 2004: Supporting Actress – Anything Goes", www.emanuellevy.com, 29 February 2004

Magidson, Joey, "The Biggest Oscar morning snubs this year", www.hollywoodnews.com, 20 January 2016

Mazur, Matt, "Best Supporting Actress Rewind 1982", www.popmatters.com, 5 February 2013

Mullen, Pat, "To Lead or Not to Lead", www.cinemablographer.com, 22 October 2012

O'Neil, Tom, "Badass Christoph Waltz leaps up to lead Oscar race in 'Django Unchained'", www.goldderby.com, 8 November 2012

O'Neil, Tom, "Julianne Moore: Drop down to supporting – That's an order!", www.goldderby.com, 12 November 2010

O'Neil, Tom, "Meryl Streep drops to supporting, takes on Oprah", www.goldderby.com, 12 August 2013

O'Neil, Tom, "Oscars flip-flop: Meryl Streep returns to lead, Julia Roberts drop to supporting", www.goldderby.com, 9 September 2013

O'Neil, Tom, "Weinstein Company confirms Christoph Waltz back in supporting for 'Django Unchained'", www.goldderby.com, 7 December 2012

O'Neil, Tom, "Weinstein Co. may push Meryl Streep back up to lead Oscar race", www.goldderby.com, 30 August 2013

Paskin, Willa, "The Oscar Recession", www.dailybeast.com, 11 November 2008

Pond, Steve, "Academy Tweaks Oscar Rules, Campaign Regulations", www.thewrap.com, 30 June 2016

Pond, Steve, "Farewell, Miramax: Oscar Will Never Be the Same", www.thewrap.com, 28 January 2010

Pond, Steve, "Sean Penn, Lesley Manville Play Category Roulette", www.thewrap.com, 27 October 2010

Pond, Steve, "What's Lead, What's Supporting – and Who Really Decides?", www.thewrap.com, 13 October 2009

Reid, Joe, "Supporting Noms That Were Actually Leads", www.film.com, 17 January 2013

Rogers, Nathaniel, "Acting Pairs and Young Bucks", www.thefilmexperience.net, 18 July 2014

Rogers, Nathaniel, "Best Actress Updates, Or: Get Right With God. Stop Category Fraud!", www.thefilmexperience.net, 7 September 2015

Rogers, Nathaniel, "Meryl Goes 'Supporting' – The Scare Quotes Are Mandatory", www.thefilmexperience.net, 12 August 2013

Rogers, Nathaniel, "Oscar Movements", www.thefilmexperience.net, 14 November 2015

Rogers, Nathaniel, "Pt 1. Oscar Editorials to Make the Blood Boil: on Category Fraud", www.thefilmexperience.net, 4 December 2015

Rogers, Nathaniel, "Yes, No, Maybe So: The Master", www.thefilmexperience.net, 21 July 2012

Sims, David, "Why Oscar Nominations Make No Sense", www.theatlantic.com, 15 October 2015

Tapley, Kris, "Ron Howard and Daniel Brühl Reflect on the SAG and Globe Success of 'Rush'", www.hitfix.com, 12 December 2012

Tapley, Kris, "Will Meryl Streep be campaigned for Best Supporting Actress in 'August: Osage County'?", www.hitfix.com, 12 August 2013

Tourtellotte, Bob, "'Baby' Oscar winners advise 'Sunshine' child star", www.reuters.com, 21 February 2007

Verswijver, Leo, "Interview with Don Murray", www.filmtalk.com, 11 December 2014

Vincent, Michael, "The disorganised state of the Academy Awards", www.abc.net.au, 24 March 2000

Whitney, Erin, "What Is Category Fraud? A Closer Look at This Year's Big Oscar Controversy", www.screencrush.com, 10 December 2015

Wloszczyna, Susan, "The Big O: Lead or Supporitng Actress? Depends on Which Category is Likelist to Hit Gold", www.indiewire.com, 24 September 2014

Zauzmer, Ben, "Oscar Nominations Odds: What The Math Says", www.huffingtonpost.com, 13 January 2016

uncredited, "Award Category Fraud", www.tvtropes.org, undated

261

uncredited, "Number 39: Jessica Lange as Julie Nichols in 'Tootsie'",
www.fritzlovesoscars.blogspot, 13 July 2011

uncredited, "Oscars double-ups predicted", www.abc.net.au, 12 December 2003

uncredited, "True Grit Exclusive", www.au.ign.com, 27 October 2009

uncredited, "Oscars: Top 20 Category Frauds", www.goldderby.com, undated

INDEX